GW00750741

TRUETA: SURGEON IN WAR AND PEACE

TRUETA:
SURGEON IN WAR AND PEACE

The Memoirs of Josep Trueta, M.D., F.R.C.S., D.Sc.

Translated by
Meli and Michael Strubell
With a Foreword by J. W. Goodfellow, F.R.C.S.

LONDON
VICTOR GOLLANCZ LTD
1980

Originally published in Catalan, in a slightly extended form under
the title *Fragments d'una Vida*, by Edicions 62 S.A., Provença 278,
Barcelona–8

Printed in Great Britain
by Ebenezer Baylis and Son Ltd
The Trinity Press, Worcester, and London

CONTENTS

*Part IV: Nuffield Professor of Orthopaedic Surgery at Oxford
(1949–1965)*

Chapter

*Part V: Retirement from Oxford and Return to Catalonia
(1965–1976)*

Chapter

LIST OF ILLUSTRATIONS

Following page 144

INTRODUCTION

PERHAPS BECAUSE HE was a doctor, I would sometimes ring up my father at moments of worry or depression and say to him "Give me an injection of optimism, please, I need one badly!" And in a few words, a few sentences, he said the right thing, exactly what one wanted to hear him say: and the injection had worked yet again. It was this very optimism, available to all, which formed such a heartwarming integral part of his character, that was to blame for the fact that he left the writing of his memoirs till so late. There were always more urgent, important things to do, and there was no hurry ... In fact, what I found when he died in January 1977 was a rather untidy, disconnected mass of papers, with a vast amount of missing words, dates, names, etc., which took me the best part of a year to put into shape for publication in Catalan. A great many people gave me invaluable help—friends, colleagues and patients. Without their help, I could not have filled in the many gaps.

We never thought to ask him if he wanted us to translate the memoirs—or reminiscences, as he insisted on calling them, since he said memoirs had to be complete and these were not—but I am sure he would have liked us to do so as Britain was so much a part of him and he had so many friends there to whom I am certain he was in many ways dedicating them. It was important to him—a Latin in scientific Oxford—to be understood, and it is precisely this desire of his that has prompted us to put these reminiscences into English.

Oxford was our home for three decades. In it we three girls were married and our children born. To innumerable people Overmead, our home, was theirs, but this can best be described in his own, translated, words, which have been slightly abridged from the original Catalan edition.

MELI STRUBELL

FOREWORD

DURING THE TWENTY years of our acquaintance I heard
most of Josep Trueta's life story from his own lips, not of
course as he eventually wrote it in these memoirs, but as disconnected episodes, out of order and context. That difference
apart I think that in this book I can hear the tone of his voice
and the turn of his phrase and see his handsome face alight with
the pleasure of the telling. He was such a good talker that there
will certainly be an audience for his collected memories among
those who, like me, have heard some of the stories before. But
this book has a broader claim to attention, an interest that goes
beyond the life history of a distinguished surgeon and medical
scientist. For Josep Trueta was born in Catalonia in 1897 and
therefore led a life which was touched at times by the great
matters of war and insurrection, by the excitement of patriotism and the sadness of long banishment. That he managed to
bring himself and his family safely through hard times to fame
in a foreign country was an achievement of which he was justly
proud and his memoirs, written appropriately when he was
once again at home in Barcelona, are a record of the resilience,
energy, intelligence and good luck without which it could not
have been done.

The eventfulness of Josep Trueta's life was not merely the
result of the geographical and historical accidents of his birth.
He not only responded to history, he contributed to it.
Certainly his ideas on how best to treat the injuries of war must
have affected the lives of thousands of soldiers in the many
conflicts that have occurred since he first tried out his methods
on the battlefield of Spain. In his special branch of surgery, the
treatment of the diseases of bones and joints, he was one of the
first to realize the importance and the relevance of animal
experiments, and he established in Oxford a school of investigators whose work still forms the basis for our understanding of
the vascular contribution to common diseases.

Trueta's teaching went beyond the normal expectation of a

teacher. To his pupil, he was also a source of energy, a fountain of enthusiasm which he managed to pass on to those who worked with him. He got them to do things which they would never have thought themselves capable of doing had he not been there near them.

The dangers of war overcome, and with the dramatic events turned all to good account, Josep Trueta enjoyed the years of his fame to the full. He travelled all over the world, met many great men and women and was generous of his time and his enthusiasm to those who were not so great. By the time he came to write it all down the bitterness had largely gone from his few disappointments but the thrill of his successes was vividly remembered.

Here, then, is the description of a long life which stretched from the end of the Spanish empire to the return of the Bourbon monarchy; an extended diary of the events both great and small which uprooted one man and his family; an insight into the alien traditions from which grew the career of a great British surgeon, who yet remained Catalan to the core.

OXFORD   JOHN GOODFELLOW
1980

PREFACE

ALTHOUGH TO WRITE one's memoirs is not usual among Catalans, with Anglo-Saxons it is exceptional for a person of even limited importance not to do so. This is probably due to the desire of the author to perpetuate his memory among his countrymen. If, apart from this wish, he has a story to tell which he considers out of the ordinary, the only matter for him to decide is the time when he puts pen to paper.

These are the reasons then why I have left the recording of my memories till very nearly my eightieth year: it has always seemed to me premature to look back while there seemed so many more urgent things to do. Now, looking at the calendar, I realize that I shall have to hurry up if I do not want my memories to disappear with me.

The years through which I have lived have been filled with wars and the upheavals which are their sequel and with which, due to my profession as a surgeon, I have had to live in close association. My experiences in the Spanish Civil War from 1936–1939 and the Second World War, which followed it, gave me such an opportunity of getting to know the immense variety of human nature that it now seems opportune to dedicate time to getting down some impressions, in spite of the fact that I know only too well how little they can do to curb the aggressive instincts of modern man, so similar to those manifested by men in prehistoric times. There is, however, yet another reason why I should like to have time to leave a written record—and that is because of the extraordinary situation which led me to live in England for nearly thirty years, many of them in a position of responsibility in affairs related to my profession, such as the direction of the Accident Service in Oxford and especially as Professor of Orthopaedic Surgery at Oxford University.

Due to my upbringing as a biologist, I hope I shall be able to be fairly objective not only as regards events but as regards the people I have known. I also hope I can be objective on the subject of myself.

During the long period of my life spent among the British I have acquired some habits for which I am grateful—one of them being that of understatement, the reverse of the Mediterranean tendency to exaggerate. Personally, I feel that the fact that the Truetas came from a part of the world where, if it did not actually originate there, Romanesque art—the architectural expression of understatement—matured and flourished, must have contributed to my easy adaptation to the British way of life. The vital experience of a people, which is its language, may also have contributed to this as both English and Catalan, although so different in structure and roots, are languages with a marked preference for the monosyllable, as though those who speak them seem anxious not to waste time in superfluous words and syllables which could be dedicated to more important matters.

Those who do not know it, may find it of interest to learn that the human being is constituted by the interplay of two elements: one, which is found at the base of our nature, is formed by genes, the intimate structure of which is made clearer to us every day by the advances of science. Genes, lodged in the chromosomes, transmit our parents' traits. However, the ancestral line of descent can be broken by the phenomenon known as mutation. The colour of our skin, eyes and hair, our height and even facets of our character have been brought down to us by chromosomes. By their appearance we can tell with near certainty the origin of a Scandinavian or a Sicilian, for instance; but it is harder to state the country of birth of a northern Frenchman, a Swiss, an Englishman etc., and often enough an Italian from Milan. Certain characteristics of peoples are explained by genetic crossings, but their final make-up is also influenced by the other factor to which I have made reference above. The second element comes to us from the outside world and is operative from the moment of conception since the development of the human embryo depends on what the placenta filters from the mother's blood. When the baby is born he is exposed for the first time to the light, heat, humidity and noise of the world around him; these will be with him to his last moment on earth. Physical activity, feeding and

very soon mimicry through education will mould the individual and submerge many of the elements he has inherited—a
large part of what is known as the genetic message. Through
this mechanism nomadic peoples move from place to place,
generally in search of food, and after settling for some time in
better lands end up behaving like the people of the areas in
which they have established themselves. This influence of the
outside world on the human being constitutes what we know
as the phenotype, and it eventually predominates over the
genotype in deciding the characteristics of peoples.

It is well known that genes accumulate vital experiences, and
so the more that "previous knowledge"—in other words,
instinct—is acquired, the richer and more varied will be the
genetic constitution; naturally I refer to organisms of similar
vital quality. It is a scientific aberration to believe that "purity
of blood" is maintained by avoiding crossings, when we know
that the contrary is the case. More than a hundred years ago,
Thomas Huxley wrote that in domesticated animals, like dogs
and horses, lack of cross breeding not only weakens the strain
but results in diminished intelligence in the animal. It is common knowledge that thoroughbred horses have had to be
crossed with "handicappers" in order that the strain may continue winning races. The cleverest circus dogs are also mongrels.
This I am sure happens as well with man; which is why I consider claims that the strain of a human group can be improved
by preventing interbreeding with another to be an erroneous
scientific concept.

These reflections may help the reader to understand what I
am made of; but it must not be forgotten that all these elements
have passed through the same strainer—the first is so strong
that for over one thousand years the Catalan phenotype has
been developed from people of very varied genetic origins. It
has also to be remembered that in this process we have, on the
one side, the mimicry stimulated by education and, on the
other, the desire of the newly arrived to resemble those already
there as soon as possible. In this influence parents, even more
than teachers, play a predominant part. It is all too well known
that even delinquency can derive from the fact that, as children, the offenders did not have the required protection or
good example of the parents.

I hope therefore that the pages which follow will be of interest, at least to my grandchildren.

BARCELONA—STA CRISTINA D'ARO   J.T.

1975

PART I

The First Forty Years

(1897–1936)

Chapter 1

MY ANCESTORS

THE TRUETAS ORIGINALLY came from the Catalan mountain regions in the Pyrenees. The root of the name is Germanic
and is found in documents of the pre-Pyrenean area of the
times of the Frankish invasions in versions such as "Truct"
(888), "Truit" (979), "Truete" (1028), "Tructa" and others
besides. Even today, a river trout ("truita" in Catalan) is called
a "trueta" in the mountain valley of Aran.* In this form it is
found in the university files in a document referring to my
ancestor, the surgeon Antoni Trueta, who was born in 1763 in
Artesa and graduated in medicine in 1790 at the University of
Osca. This document vouches for the fact that the blood of the
candidate, son of another surgeon and of Raimonda—herself
the daughter of a surgeon—was "free from all contamination
by Moorish, Jewish, Lutheran and all other bad and repre-
hensible sects", as was the case, it goes on to say, with the
grandparents of the candidate, and that all concerned were
born legitimate. "State whether the candidate and all his
parents and grandparents on both sides are and have been
good Catholics, Christians of long standing . . . and have never
been arraigned before the Illustrious Tribunal of the Faith . . .",
is one sobering requirement in the document. The Tribunal of
the Faith, in other words the Inquisition, was still operating in
Spain in the eighteenth century.

Antoni Trueta had still been christened in Catalan,† as
recorded in the parish records. He became surgeon to General
Lancaster's army in the Rosselló war of 1795, and the family
still has the original written commission.

* Vall d'Aran—Catalan Pyrenees—Lleida.
† Shortly after it was decreed that all official documents had to be in
Castilian and Christian names in Catalan form were prohibited in
baptisms.

The Truetas continued to live in Artesa until shortly before my father was born in 1870, when his father, my grandfather Josep, opened a chemist's shop in nearby Lleida. He soon became possessed of an uncontrollable urge to meddle in politics. This addiction took hold of him when he was studying chemistry at Zaragoza towards the end of the reign of Isabel II, and he joined the "Progressivist Movement", which was a Republican party. A Republican experiment, in which many famous Catalans took part, proved unsuccessful and this failure left my grandfather, and many others of his generation, with the memories and nostalgia as it were, of one's first love affair.

My grandfather considered those who were trying to intensify the Catalanization of the country, and they were many, to be suffering from some sort of mania, but he always used Catalan except when he was referring to something which had been said in a foreign language, whereupon he inevitably switched to Castilian. I remember him, for instance, telling us at the beginning of the First World War, how the Kaiser had preached to his son warning him: "My son, you will have to suffer greatly before your dreams come true and you are emperor, etc."—all this in Castilian. I think he thought it would not have been sufficiently dignified for an emperor to address his son in the idiom of a chemist from Lleida or any of our neighbours in Barcelona.

Among the political experiences of my grandfather there is one which stands out because it left an indelible mark on my own father. When my father, having passed his final school exams in Lleida, wanted to show his diploma to his father, he had to take it to the famous gaol in Lleida, where grandfather was paying with his own liberty for his efforts to see freedom extended to the working classes.

Because of the coincidence of the dates, I infer that my grandfather's imprisonment must have been connected with a revolt which took place in 1886. By then, he had already lived in exile in France for many years—which enabled him to teach me French thirty years later.

Due to all the misadventures which befell my grandfather and consequently the whole family, my own father always had such unpleasant memories of politics that the very mention of the word used to drive him into a state of frenzy. This phobia had a great influence on me.

My grandfather was married to Júlia Secchi, a Valencian lady of Italian descent whose grandfather had had to flee from Austrian persecution in Italy, and had landed by sea in Valencia. Josep and Júlia had two children: a son, Rafel (my father) and a girl, my Aunt Empar who, at thirty-five, married a Mr Moss, an English engineer with the "Canadenca"* whom she met when he was working on the electrification of Camarassa—the first of the Pyrenean reservoirs—soon to be followed by others.

From the photographs which we have and from the reports of those who knew her, grandmother Júlia must have resembled a beautiful Italian madonna, a similarity which, like her name, has fortunately persisted in my family. My Aunt Empar had very high-falutin' aristocratic airs. She never tired of telling us children of how her uncles had claimed rights to a noble title in Italy, which however were not granted.

What with the little time he dedicated to his chemist's shop in Lleida and because of his support for "the Cause",† grandfather's income steadily declined. Nevertheless he still managed to send my father to Barcelona to study chemistry, on the understanding that he would return to Lleida to take charge of the chemist's shop when he had finished his studies. My father went to Barcelona in 1890 with his childhood friend Romà Sol, and together they lived in a boarding-house near a famous street called the Paral.lel. Sol studied law, in which he was to distinguish himself later—it was said he never lost a case. Already very short sighted as a child, Sol ended his life almost blind. He had however a fantastic memory which enabled him to remember with the utmost detail facts from documents which had been read to him only once. He might have become the second President of the Catalan Mancomunitat,‡ had it not been for his bad eyesight. As a child he had had tuberculosis and never enjoyed very good health; notwithstanding, he lived to be eighty-one. During the Civil War his prestige

* A Canadian company—the Barcelona Traction Company—the main Barcelona electric company.
† Republicanism.
‡ See page 44.

protected him in Lleida from which he never moved, and he was unmolested by either side. He was best-man at my wedding.

My maternal grandfather—and godfather, also Josep but whom we called grandfather Pep—belonged to a family originally from southern France, probably Roussillon, whose surname was Raspail, later changed by my father to Raspall.* He was a beret-maker in Sabadell when he married Paula, the daughter of a textile manufacturer in the same town. Paula's family bought a house in Barcelona, in the suburb of Poble Nou, where my grandfather Pep installed a workshop on the ground floor. This eventually became the haberdashery shop for that part of Poble Nou. It was here that my parents first met.

My Raspall grandparents had three daughters: Mercè, my mother; Joaquima, seven years younger who was extraordinarily dedicated to teaching; and a younger sister, Teresona, who contracted encephalitis as an infant and remained subnormal for the rest of her life.

Aunt Quimeta, as we called Joaquima, was known and loved by everyone in Poble Nou where she taught uninterruptedly four generations of girls whom she not only instructed in the three "Rs", but to whom she imparted the high moral standards which have always been one of the virtues of Catalan girls. She married Dionís Monton, a sculptor, and they had three children—two girls and a boy, Dionís, to whom I was godfather when I was nineteen years old; he later became a doctor and a very distinguished anaesthetist. Aunt Quimeta died at ninety-one, still at the head of her school, in 1970. Physically she greatly resembled my mother, which may be one reason why I loved her as if she had been.

The shop in the house (where I was born in 1897) was my playroom until I was six or seven years old. Aunt Quimeta and her husband allowed me to take all sorts of liberties with the objects on sale. The stock was always increased for festive occasions such as Christmas and Epiphany, when toys were even imported from abroad. I well remember a little ship, sailing on a stormy sea of cotton-wool in the shop window. When the shop was closed one day, and when no one was

* Raspall is easier to pronounce in Catalan than Raspail.

looking, I started to rip the vessel apart with the crude instruments at my disposal until I arrived at the very core of the toy: this must have been my first dissection. To the great consternation of my grandfather and uncles, it had no beneficial effect whatsoever on the toy.

Grandfather Pep was small with the agility of a former classical ballet student. All who knew him agreed that he was extremely intelligent and good-natured—virtues which he passed on to his two elder daughters. He was a great music lover and, although of modest means and scant culture, he had a certain natural refinement. It is to him that I owe my first real contact with nature because he showed me the marvels of Montseny, the beautiful mountain near Barcelona, when I was six.

One trek I remember in particular: when he took me in midwinter to spend a few days with friends at a farmhouse high up on the Montseny mountain. By train and horse-drawn trap we reached a point where the final half mile had to be covered on foot. Half way up it started to snow heavily and to reach the farmhouse before nightfall my grandfather took me by the hand and warned me to keep going by pointing out where elephants had gone before us. I was too young then to distinguish cow pats from the tracks of pachyderms, and I know that I needed no further urging on.

For years to come, this part of Catalonia typified for me the romantic side of nature with all its mysteries and beauty—the arrival of herds of sheep and goats returning from days of grazing on the slopes, the winter nights with farmers and shepherds eating round the hearth and, above all, the awe-inspiring panorama of the valley of the Vallés, with the sea in the distance, riding, as it were, the saddle of the low hills of the Maresme. Beyond all doubt, it is to my grandfather Pep, the modest beret-maker from Sabadell, that I owe the discovery of the beauty of my country. With the passage of the years, and after travelling to so many lands whose mountainous grandeur —the Alps, the Andes, the Rockies and other ranges—has so impressed me, revisiting the Montseny some sixty years after I first saw it finally revealed why it has had such a great attraction for me. It is simply because it is a mountain on the human scale. I was surprised that the memory of it had remained so faithful to reality. Everything was the same as the last time I was there, thirty years before. Only the large oaks over the water chute beside the threshing floor, where we used to bathe as children, were missing. I was told they had been sold when the heirs went to live in a nearby village.

Recently I had the chance of going right up to the old farmhouse without having to get out of the car. A network of roads, the result of intensive property development, leads directly to the old farmhouse, which now resembles a witches' castle from a Grimm's fairy tale; thus most of the magic I remember from my childhood has been swept away.

This then briefly is what I know of my family roots. I have often thought that if what goes to make up one's personality, instead of being genes, were water colours, in which the final picture depended on the blending of various tints and not, as with oil paint, the effect of their superimposition, the result in my case would be a quite indefinable colour due to the diverse ingredients that have gone into its make up—from peasants to university graduates, including tradesmen and industrialists, some of whom enjoyed financial security and social eminence, while others had to work hard merely to survive.

Genes, which are the basis of one's character, are subject to variations or mutations—this we know. However, there are certain predominant genes which are affected by external factors and no doubt the stimulation of education through mimicry is one of them. I attribute my decision to study medicine to the fact that since the eighteenth century the Truetas had successfully been surgeons or chemists, right up to the time of my own father, who was a physician. From my father I inherited the physical characteristics of northern Europeans, the colour of my skin and of my eyes, and also my height. To my mother I owe in great part the nature of my character—which tends towards compromise rather than the asserting of one's will. The same could not be said of my father—which may explain the restricted circle of friends he had.

Chapter 2

FROM LLEIDA TO BARCELONA

WHY MY FATHER did not go back to Lleida is not certain; probably the fact that he had met my mother was decisive. Without telling his father, and instead of taking his chemistry finals, he switched to medicine. He studied with a friend, younger than himself, August Pi i Sunyer, who, like him, was in a hurry to become a doctor and together they achieved their goal in 1898. In 1895, thanks to the financial help of the Raspalls, my parents were married, and by the time my father qualified as a doctor my sister Júlia was already one and a half years old and I had been born a few months before.

As soon as he qualified, my father installed himself in the working-class district of Poble Sec, where he had lived as a young man. This district already extended at the end of the nineteenth century from Barcelona harbour towards the mountain of Montjuic, where it became too steep for large buildings. From there it became a mass of vegetable gardens and small huts where the more modest inhabitants of the Poble Sec lived. The popular part was "La Font del Gat" (the Fountain of the Cat); whereas the more affluent went to the clay pigeon club at the top of the mountain. My paternal grandfather was friendly with the manager of the club who, like him, came from Lleida, and ever since his arrival in Barcelona in 1904 he had got into the habit of going to drink water from a fountain inside the club grounds. According to him, this water was unequalled by any in or around Barcelona. Every day, even when he was almost eighty, he walked airily, stick in hand, with agile, rhythmic step from our house to the fountain and back—a walk of nearly five miles, much of it uphill.

Many times I heard the story told of an escapade of mine at the age of about two when, taking advantage of my mother's momentary distraction, I set off all alone to the house of some clients of my father's, where I had been taken on one or two occasions. This adventure, together with some rather more boisterous ones, gave me the reputation of being a mischievous if not wilful child; which probably accounts for my father's just but never excessive severity towards me.

I well remember the day when at the age of about six, I appeared before the grown-ups, to the great distress of my mother, with long moustaches acquired at the expense of her hair-piece. Nor was I any more successful when I put on my sister's new, white, wide-brimmed hat, the shape of which was normally held by wire, which I had twisted under my chin. The yell my sister Júlia let out when she saw that I had destroyed her new hat brought my father headlong out of his study to give her a thoroughly undeserved smack. I emerged from my hiding-place rather shamefaced at the injustice I had just witnessed, it being obvious that the one deserving the spanking was me.

These are not by any means the only theatrical scenes I remember as a child—I could go on for ever. However I make one exception: it concerns the disgraceful way my sister and I treated our young brother Rafel. Júlia and I both liked having our backs scratched. We had a contract with Rafel whereby he scratched our backs in return for some five centimos per quarter hour. That was in theory though, because in fact we never seemed to have any money to give him. Rafel therefore kept an accounts book—I remember it well—in which he would write down our debts. I do not recall that either of us ever paid him anything though. Be that as it may, he somehow managed to acquire a few centimos and one day, to the great astonishment of my mother, he appeared with an enormous plaster statue of the Venus de Milo. When asked why he had bought such a monstrosity he answered, unperturbed: "Aha— perhaps one day we shall need one and then we may not be able to find it!"

About this time I had an illness which left me marked psychologically more than physically. My father arrived home one day and I rushed to kiss him as usual only to be kept at arms' length, to my great surprise until he told us that he had just visited a small patient with smallpox. Although I had been vaccinated several times, the vaccine had not "taken" and as a result I caught smallpox, though not too severely. I was not left with many scars—although enough for one or two of my schoolmates, with the cruelty so often found in children, to call me "poxed". With the passage of time, the small marks on my face practically disappeared but they left me with a feeling of shame which made me reluctant to show my face, and which took me years to overcome.

When I was born my sister was sent to Lleida to be looked after by my Aunt Empar. Later, on the birth of my brother Rafel, when I was five, Júlia was brought back to Barcelona to meet him. It was with amazement that we discovered that not only did she not speak Catalan but that she did not even understand it. For some reason, Aunt Empar had always spoken Castilian to her. My father therefore forbade her to go back to Lleida. For some time we were kept at home together, which may be one reason why we always retained the greatest affection for each other to the end of our lives. Later she attended school and I went daily to a nursery school of which I have no memories.

My father achieved a good position for himself as the physician of the Poble Sec—everyone knew him as Don Rafel— and so we moved to better appointed flats as his financial position improved. In those pre-pharmaceutical days, the fact that he was a chemist as well as a doctor came in useful, as not only was he able to prescribe medicines for his patients but also to dispense them.

In the basement next to one house where we lived for some years was the chemist's shop of Pompeu Simó, ex-resident of Cuba who, like so many others, had seen with sadness the last of the Spanish colonies achieve its independence. Simó was a kind, generous conversationalist who used to give us sweets. It was through his discussions with my father that we first started to grasp the importance of the end of the Cuban war and the loss of the colonies. Although these events meant the ending of the imperial Spain created by Castile, youth in Spain was brought up in the heroic military tradition for many years to come. I remember the excitement with which we opened chocolate bars to find pictures of the Russo-Japanese War of 1904 inside the wrappers. This glorifying of all things military went on until my adolescence as the centre of heroic activity was transferred from Cuba to the Rif zone of North Africa.

The loss of the Spanish colonies occurred when I was scarcely a year old and it altered the course of the life of the whole country, moving the centre of political gravity from Madrid, where it had been maintained for four centuries, back towards Barcelona and the Mediterranean where it had formerly pivoted before the colonization of America. With my contemporaries therefore we are the so-called Catalan generation of '98, a privilege for which we have had to pay dearly. The loss of the last remaining territories, to which the poor of Spain had previously emigrated, together with the growth of industry in Catalonia, resulted in the discovery first of Barcelona and later the whole of Catalonia as the new land of promise for the disinherited of the rest of Spain. This phenomenon was to have a decisive influence on the whole of my generation in Catalonia.

Chapter 3

THE EFFECTS OF INDUSTRIALIZATION
IN BARCELONA

INDUSTRIALIZATION IN THE Poble Nou was already in full swing when I was born. It all started with the opening of the railway to Mataró in 1848 and was followed by the building of the main railway station and the factory making railway equipment. A sector of this quarter was known as Little France due to the nationality of some of the factory owners and workers. On the other hand, there was not one single important factory in the Poble Sec, populated as it was by mechanics, shopkeepers, artisans and some port workers, except for an electricity plant and a bell foundry (owned by a family of French descent related to the Catalan musician Frederic Mompou, whose talents were used for adjusting the pitch of the bells cast in the foundry).

This limited industrialization gave the quarter its character. The growth of the district was largely due to Catalan immigrants or people from neighbouring regions such as Valencia and, even more so, Aragon. The economic advantages were not as yet strong enough to attract peoples from further afield. However labour was soon required to work on the Barcelona tramways—a company controlled by Belgian capital—and this led to the vast immigration of workers from Murcia, many of whom settled in the Poble Sec.

In 1909 the burning of churches and convents by youngsters trained in the principles and beliefs of anti-clerical "lerrouxism",* brought into headlong confrontation the two largest social groups in Catalonia, an occurrence which, apart

---

* Followers of Lerroux, a corrupt, opportunist Andalusian demagogue, anti-socialist, anti-clerical and anti-Catalan. During the Republic (1931–1936) he became Prime Minister of a very right-wing government, and was later a supporter of Franco.

from the Carlist Wars and the uprisings of the nineteenth
century, had not happened since the fifteenth century.

The Spanish army was called in to re-establish order
following the disorders which occurred immediately after
Catalan reservists had been sent to Morocco. The division of
Barcelona society into two classes, split by an antagonism
which was not to diminish until the outbreak of the Civil War
in 1936, began, as I see it, with the arrival of Lerroux when I
was three years old, at the very beginning of political
Catalanism.

Much later, when I was already the doctor of a workers'
accident insurance company, the construction of the under-
ground Metro and later the 1929 International Exhibition
buildings, many of whose workers I treated medically, attracted immigrants from further and further afield and became,
with the Civil War, a continuous flow which has not dried up
to this day. It is principally to this vast immigration that we
owe the extraordinary growth of Barcelona.

My generation has been deeply affected by this nomadic
invasion to which is due, on the one hand, the growth of the
city and, on the other, the tendency for it to lose its own
identity, a factor which finally provoked Catalans to a sustained effort to preserve their own national characteristics. I
believe the exuberant flowering of Catalanism and its evolu-
tion from historical romanticism to political action, is related
to two events arising out of the loss of the colonies. First, the
discovery of Catalonia as a place where it was possible to work
and prosper; and secondly, the resistance of Catalans, first in
Barcelona and later all over Catalonia, to having their identity
submerged by the newly arrived. This reaction is by no means
exceptional; it is common enough in countries with vast
immigration currents.

Another consequence of the loss of the last Spanish colonies
was the vast repatriation of army officers who became redundant once the Cuban war was over. In 1907, according to the
American historian, Joan Connelly, there were thirty lieuten-
ant-generals for only eight army corps, sixty major-generals
for sixteen divisions; three colonels for each regiment and
nearly 15,000 officers for an army of 80,000 men. These
officers soon found full-time work in the Moroccan Rif

campaign, which lasted until 1926 when, through the joint efforts of Spain and France, the Rif was finally subdued.

At the beginning of the twentieth century, Catalonia was riding on a wave of creative activity difficult to find elsewhere in Europe at that time. The architecture of Gaudí, Domenech and Puig i Cadafalch; the paintings of Nonell, Picasso, Torres Garcia, Mir and Anglada i Camarasa; the music of Granados, Albéniz, Morera and Casals; the sculpture of Blay, Clarà, Gargallo, Hugué and Llimona; the writings of Maragall, Guimerá, Iglesias, Victor Català, Josep Carner and others; finally the statesmanship of Prat de la Riba, Cambó, Abadal, Carner and Sunyol. These contributions show how the centre of gravity in Spain was increasingly moving from Madrid towards Barcelona, causing an inevitable anti-Catalan reaction. The Catalanist movement was in the ascendant whereas repressive centralism was slowly losing the sole power of decision and becoming more and more intolerant. The conservative heads of the Catalan movement tried in vain to assure the rest of Spain that all they were trying to achieve was the awakening of the same creative impulses which they were certain existed throughout the Spanish State.

This Catalan renaissance terrified the leaders in Madrid, creating in their minds a horrifying phantom dressed in a great big sheet with "Separatism" written in large letters on it. They gave this name to any manifestation—even if it was only in support of our native language or our own way of life. As a brake on anything which might seem to promote the Catalan movement they took advantage of the arrival of Murcian and Andalusian peasants, attracted to Barcelona by the boom in the building industry and the increasing number of new factories in the city. The immigrant workers in Barcelona were Castilian speakers feeling as though they were in another country, and were fertile ground for the experts Madrid sent to Barcelona for the purpose of putting obstacles in the way of Catalan revival.

This is where Lerroux came in. I was, as I say, about three years old when he made his first visit to Barcelona. He was the son of an army officer but was turned down when he applied to enter the Military Academy in Toledo. He came to Barcelona in 1901 and, according to what I picked up at home when I was old enough to listen in to family conversations, he received economic aid from Madrid to enable him to exploit to the utmost the flood of mostly illiterate immigrants in obstructing the growth of Catalanism.

At first Lerroux's activity centred around the historic republicanism which had evolved in Catalonia. At that time, my grandfather still felt himself to be a Progressive Republican. He met Lerroux and once or twice even went to one of the "Houses of the People" he had established. Nevertheless, it was not long before, thoroughly disillusioned, he gave up all political activity.

All this had its effect at home, notwithstanding my father's continuing allergy to all things political, which was such that he refused even to discuss politics. As though presaging the troubles which were to follow one another throughout the course of my life, on 8 August 1897, a few weeks before I was born, Cánovas del Castillo, prime minister at the time, was assassinated by an Italian anarchist as a reprisal for the execution of the Catalan and Italian anarchists accused of having set off a bomb which had killed twelve people shortly before.

The other event which I consider to be representative of the problems which in various forms were to be repeated all my life was the refusal of the Catalan bourgeoisie to pay newly imposed taxes. These were required by the State to make up for the loss of revenue from the ex-colonies. It can be said with truth that, for the first time in centuries, the interest of the Spanish State centred on the country itself, although not for long, since shortly afterwards the army, concentrated in the Moroccan Rif on its return from Cuba, was to restart fighting. The Catalans thought, ingenuously, that "he who pays commands"—an error which was to cost them dearly. Although a very high proportion of the State revenues came from Catalonia, this did not mean that the Catalans could exact any concession in return.

In my childhood, anarchy played a prominent part in the troubles we lived through. The first anarchist activity in the Peninsula began in Andalusia with the assassination of landowners in 1882 by the members of a sect known as The Black Hand. In Barcelona, due to the Catalan character, anarchy took on an individualistic form. The city at that time was a

simmering cauldron, and with lerrouxism and anarchy working like some dread epidemic within a city badly guarded by
inept and apathetic police, a series of events began similar to
the current terrorist atrocities of today. Bombs went off in the
streets with no apparent motive. Some, near our home,
accounted in one night for so many dead and injured that the
chemist's shop of our neighbour Simó was filled with casualties.
Some of the bombs were detected in time, others exploded. The
strange thing is that, apart from two in the opera house, these
bombs always seemed to be in places occupied by people of
modest means, which made it hard to understand what kind of
social injustice the terrorists were fighting against. The reputation of the city certainly suffered; it became known as the City
of Bombs.

One conversation I overheard between my grandfather and
my father made a great impression on me. My grandfather had
just been told by an old friend of his, a police inspector, that
some Catalan members of the bourgeoisie had proposed that
they employ him with a view to his finding out who was behind
all the bombs and why the assassins appeared to enjoy a certain
immunity. My grandfather's police friend had had to refuse
the job as, he said, he could not obtain the necessary permits
to go into official buildings such as the Civil Government. It
was then, in July 1907, that a former Scotland Yard detective,
Charles Arrow, was commissioned to investigate the affair by
private citizens under the leadership of Puig i Cadafalch.
Unfortunately, Arrow went back home shortly after his arrival
without having been able to solve anything, as it appeared that
at every step he found his way blocked by Lerroux and his
adherents.

After so many years in England, I regret never having been
able to find out what Arrow really thought. In his book,
Rogues and Others, published in London in 1926, he mentions
Catalan terrorism, but without going into details. The bombs
stopped when a certain Rull was gaoled, which incidentally
coincided with Mr Arrow's arrival in Barcelona, but Rull
refused to say whom he worked for. One of the lawyers in the
case told my grandfather that Rull thought he was going to
have his death sentence commuted; it was not, and by that
time it was too late for him to speak. There is little doubt that

2

Rull and members of his family planted the bombs and were then paid by the police for every one that they "discovered". With the execution of Rull the bombs came to an end. Francesc Cambó* in his book *Per la Concordia*, published in 1927, said: "If one day it were possible to determine the origins of the successful attempts on the lives of Cánovas, Canalejas and Dato,† we should surely find that the anarchist plots which both conservative and liberal governments fomented in Catalonia to combat Catalan individualism were not totally dissociated from the conception of these crimes."

* Cambó—a prominent Catalan conservative financier who became minister in Madrid during the reign of Alfonso XIII. He died in exile in Buenos Aires in 1947.

† All three heads of government assassinated while in office between 1897 and 1920.

Chapter 4

MY EDUCATION

WHEN MY PATERNAL grandfather came to live in Barcelona he was sixty-five years old. He rented a flat near ours and, together with the concierge of his house, in the autumn I made my first excursions with him to the woods near Barcelona looking for a special kind of mushroom. We would set off at dawn and I would get back exhausted. I was infected by the Catalan enthusiasm for this pastime by the age of eight. In my case, as no doubt in many others, this hobby developed my intuition, which is simply experience based on previous observation. I have seen this same faculty in doctors with a "clinical eye" when it comes to making a diagnosis; what they possess is the experience to clear the path and eliminate errors. My youthful addiction to mushroom-hunting, acquired at the expense of much exhaustion, perhaps developed in me the urge for research—the same urge which induced me to disembowel the cardboard boat in my uncle's shop—and which led me to work in scientific laboratories. I remember the Nobel Prize winner Ramon y Cajal recounting in his memoirs his excitement on reading Defoe's *Robinson Crusoe* and how he managed to convince a few of his equally youthful friends to explore with him a mysterious island which lay in the middle of a river. They stayed there until hunger drove them home to their village. When Cajal was already a world-famous scientist he once said that he carried on his search for new scientific data with the same excitement that he had felt as a boy exploring the mysterious island. I feel as though I were looking for mushrooms in the forest when I search for the path which I must follow in order to reach the "measurable truth", which is the aim of science. On the other hand, this custom of mushroom-hunting is very old in Catalonia, and my daughters and grandchildren have inherited it—which does not imply however that they have all made scientific discoveries.

In order that I should improve my education I was sent to the Escolapis, a school with a good scholastic reputation which took children from all classes. The "rich" were separated from the "poor" by the width of the street. On the side of boys of well-to-do parents or those with a "recommendation", we were privileged to have a large playground, where we were allowed to mix with the "others" during the breaks known, quite wrongly, as "rest time". I was lucky enough to be taught by very good teachers—priests with a reputation for humanism and liberalism which no doubt influenced my parents' choice of school.

In May 1909 I took my first communion, and was made to wear the latest fashion for small boys, a thick white cotton sailor suit. This contrasted with the dark suits worn by all the others and gave me a complex, as if I were wearing the "Sanbenito" instituted by the Inquisition. I remember this so well because ever since I have been terrified by the thought of being the centre of attention, even when I have had to speak in public. This may surprise some of my friends, but only I know how much it has cost me to hide this shyness which, fortunately, has slowly diminished with time. It may seem a paradox, but the greater my responsibility and the larger my audience, the easier it became for me to overcome my natural shyness.

I carried on at the same school even after it was burnt down in 1909 and moved to another street, but not for long as, to the great consternation of the whole family, I failed in mathematics right at the beginning of my "batxillerat."* My father then decided it was time I put less trust in the little altar in my room that I had dedicated to the Virgin Mary, and more in the contents of books. My optimism, if not my truthfulness, in those days must have been unbounded since, when I arrived home after my exam, I told my father I was quite certain I had passed it, whereas my grandfather Trueta, who had been present, though out of sight, at my exam, had reported that I had not answered a single question. My father asked me if I believed in the miraculous power of Holy Pictures and I said firmly: yes, I did—even though on that occasion they had let me down. Hence the change to the Institute of Secondary Education. I must make it quite clear though that my failure was in no way

* Equivalent to a sort of GCE "O" Levels.

the fault of the good fathers. It was simply due to a tendency to let my imagination run away with me and to a lack of concentration which was sometimes so obvious that people speaking to me often had to shout at me to get my attention back. Any book or magazine that described adventures, however fantastic, I could not leave alone.

At a time when scarcely anyone interested himself in the education of the poor, the work of Calasanç, founder of the Escolapis, was obviously bound to prosper. This makes it incomprehensible why during the "Tragic Week" between 26 July and 1 August 1909, a school where the poor were educated should have been burnt down by a mob of young hooligans. It has been suggested that the burning was carried out by rivals from another school, instead of the "young barbarians" of Lerroux who were undoubtedly to blame for most of the burnings of convents and churches in Barcelona. What is beyond all doubt is the innocence of the owner of the rival school, Ferrer, who was accused of leading the revolt as a protest against the sending of reservists to the Rif, where Spanish forces had suffered heavy losses. Notwithstanding his proven innocence, Ferrer was executed as a scapegoat. As for Lerroux, who had recommended his followers to "lift the novices' veils and turn them into mothers"—he was untouched; when the rebellion broke out he was safely in Argentina.

Although we children were spending the summer out of Barcelona, I remember the "Tragic Week" very well. Most of the destruction took place near our house, and my father had to stay in the city to work. My parents were thus out of touch with each other for several days, and the rumours of what was happening near our home terrified us until finally my father was able to come and fetch us.

It was with great excitement that we saw the bullet holes in our house and the spent bullet which had fallen on my parents' bed. I remember too that a balcony from which the soldiers had been fired on had been wrenched away from the wall of a near-by house.

The wilful destruction of my school by fire had a tremendous effect on me, more so even than the bombs, and awakened in me a repugnance against human cruelty and stupidity which has never lapsed.

Probably due to the fact that from an early age I had sensitive hands and also was ambidextrous—I was born left-handed but was made to use my right hand, fortunately as it turned out, with equal facility—I used to make all sorts of objects out of wood and cardboard, such as boats and houses. When I was eight years old, my father brought me a small carpentry set from Switzerland. I thereupon decided that I was going to become a carpenter.

My father, though, already had high hopes that I would follow the family tradition and become a doctor or even, with my dexterity, a surgeon. One Sunday morning after Mass and not having yet breakfasted, I was taken by my father to a nursing home where a friend of mine was to have an abscess lanced. Without being asked, I was led to the operating theatre, where my little friend was already on the table, crying with fear. As it was only a question of a small incision, anaesthesia was not considered necessary provided a male nurse were just to hold the child still. In no time blood and pus were pouring down the little hand, while my friend let out a heart-rending scream—or so I was told later, as by that time I had already passed out cold on the floor. I need hardly say with what pessimism my father viewed my prospects as a future surgeon, but the incident was blamed on the fact that I had had no breakfast. . . . I never fainted or lost consciousness again in my lifetime with the exception of two hours with concussion caused by cracking my head against a tree when cycling head-long down a hill with no brakes. Not that I had had no occasion to hurt myself before then—on my frequent explorations of the Poble Sec I had often joined up with a gang of young ruffians who used to throw stones at rival gangs from other streets. Once or twice the tell-tale lump on my forehead gave away what I had really been up to when my parents had sent me for a quiet walk down the Paral.lel.

These pastimes alternated with others more conducive to the formation of the intellect. In one of the flats in our block there lived a boy whose father was connected with the Apolo Theatre. This enabled me to spend many Sunday afternoons watching the show from the wings. I remember seeing over and over *The Sun of Humanity*, in which the author tried to put across his views on social justice to a noisy audience. This privilege of going to the theatre for nothing lasted several years—so much so that I even knew by heart whole pages of romantic plays, which probably explains why I fell in love with an actor's daughter who, like me, was just ten years old.

The semi-suburban street known as the Paral.lel was a strange phenomenon. From the end of the nineteenth century its activity steadily built up from the evening until well into the dawn. There were cabarets and theatres of all kinds: pantomime, tragedies, comedies, vaudeville. The Café Arnau, where the famous Raquel Meller made her début in 1911; the New Theatre, the Moulin Rouge and many others. At the same time as Raquel Meller was exciting the shouting audience while looking for "a flea" which, although never found, gave her an opportunity to show off innocently a limited amount of her anatomy, a few metres away the audience was being carried away by *The Sun of Humanity*.

The Paral.lel was by no means restricted to light theatre. My father always went to the plays in which the great Italian dramatic actress Vitaliani took part—around 1903.

I remember most clearly the celebrations held on the eve of St John and St Peter, and Carnival, with the mass of the people, the colours, the noise, fireworks, catherine wheels and the rest. My sister and I would have our own firework display on the balcony and, modest though it was, we usually attracted an admiring audience.

This phenomenon of the Paral.lel has often been compared to Montmartre in Paris. The discovery of Paris made by our artists towards the end of the nineteenth century may explain how the influence developed. However, Montmartre is a whole district where artists of all kinds live and work, whereas the Paral.lel is just a quarter-of-a-mile section of a wide avenue. The remaining mile or so of the avenue had no connection whatever with this nucleus where the aim was solely to amuse and be entertained.

My move to the institute opened up a new world for me. On the one hand I felt free from the supervision of the Escolapi Fathers, which represented a certain liberation, but on the other, I was now placed under the control of my grandfather Josep, who acted as tutor to me for some years. He taught me

French, so that by the time I was twelve I could speak Italian and French fairly well, as well as Catalan and Castilian. I soon made friends at the institute, especially with Josep Cabré with whom I used to walk to and from school reading the latest instalment of *Nick Carter*, *Sherlock Holmes* or *Arsène Lupin*.

I often used to get home filthy, with my shoes scratched and buttons missing, from playing football on the wide pavement outside the institute—much to my mother's distress. My life-long love of sport must have started at this time. My father encouraged it by taking me to football matches and making me a member of Barcelona Football Club in 1909. I remember the excitement of watching the stars of the day play. Cabré and I decided that we wanted to play football on proper pitches and joined a club on the outskirts of Barcelona where, for the first time, we wore the heavy football boots in use at the time. I remember our colours were yellow and blue in three wide bands. Because of my height, I played centre-half, while Cabré's dashing personality fitted him to be a perfect forward.

My father, who in so many ways was far ahead of his time, sent us out of Barcelona for the summer holidays from 1905 on. One year we went to St Pol de Mar, just north of Barcelona, where we were received, not as welcome money-spending visitors, but as intruders. This antagonism actually became violent where we children were concerned, as I remember to my cost one evening when, sitting outside the front door of our rented house and minding my own business, I was struck on the nose by a flying rock which broke a bone and caused an alarming nosebleed. As a result, the right side of my nose was slightly dented and required manipulation, which was reasonably successful.

In 1914 we went to Blanes, the first village of the Costa Brava and made friends with two French boys, both of them good swimmers, who helped my brother and me to improve our style a great deal. While we were in Blanes the two French brothers left to join the French army on the outbreak of the Great War. The next year we again went to Blanes and I fell head over heels in love with the daughter of a colleague of my father for whom he felt no great liking, a feeling which was heartily reciprocated. The courtship came to an abrupt end when, after meeting on Sundays after Mass at Santa Maria del Mar in

Barcelona, the young lady told me we could meet no more. Shortly after, she married a distant relative. It was my first sentimental heart-break, which took me some time to get over, although I realized that without my family's help I could not possibly expect the young lady to wait six or seven years until I finished my studies and was able to keep us both.

No doubt the beauty of Blanes, the music, the dancing in the moonlight all contributed to my attraction to the blue eyes and pretty figure of the young lady responsible for my first senti-mental set-back.

My medical books apart, I had by then already given up adventure books for works on travel and history, especially those dealing with social problems. Among the books which my grandfather Josep had brought with him from Lleida were some twenty large volumes of voyages and exploration. I was fascinated by the story of Stanley finding Livingstone in darkest Africa, and Simoine's tales of the American Far West where the Sioux and the Cayenne tribes still scalped the white man. I preferred Charles Dickens, Dumas fils and Walter Scott to Goethe, and by the time I was eighteen I had already read all the works of Tolstoy, Turgenev, Dostoievsky and any other works by Russian authors which I could find in Castilian or French; in particular I shall never forget the effect that Kropotkin's *The Conquest of Bread* had on me. I read prac-tically the whole of the Portuguese Eça de Queiróz, and of the Spaniards Galdós and Pio Baroja, a lot of whose work I could recite from memory. I used to read in bed, lighting my lamp as soon as I thought the family were asleep and reading some-times until dawn or until sleep overcame me. My father always encouraged me to read. He had a good knowledge of literature and a fair library, as well as being a member of the Barcelona Athenaeum where he used to go whenever he had time, spending as long as he could in the vast library there.

I never came across Karl Marx until much later. There was a copy of the first edition of *Das Kapital* at home belonging to my grandfather Josep. However it was in German which prevented me from reading it. When years later I did read it, I found Marx excessively dogmatic and authoritarian for my taste. By then I was well on the way to becoming a doctor and I was aware of the foundations of the great scientific revolution which

2*

had been started by Charles Darwin, Claude Bernard and Louis Pasteur, among others, none of whom had resorted to dogmatism, an attitude of mind which I find totally incompatible with science. It seemed to me that Marx was a bit of a demagogue, that he took advantage of the credibility achieved by the great biologists and wanted to make "his truth" unquestionable. It has taken me many years to find the necessary evidence to satisfy myself that I was not far off the mark in suspecting that Marx and Engels were influenced by the great prestige in which biology was held at the time and advanced their theory of, for them, the inevitable collapse of what they called capitalism and its simultaneous replacement by communism as if it were a biological law. Later in England I came to see how, as Germans, both Marx and Engels were attempting to impose on society a philosophical system of an authoritarian and State-dominant type very similar to Hegel's. But, as a Jew, Marx introduced into his theory a prophetic element which sought to make it untouchable. Engels, who lived in Manchester where his family owned a textile factory, superimposed the scientific varnish by his conversancy with Darwin's work. Engels himself demonstrated this in the preface of the *Manifesto of the Communist Party* by Marx and himself, published in London in 1888, where he says: "This proposition [the economic theory of history] which, in my opinion, is destined to do for history what Darwin's theory did for biology, we both of us had been gradually approaching for some years before 1845." It could not have been for many years since Engels and Marx only got to work together in 1844. When *Das Kapital* was published in 1867, Engels sent a signed copy of it to Darwin. The worst thing was that the theory and its dogma did away with man's freedom, leaving only that of the philosopher-prophet Marx. Rosa Luxemburg, the German Communist, saw this threat before she was murdered in a Berlin gaol in 1919 when, speaking of the recent Bolshevist Russian revolution, she stated that the liberation of the Russian people would rapidly lead to the extinction of their freedom, as has been the case in Russia and indeed wherever communism has taken hold.

In 1919, Rafel and I became members of the swimming club in Barcelona and from then on we both became ardent swimmers, Rafel becoming the 100 metres free-style champion of Spain in 1922 and winning several relay titles. We also used the gymnasium at the Barcelona Athenaeum and even fenced. We combined physical exercise with chess—as if trying to find a balance between the body and the mind. I used my right hand for fencing, my left for tennis, both in drawing and painting, and later on was able to use a surgeon's scalpel and to suture with either hand.

The existence of Catalonia as an entity was practically unknown to me since, at home, my grandfather Trueta was a fervent classical Spanish republican. When I started catching the feel of the Catalanism which was palpable in the street, my grandfather was very cross indeed. As for my father, although intrinsically he was, and felt, deeply Catalan, he was not pleased by any display on my part of this Catalan spirit which, he maintained, if there were a good central government (a thing which, ironically, he found quite impossible), would be redundant. I was still at school when I started attending Catalan public demonstrations, so frequent in those days in Barcelona. I soon learnt how to run in front of the police horses, a training which stood me in good stead until well into my medical studies. I was finishing at school one Christmas holiday when I witnessed and participated in the throwing of rocks at the train which used to pass noisily, in the open, down one of the main streets in Barcelona. The procedure was very simple: we took up some paving stones on the next street and lobbed them on to the rails. This provoked the fury of the mounted police who proceeded to charge us. This in turn led later to public accusations of police brutality. Two or three days of disorders and bruises and my classes were suspended till after the Epiphany. I was never able to discover who started this annual commotion, but it happened every year in December. I suspect that someone had had enough of listening to teachers continuously for ten weeks and wanted a rest. None of us had ever heard of Trotsky nor, of course, of Mao. . . .

I was greatly influenced in 1913 by Canalejas' acceptance, as Spanish prime minister, of the proposal of the four Catalan municipalities* to group themselves into what was called the

* Barcelona, Girona, Lleida and Tarragona. They were granted a limited form of self-government.

"Mancomunitat"—Commonwealth—under the presidency of Prat de la Riba. Each municipality sent representatives to Barcelona, and Lleida chose my father's old friend, Romà Sol, who came every week. He used to stay with us when he came to Barcelona, and I would act as guide and secretary to him, reading his mail and so on. He was terribly short-sighted even then and had trouble reading even with the thickest glasses. Sol would enthral me with stories of what was being achieved in order that Catalonia might have the services it lacked. What most amazed me was that although the "consellers" (or ministers) differed widely in their ideologies, they seemed to be able to discuss things without quarrelling—something which seemed incredible to me then but which I was to discover much later was quite normal in Great Britain. Unfortunately, good things do not seem to last for long in my country and the untimely death of Prat de la Riba was a tragedy for us. It was Sol who was chosen as his temporary successor, until the election of Puig i Cadafalch, and he led the whole of Catalonia in mourning Prat de la Riba at the funeral.

But although one was aware of the improvement that was going on in Catalonia on a European scale, with the opening of the Nurses' School, the School for Librarians, the Institute of Catalan Studies, mobile libraries, the Library of Catalonia, the asphalting of roads, the linking of Barcelona by telephone with surrounding towns, etc., it was not until everything was lost that one came to realize how much had been achieved at that time when I was in daily contact with Romà Sol.

Before I finished my schooling, I started taking drawing and painting lessons. I must have been around sixteen at the time and I covered many canvasses. I have managed not to lose three of them; they do not seem too bad even now. As I look at them I think to myself how near they came to changing the course of my life. The fact is that when the time came for me to choose a career, carried away by my artistic efforts, I wanted to be a painter. I told my father it would be a waste of my valuable painting time for me to do a university course as I was going to be a professional painter. My father said he found the idea interesting but thought it would be a good idea for me to have a university degree to fall back on should time prove me wrong. He convinced me, so I decided to read law, which I thought would be the easiest. "You are wrong," he said. "If you read law, I cannot help you at all, whereas if you decide to read medicine all the professors at the faculty are friends of mine. They will be kind to you. Leonardo was a great painter because he studied human anatomy. You can still do the same."

So, without further discussion, it was decided I should read medicine, and after the first few days of getting used to the depressing smell of phenol and decomposing flesh so characteristic of the anatomy departments then, I managed to do well in dissection no doubt due to my manual dexterity and artistic facility. My predestination as a surgeon was thus fulfilled.

I was not yet seventeen when the Great War began. For various reasons Spain remained neutral, probably in part due to the fact that Alfonso XIII was pulled both ways—his mother, Maria Cristina, being of Austrian origin, and his wife, Victoria Eugenia, half English. Generally speaking, Spain as a whole was pro-German, but in Catalonia there was a vast consensus of pro-Allied feeling. At home we had a curious situation: my grandfather was a passionate Francophile, whereas my father was inclined towards Germany, though less passionately; perhaps it would be more exact to say he was anti-French. As the war went on, though, he became more and more neutral.

When the Great War broke out my brother Rafel, who was then twelve years old, was starting his "batxillerat". Shortly after, it seemed to be agreed that he would become an engineer. The reason for this decision stemmed from the fact that my father had a client, Josep Barret, owner of a metal-lurgical plant producing munitions for the French army and godfather to my brother. When Sr Barret was later assassin-ated in 1918, shot down by a gang of mercenaries led by an ex-policeman, Bravo Portillo (who was said to be in the pay of a German agent known as Baron von Koenig), the whole course of Rafel's studies was changed. Without the encourage-ment of Sr Barret, Rafel decided that he would rather read medicine.

Bravo Portillo's gang served as the model for other gangs financed by Barcelona industrialists, and their activities resul-ted in more than six years of bloodshed in Catalonia. The unexpected, senseless bombings had stopped in Barcelona, but now people of all classes were being murdered in the same streets, victims of the most primitive instincts, and there seemed no way of stopping it.

The war was a source of great prosperity for Catalonia, which turned out vast quantities of material for the Allies, such as uniforms, boots, leather and steel goods. The fortunes made by Catalan industrialists were unprecedented and were certainly unequalled in the future; however, they were the cause of great social unrest when the workers' demands for a greater share of the profits and an eight-hour working day were turned down. This resulted in a strike, in 1919, of the workers of the Canadian electricity company—La Canadenca. It was during this strike, which threatened to disrupt civil order in the city, that I first heard the name of Salvador Seguí. He was a Catalan workers' leader who was to remain forever inscribed in the history of the Catalan workers' movement, and whom later I was to remember for more personal reasons. I recall the enormous interest which we felt at home when this self-educated militant anarchist confronted thousands of strikers at a meeting in a Barcelona bull-ring and convinced them to return to work. A few weeks later Romà Sol told us how, when he was travelling between Lleida and Barcelona by train in a compartment occupied only by himself and a friend, a tall, robust young man entered their compartment. Romà Sol and his friend continued talking and happened to comment on the personal qualities of leadership of Seguí and the possibility that he might lead the Catalan Syndicate Movement along the same lines as the Labour trades unions in Great Britain, thus turning aside from "anarchic communism". The surprise of both Sol and his friend can be imagined when their travelling companion, on leaving the train at Barcelona, said to them: "I am most grateful for your praises. . . ." It had in fact been Seguí himself. A few years later, the evening of 10 March 1923 to be exact when I was already a fully-qualified doctor working at the Hospital de la Sta Creu, two victims of a shooting were brought in. One of them, already dead, was Seguí.

I have often asked myself what would have happened if Seguí had not been shot, though it is time wasted to speculate on what is irreparable. However, when years later the syndicates came to be controlled by the anarchists, thereby reducing the workers' movement to complete sterility and resulting largely in the developments which culminated in the Civil War, I felt that had Seguí been alive, Spain might perhaps have been spared the cruellest fratricidal war of modern times. When Seguí was assassinated I was already working as a surgeon in the Workers' Accidents Association ("Caixa de Previsió i Socors, Anónima d'Accidents"), and found myself in the middle of the contentious world known to sociologists as capital and labour.

Chapter 5

MEDICAL STUDENT

FOLLOWING THE FAMILY tradition then, when I finished at school it was decided that I was to study medicine. After my unfortunate start in the "batxillerat", I managed to pass all my exams, and in 1916 I was admitted to the Faculty of Medicine in Barcelona together with my friend Josep Cabré. My father gave me a great deal of useful advice, but there was nothing he could say or do to help me overcome my distaste for the autopsy and dissection room when I started studying human anatomy. I had a deep feeling of disgust, sadness and despair at seeing at such close quarters the decomposition of human matter—which was so much at variance with the concept I had formed of the spiritual nature of man. The hours spent dissecting extremities and entrails taught me to understand the truth of the substance of which we are made, dispelling the fog of Utopian idealism to which I inclined, probably because of my artistic sensitivity.

In the course of my second year of medicine, Prat de la Riba died. His death made a profound impression on me. Prat died at the height of his mental capabilities, leaving no successor since he was a statesman, a man who saw his country in the perspective of several decades as did Churchill, for example, whereas even the best of those of his time, reasonably able men, were merely politicians.

Meanwhile, the social situation was steadily deteriorating, with tension and hostility building up from successive strikes and lockouts. In March 1919, following a call for a general strike, a State of War was declared. The sons of the bourgeoisie, armed with rifles and wearing red armbands, patrolled the streets of Barcelona like the "Sometent" (a kind of Vigilantes) of old. Cambó proposed in the Madrid parliament that the two sides should get together and discuss the situation; but on

4 January the first attempt against the life of Salvador Seguí was made. Other union leaders were in fact assassinated, which made discussion between the two sides impossible. On 8 November, General Martinez Anido had been appointed civil governor of Barcelona, and as a result of this appointment no less than twenty-two Barcelona citizens were assassinated in the last three weeks of the month. Anido put into practice the infamous "Ley de Fugas", whereby many detained prisoners were shot "while trying to escape". Hundreds of victims fell in this way until Anido was removed in 1922. In the meantime, on 8 March 1921, the prime minister, Dato, had been murdered in Madrid by three Catalan anarchists.

In the same old university building where future doctors and chemists met each other, as the two careers were studied together, I went on studying with my old friend and colleague Josep Cabré and with other friends we passed our exams, were admitted as medical students and, for the first time, came into contact with anatomy.

During the spring of 1918 and the whole of 1919, an influenza epidemic spread throughout Spain—which gave it its name—and the rest of Europe. It was extraordinarily virulent and frequently—this was of course long before sulphanilamides and antibiotics—turned into bronchial pneumonia. My grandfather Josep, my sister Júlia and I caught it. Theirs turned into pneumonia and my grandfather, nearly eighty years old, died of it. I had a less serious complication, but for a month, just before my examinations, could not attend classes. As there were hundreds of students in my situation, the examinations were postponed until August. I was sent to recuperate at a hotel on Tibidabo, the hill overlooking Barcelona, where I spent several weeks studying. On the day of the exam I overslept and had to run part of the way to the hospital, proof if it were needed that I had fully recovered. My examiner, August Pi i Sunyer, of international repute, asked me several questions, and I remember that he concentrated on the function of the kidneys. I was able to describe enough about renal reabsorption, the power of concentration of urine and the pathology of kidney failure for him to give me a credit, although my knowledge was hardly creditable in my view.

Years later in England, on the occasion of the International

Physiology Congress in 1947 which was held in Oxford, I was exhibiting the studies we had carried out on renal circulation and Pi i Sunyer asked me to tell him and his group all about our research. I was able to remind my ex-examiner of the physiology exam, which caused him no little amusement.

Due to the influenza, my father decided that my sister and I, accompanied by my mother and Rafel, would spend the summer at Castellterçol, a mountain village to which patients were often sent. We had great fun there, and made a full recovery. We met a whole lot of new young people, as well as old friends of our childhood; so much so that we went back again the following year and spent three months there. This was a very important period in my life as it was during this summer that I met Amelia, who was later to become my companion for life.

In 1919 I did my military service. It only lasted three weeks, the minimum time considered necessary to learn the basic elements of military instruction.

That summer, before I was demobilized, I was able to parade in my uniform in Castellterçol. I do not think my arrogance influenced Amelia's decision when I later proposed to her. An amusing anecdote regarding our military service comes to mind. My friend López-Soler, a thin little man, on the day we reported for duty presented himself in his new uniform, but, having forgotten his regulation cap, went on parade wearing a straw hat—a typical boater. When his name was called out the reaction of the training sergeant can be imagined. It was not surprising that López-Soler was immediately despatched to the guard-room, but how he managed to get out as soon as he did we never found out.

It may seem odd that this period of three weeks in military uniform is the only time in my life in which I have had to wear one, considering that altogether I spent almost nine years directly involved in war later. The fact is though that I never wore a uniform again, for which I was thankful.

When I met her, Amelia was nineteen years old, and pretty, without being a striking beauty. She was very vivacious, danced well both the Catalan dance, the Sardana, and the dances in vogue at the time, and we soon became good friends. This liking was fostered by her close friendship with my sister, so that when we returned to Barcelona the relationship continued. It was intensified upon the tragic death of Amelia's mother, leaving her at nineteen in charge of home, an already elderly father and three brothers of whom only one, Guillem, was younger than herself. She had been educated at the French school of the Loreto, where she had learnt French and a lot of *savoir faire*, but not very much about arithmetic. . . .

Step by step our feelings for each other deepened so that I soon came to the conclusion that she was the girl for me, notwithstanding the warning of a friend who knew her and told me "Trueta, you are getting engaged to a very superficial girl". This was because she went to the races, played tennis (and indeed won the championship at the Polo Club in 1919) and, in short, had been educated in the way girls of the Barcelona bourgeoisie of those days were brought up. I told my solicitous friend that I knew her well, that I did not know if he was right or wrong but that I was certain the raw material was excellent and that I did not think it would be difficult to remove this "superficiality". In the course of more than fifty years that we have lived together I must say, at the end, that I was not able to remove it altogether; but this must have been a favourable factor since, with my rather introvert character, Amelia's ability to win people's sympathy has been a great help to me in my life. Maybe if she had been a bit more timid I would not have made the same progress in my career as I am at heart rather an unsociable person.

I proposed to Amelia and was accepted in a cinema in 1920. I still had two years to go before qualifying, and together with two friends decided to make a real effort to try and do the two years in one.

We used to study in my home, where we were joined by a cousin of mine who divided his time between reading chemistry and finishing off my father's cigars. We worked very hard indeed, so that by 1921, instead of 1922, we were all three doctors. I had previously discussed with my father where it would be best for me to do my clinical training and with an immature sense of reality had told him that, as I wanted to be a surgeon, I supposed the best course was to enter the surgical department. My father however considered this would be time wasted, as lancing and suturing would not be difficult for me to learn. He also pointed out that if I went straight on to surgical techniques, I would lack a clinical formation. His suggestion was that I should enter the internal medicine department, where it so happened that Dr Ferrer, the best possible expert in symptomatology and diagnosis, taught. As so often happened in my life, my father's better judgment convinced me.

As my fellow-students were all going in for internal medicine I joined their group and we were all admitted, first as provisional and later as regular interns, until we were fully qualified. This allowed me three years, between 1918 and 1921, in the department of Ferrer, learning how to interpret a cardiac puff or a pleural friction, something which I would never have learnt if I had started to cut and sew while training. This formation under Ferrer has been of the greatest benefit to me. It has allowed me to study patients as if I were an internist, one who could operate if necessary. Ferrer was a splendid teacher. I do not know what he thought of me, as he knew I wanted to be a surgeon. I think at heart he thought to himself: "It is good that he should have clinical knowledge, but perhaps he doesn't need so much."

When I finished studying medicine in 1921, a place as a surgical trainee was already waiting for me. My father used to send patients requiring surgery to Dr Corachan, still a young man of about forty then, who already stood out as one of the two or three leading surgeons of Barcelona. In 1921 he was appointed Director of Surgery at the Hospital de la Sta Creu and my father asked him to keep a place for me. So as soon as I finished my studies I went to Corachan, who really taught me how to use a scalpel, how to treat patients, how to suture a wound and generally how to heal.

Apart from studying, I found time for other interests. My friend Alfred Rocha was already in those days a good violinist and, although I had scant knowledge of music reading and the piano, having only studied two years of each, I have always had a great love of music. As students we used to go to the opera house in Barcelona, the Liceu, whenever they had Wagner or French operas, and on a particularly memorable occasion, for the first performance of Charpentier's *Louise*. Being short of money, we used to queue early in the morning to get a ticket of admittance to the gallery, then return in the afternoon and climb the stairs to the "gods" on the fifth floor to claim seats. My athletic preparation and the length of my legs made it possible for me to arrive there among the first and get a good seat which I shared with Rocha. In this way we also both saw *Parsifal* for the first time.

I must have inherited my love of opera from my father, who was passionately fond of the bel canto. Early on in his life, in order to get together the one peseta for his ticket, he frequently had had to borrow ten centimos from the necessary number of friends. This lasted until he was appointed a member of the "claque" and eventually attained the post of one of their cheer-leaders. He had a good tenor voice, and could sing whole arias from *Lohengrin*, although in Italian, his better efforts mainly coming from the bathroom.

When we finally finished our studies in 1921, we had to go to Madrid to be examined in four subjects before we could each present our doctoral thesis. Our plan was to prepare ourselves calmly—perhaps too calmly—in Barcelona and then go to Madrid in the spring, three or four months before the exams. We were not yet able to pay our own expenses, and we all depended on financial help from our families. Needless to say, this system precluded the students of more modest classes from getting their doctorates, which some thought of as only of academic value. Every Spanish graduate in medicine can call himself a doctor whether or not he has submitted a thesis.

Amelia arranged to go on a long trip to Italy with her father while I was in Madrid. With Corachan's permission some other graduates and I left for Madrid where we stayed in a tumble-down old palace of a boarding house in the centre of town. At the entrance of the boarding house there was an enormous, almost life-size photograph of a very stern, condescending-looking gentleman, in tails, at the foot of which there was a large "YO". We immediately christened the pension "Chez Yo", which was all wrong as Yo was merely the name of the photographer. The rooms were enormous, with very high ceilings; the floors were uneven and the door which separated our room from our neighbour's had a space of some two inches at floor level through which the light poured in. We soon discovered that our neighbours were two pretty teenage girls, and, without giving it a second thought, we took down the mirror from the bathroom wall and placed it at an angle of about forty-five degrees against their door in such a way that we could have a comfortable lesson in comparative anatomy when the two innocent girls undressed. The only problem was that the mirror was not wide enough for more than two of us to admire the view at one time and we were five! The whole affair was more in keeping with fifteen-year-olds than aspiring doctors.

We spent the first few days getting to know our way around Madrid. It did not take us long to decide on our favourite haunts: the Prado Museum, to which I was drawn by my old love of painting, and the two large parks. Sometimes we would study in one or other of the parks, one of us reading aloud while the others listened, and, if we were sitting, I would get a stick and trace on the sandy paths the chemical formulae which the reader was talking about. Needless to say we were soon conversant with the cheapest "tascas" or small bars, and the towns around Madrid.

We decided to spend a night in Toledo and as our visit coincided with a full moon, we waited until night-time before walking around the old city.

Although during the day we had covered a lot of ground in visiting El Greco's house, the cathedral and other treasures, scarcely ten minutes after starting out at night we lost ourselves completely. The worst of it was that there was no one about to ask for directions, and we seemed to be going round in circles. Eventually a man of peasant appearance turned up. He looked at us in some alarm; it was well after midnight and all that could be heard was the regular toll of bells in the distance. The man followed us for a time, and, realizing that we were lost, offered to help us. We told him we were students marvelling at the beauty, silence and contrasts of light and shadow of night-time Toledo, but that we now found ourselves unable to get back to our hotel. In the most natural way—probably he was happy to come across some Catalans so obviously impressed by seeing Toledo by moonlight—he offered to take us back to our hotel, but not before we had seen more of the golden marvels of an historic city which had been the centre of a Gothic empire more than a thousand years ago, and was now shown to us not as a dead city but rather one asleep. We wandered around until nearly daylight. When our new-found friend took us to our hotel he made it plain he would not welcome any recompense; the mere movement of a hand to one's wallet made him draw back with such dignity that we realized at once that we would be insulting him if we insisted. We shook hands and said good-bye for ever. He could not possibly realize that we would never forget him and from that day this kind, humble Toledano symbolized for us the character of the quiet, obliging, dignified Castilian, who has so little in common with the arrogant grandiose chatter-boxes, their heads full of abstract ideas about the grandeur of Castile. The paradox is that the real period of Castilian splendour—the Golden Age of its literature—was no longer the era of grandeur but of decadence.

We also visited the Escorial, and there we were able to sense acutely the spirit of confinement which dominated the soul of Philip II, who not only introduced into Castile the pointed slate roofs common in northern Europe at that time, but blended these into an exaggerated Castilian austerity. The result suggests a fear of the outside world, as if he were trying to isolate himself from it with granite blocks. What impressed me most was the immensity of the building inside which Philip moved about as though in another world. It is not surprising therefore that a naval operation of great complexity such as the one aimed at the invasion of England—the Invincible Armada —went on the rocks and foundered, and that control of the seas passed for ever from Spain to England and Holland. This isolation, together with the distance of Madrid from the sea, the only means of communication with the empire, begins to explain why the expedition was planned so superficially and why the command of the Armada was placed, at least officially, in the hands of the Duke of Medina Sidonia, who it appears suffered severely from seasickness. Alvaro de Bazán, a good sailor, must have gone through a great deal to try and save what he could of this great maritime adventure, from which the beginning of Spanish decadence can be said to date.

When we went to the country we were impressed by the immense plain of La Mancha and the poverty of the villages we saw, notwithstanding their proximity to Madrid. Having seen the Escorial partly explained this because it seemed obvious that those inside the enormous cloister could not be aware of what went on outside, not even if it happened within view of the topmost towers of the Escorial.

On returning from Toledo, with our spirits satiated with history and moonlight, I wrote such a romantic loving letter to Amelia, who was with her father somewhere between Milan and Venice, that she kept it for many years. When I re-read it some years later I was convinced that it had been influenced as much by the shining light on the golden stones of the old city as by my profound love for Amelia.

Eventually the time came for our examinations and I passed them more or less successfully. Whereas in chemical analysis and urology my results were only sufficient for a pass, I got good marks in parasitology and history of medicine. On 3 June we finished our exams and with them our stay in Madrid, always to be a valuable experience while Madrid still remained a small city full of grace and ingenuousness.

Fifty years later, on visiting Madrid where I now have family living, with its chaotic traffic, pollution and noise, I remember with nostalgia the welcoming city of my youth, where time went by unhurriedly and life began late in the mornings.

When the time came for me to consider getting married—I was beginning to earn my living as a surgeon—Corachan helped me by appointing me as a "finger-healer", with a fixed salary of Ptas.250, (about £10) per month, at the Caixa de Previsió i Socors—the Italian workers' accident insurance company established in Spain very successfully with its headquarters in Barcelona. I used to go two hours every day to attend to cut fingers and wounds which did not require inpatient treatment. They had a contract with the Remei Clinic, a newly formed nursing home looked after by the St Josep nuns, if any worker required to be admitted to hospital. The nuns at the Remei Clinic were to play an important part in my life. Thus it was that shortly after I started to work with Corachan, he initiated me in the treatment of wounds and complaints of the bones and joints, a speciality which in other countries is called orthopaedics. Slowly, I went on preparing myself and specializing in the surgery of the skeleton.

In connection with my work there, I remember a case which

reflects the state of anxiety which gripped the city in those days of street murders. A Catalan worker came one day with a wound on his hand. It gave the impression of being a blister rather than a recent wound—I was a bit perplexed. I tended the wound, and he left after thanking me politely. He came for several days and I noticed that, notwithstanding my treatment, the wound did not heal. I started to suspect that he was tampering with it to prevent it from healing; malingering was nothing new. I therefore put on a plaster cast covering the whole hand—but even so, when it was removed, the wound was still unhealed. At a loss to know what to do, I told him I would have to keep him in hospital under observation. As several days passed without him putting in an appearance, I told the almoner that this particular patient was not coming for treatment any more. I was surprised several days later to see him waiting in my private consulting rooms. He said to me: "Doctor, I have come to thank you for not letting the insurance company know immediately that I had stopped coming. My name is not what I told you, and, as you suspected, I have been tampering with my wound. My name is Riera. I have been warned that I am on the list of those to whom the 'Ley de Fugas' is to be applied and so I swapped places with a friend of mine who hurt his hand, and he lent me his papers so I can get around. If you had told the company that I was interfering with my wound, they would have found out I was not the person I was pretending to be and I would not be here now. So I have come to thank you and to tell you that this evening I am leaving for France and I am not coming back until order is restored in this country." I asked him why he was confiding all this to me while there was still time to call the police. "I know you would not do that." He went on to say that there had been around 800 murders committed of which a detailed report had been made and a copy of which was in the hands of a public notary in Paris. One day all this was going to be published, he said, and then the world would know the horror of the years during which Martinez Anido had held office as civil governor. I must say that, so many years later, I have never seen these records published. I do not know if the information has somehow vanished or whether the time has not yet come for it to be published.

On 13 September 1923, Primo de Rivera triggered off his coup d'état in Barcelona, where he was captain-general. It was another instance of how Barcelona, rather than Madrid, still motivated Spanish politics. Primo de Rivera promised that the aim of the coup was to establish a lasting peace in Spain, based on recognition of regional rights. It was a promise which the dictator forgot as soon as he arrived in Madrid.

Some people think Primo de Rivera was a man of good faith, and that he even felt a certain sympathy towards things Catalan, since, when he left Barcelona, he did not seem to have had it in mind to start a systematic persecution of everything essentially Catalan. Notwithstanding his good intentions, if he had them, no sooner had he arrived in Madrid than two decrees were issued—one against our language and the other against our flag. The flag of the kings of Aragon which had flown over so much of the Mediterranean was from then on forbidden in Catalonia. The reason for this sudden *volte face* has never been fully explained. My personal opinion is that it was due to King Alfonso XIII.

The king was an intelligent man, well endowed by nature, who had suffered the misfortune of having been born after the death of his father. His mother, Maria Cristina, an able queen regent, brought up her son in the Teutonic mould, educated from birth in the royal palace in Madrid and surrounded by no one but servants. From them he derived his concept of the people: submissive, friendly, whom it was best to patronize, but who were destined never to rise to a category superior to the one in which they found themselves. He had no sympathy or understanding of the Catalan cause. An indication of this is that having promised, on his first visit to Barcelona in 1904, to return speaking Catalan, he regrettably never fulfilled his promise and died without having made the effort to learn a word of it.

Cambó, the famous Catalan politician, has acknowledged this by writing that this one sole action by the king might have successfully suppressed the assimilitative instincts of the Castilian race: "Just think how resistance would have disappeared, how many bridges would have been thrown up over the chasm if the king had but kept his word, given in 1904, and come back to Catalonia speaking Catalan. The most prickly issue, the

seemingly insuperable obstacle would have simply vanished."
There are three other reasons why I believe that Alfonso XIII
directly influenced Primo de Rivera's change of attitude.

Towards 1927, Corachan was offered the direction of the
Sabadell Workers' Accident Association. Not having time to go
every week, he sent me to act as his assistant and later on as
head in my own right. One day, one of the foremen of a textile
factory came to say good-bye to me as he and some others were
going to Seville where the government was establishing textile
factories in competition with the Catalan centres of production,
Terrassa and Sabadell. Less than two years later he was back
in Sabadell. "Are you on holiday?" I asked him. "No," he
said, "I have come back for good." He told me the attempt
had been a complete failure. They had not been able to do
anything as no one there seemed to realize that work meant
regular hours. He was never going back there again. It would
not surprise me if the decision to divert to Seville part at least
of the textile industry of Catalonia was inspired by Alfonso
XIII.

This conviction was later confirmed in Oxford. Through my
friendship with Lord Nuffield, I learned that in 1926 he had
wanted to build a Morris car factory in Barcelona, with the
idea of taking advantage of the preferential trade agreement
which Spain enjoyed with South America. Nuffield sent
technicians to Spain who prepared a report for him. Their
findings recommended that the factory should be built in
Barcelona because, apart from its large port, it was already an
important industrial city and was producing in particular a
car of the category and international fame of the Hispano-
Suiza.

The report was submitted to the Spanish government, who
returned it saying that it would be willing to support the
setting up of the factory in Guadalajara (some twenty-five miles
east of Madrid) but not in Barcelona. Primo de Rivera had
already ordered the transfer to Guadalajara of the assembly of
army lorries which up to then had been carried out at
Hispano-Suiza in Barcelona. The English studied the counter
proposal and decided that the project was no longer a feasible
proposition, Guadalajara being too far from the ports through
which unassembled units would have to be imported and the

assembled cars exported to South America. Nuffield offered the necessary funds to establish a chair of Hispanic Studies at Oxford, to bear the name of Alfonso XIII, and even went to see the king in Madrid but to no avail. Nuffield told me personally that although he brought up the subject of the car factory, the king was adamant that it should not be in Barcelona.

The third reason for my contention derives from a visit by the king to Catalonia in 1924 where, in front of 1,100 mayors from all over Catalonia, he said: "There are no conquerors or conquered in Spain in the work of national unity. There have however been fights for ideals and interests which may have left painful impressions behind, as also painful measures . . . which governments have been obliged to take. And the memory of some of them, such as those taken by my ancestor Philip V, have been maliciously distorted, totally overlooking the fact that they were adopted for the good of Catalonia, indeed to save Catalonia."

I ask myself, why did he have to mention Philip V, who took away all our liberties? What did Philip V save us from? Was King Alfonso trying to make excuses on behalf of his ancestor? Personally I think it was meant rather as a deliberate reminder of what had happened before and could happen again.

Primo de Rivera's dictatorship was established to cover up an error of the king in ordering direct intervention in Africa, a move which resulted in the annihilation of General Santiago and his army in a badly prepared attack against the natives. This defeat had a resounding reaction in Spain as the question on everyone's lips was how such an attack could have been launched without due preparation. There was an impression that the king had personally ordered General Santiago to attack and to finish with the Rif resistance at all costs. The popular outcry reached such extremes that the matter was brought before parliament, which appointed a committee to investigate the affair. Significantly, the coup d'état took place before the findings of the committee could be published.

Chapter 6

MY MARRIAGE

AMELIA AND I were married on 29 December 1923. My father-in-law lent us a flat to live in at a house he owned in the centre. There I opened my consulting rooms, although I still shared my father's with him.

Instead of having a large reception, my father-in-law gave us the money it would have cost him, which did not please my traditionalist father at all. We started our honeymoon, however, a day late as we missed our train. We hoped this embarrassing situation had gone unobserved and took a taxi back to our new home. However, next day when I ordered some food to be sent up from a near-by restaurant we were thoroughly discomfited to find that the waiter who served us our lunch was Amelia's youngest brother, Guillem, in disguise!

Twenty-four hours late, then, we set off on the "grand tour" of Italy, Switzerland, Germany, Belgium and France. In particular I shall never forget our standing together in the central square of snow-covered Bruges on a January morning, under the vast bell tower with the carillon in full peal, the sound somewhat muffled by the cold. As our money was running out we had to leave the rest of the world for another time and, after spending four or five days in Paris, got back to Barcelona with twenty-five pesetas between us. This must have presaged later journeys we were to make, often further afield, with not much more in our pockets.

On returning from our honeymoon I went back to work at the Hospital de la Sta Creu in Dr Corachan's department. I was put in charge of the ward in which patients contributed financially as far as they could. There was a small single room where we used to place gravely ill patients or anyone requiring special attention. It was in this small room that the brilliant, if controversial, architect Gaudí died in 1926. Gaudí was run over by a tram and, unidentified, was taken directly to the emergency ward. When my assistant arrived at the hospital just before 8 am, Gaudí was already being operated on. I arrived a few minutes later when he had already been identified. It was then decided to move him to the small single room as many visitors enquiring after him were starting to arrive. Gaudí died three days later without having regained consciousness.

The burial of the great architect was the signal for a manifestation of popular grief. He was an extremely religious man and I am sure would have been quite happy to know that he died within the walls which for 500 years had been the hospital of the poor of the city. Notwithstanding its age, the hospital impressed such an acute observer as Joseph Townsend who, in his book *A Journey through Spain in the years 1786 and 1787* (Dublin, 1792, p. 85) wrote: "No hospital that I have seen upon the continent is so well administered as the general hospital of this city. It is peculiar in its attention to convalescents, for whom a separate habitation is provided, that after they are dismissed . . . they may have time to recruit their strength, before they are turned out to endure their accustomed hardships. . . . Nothing can be more useful, nothing more humane, than this appendage."

My routine was established for me by Dr Corachan, an early-riser and a very punctual man, strict but extremely humane. From 1921 on, when I started working in his department, Corachan put me in charge of the treatment of the locomotive system. There was still no separate department of orthopaedics, although there was one for traumatology. By 1928 my experience of this type of injury was already considerable, and among the patients I had under my care were those with chronic osteomyelitis, or persistent bone infection, which took up a great deal of hospital beds.

In 1924 an article had been published by an American doctor, Winnett Orr, of Nebraska, recommending a new technique which enabled the patient to make an earlier recovery. The method consisted in making a large incision directly over the infected bone in places appropriate for the drainage of pus, packing the wound with gauze soaked in

vaseline or paraffin, and finally—and this was the revolutionary
feature of the treatment—Winnett Orr recommended covering
the wound and the two joints above and below the affected
part with a plaster of Paris cast. This technique immobilized
the infected zone, thus localizing the infection and at the same
time permitting the pus to drain outwards. Its disadvantage
was that the plaster cast soon stank unbearably from contamination and consequently the technique could only be
used in cases of chronic infection. The results, though, were far
superior to those of the common treatment of the time which
involved the use of antiseptics, especially Dakin's, whereby
with each change of dressing new entries were opened up for
the penetration and diffusion of toxic germs. This meant a long
drawn-out treatment, not to mention much suffering for the
patient.

Towards the end of 1929, and after having treated a considerable number of osteomyelitis cases in this way, I decided
by simple reasoning that if this method of treating chronically
infected bones nearly always worked there was no reason why
it should not be successful as a preventive treatment of infection in recent open wounds; that is to say, applying the plaster
treatment to wounds before they became infected, bearing in
mind that there is always an interval between contamination
and infection, its length depending on the ease or difficulty
which the germs encounter in creating invading colonies. This
reasoning was made viable by the fact that by then I was well
aware of the importance that dead tissue and "dead bodies"
have as sources of bacterial cultures within wounds. I was also
aware that the benefit of excising tissue which had come into
contact with the exterior and was therefore contaminated,
although otherwise healthy, had already been proved in World
War I, often for incorrect reasons. This is why it was common
for the surgeon to remove the minimum amount of contaminated tissue, avoiding the enlargement of the wound for fear of
further increasing the contaminated part. This erroneous
concept was widely accepted after the German surgeon P. L.
Friedrich published an experimental work in 1897, from which
stemmed belief in its supposed advantages over the elimination
of contaminated tissue in the avoidance of infection. The concept
is erroneous because the surgeon's concentration is distracted

from the most important issue: i.e. the state of vitality of the
wounded tissue.

My own idea was that infection would not take place at all
if all the dead tissue and matter which served as germ culture
were eliminated. In tissue devitalized as a result of impaired
blood circulation infection is produced systematically, whereas
if the tissue is merely contaminated infection does not occur
provided the right treatment is carried out. Therefore, the
important thing was to stop fearing contamination—which in
any case is always present in all open wounds—and concentrate
instead on exploring and cleaning the wound with scissors,
after having opened it up with a scalpel, according to the
gravity of the wounds.

In peace time, if a wound is well operated on within six hours
of the accident, and if the muscular tissue is not excessively
damaged, it can be sutured subject to three reservations: that
the patient remain under the direct charge of the surgeon who
has performed the operation; that the suture does not result
in any constriction that might diminish the local circulation
and thus facilitate infection; and lastly, that the wound can be
inspected frequently. In war surgery, these conditions for
suturing the skin hardly ever exist, and the dangers are too
great for the risk to be taken. When the wound is left open,
even if the operation has been performed within six hours, it
must be drained so that it remains free from blood and lymph—
not through gravity, as Orr recommended for the draining of
pus in chronic bone infections, but by the absorbent action of
thick-meshed dry gauze packed in every corner of the wound.
Before the operation, the wound and the surrounding skin are
thoroughly scrubbed using soap, water and a nail brush. After
complete excision and drainage, a plaster of Paris cast is
applied for immobilization purposes. This last stage is really
the only point of resemblance with Winnett Orr's method, as
he repudiated the practice of excision believing it to be
dangerous.

My having complete responsibility for the treatment of injured
factory workers and road casualties at the Remei Clinic, where
insured patients were interned, allowed me to experiment on
the possible difficulties and dangers of the treatment. I doubt if

I would ever have tried it out if I had only had hospital patients under my care, even under the enterprising guidance of Corachan, who was always ready to try new things. At last, one day in 1929 I had my chance. Amelia and I were in a box at the Liceu Opera House when our maid came from home to tell me that I was required urgently at the Remei Clinic where a patient had been brought in with a badly mangled hand which he had caught in a gear mesh. My wife insisted on accompanying me to the clinic and, perhaps stimulated by her moral support, I decided to try the complete method, suturing the wound for aesthetic reasons and finally encasing the arm in plaster halfway up to his shoulder. The hand and arm were kept elevated in bed. Next day the patient's state was very satisfactory, and a most encouraging sign was that he was totally free from pain. The progress of the patient was completely normal, which prompted me to treat more and more serious cases in the same way.

In the course of the years, the number of patients attending the Workers' Insurance Association increased greatly, and I usually only saw the more serious cases. In 1933 the Italian Insurance Company opened up a branch in Madrid and I was asked to recommend a surgeon to take charge of it. I recommended d'Harcourt, a military surgeon I knew well, and he came to Barcelona to see how the association was run and attended many operations in which I was using my new method. In October 1934, the violent armed rebellion of miners took place in Asturias and casualties were transported to the Military Hospital where d'Harcourt and his teacher, Bastos, worked.

I thought this would be a good opportunity for them to try out my new method, and wrote to d'Harcourt. Unfortunately he told me that, as he was not the head of the hospital, he was afraid of the possible complications which might arise under the plaster casts in recent shot wounds. Bastos himself was refusing to cover wounds with plaster until, at the earliest, twenty days after they had been inflicted. This attitude, which Bastos continued to defend in a book on war wounds published in 1936, was so inflexibly maintained that when, two years later the Civil War broke out and thousands of casualties had to be treated, there was no way in which the Republican military

3

authorities could be persuaded to depart from it. It was not until d'Harcourt became head army surgeon in Barcelona in 1937 that my method was put into practice on casualties from the Republican assault on Teruel, where d'Harcourt and his assistants treated some one hundred casualties in strict accordance with my five points. On returning to Barcelona my friend told me how satisfied he had been with the results.

Meanwhile, my progress in the years preceding the Civil War had been very satisfactory. At the hospital I was learning more and more from Corachan's wonderful technique and acquiring the experience of a long series of cases.

Two of these stand out most in my memory. A young boy of nineteen from a small Andalusian village was brought to my department one day suffering from Pott's disease, or tuberculosis of the spine. When I made out his clinical history he told me he was one of nine brothers and sisters, two of whom had died in infancy, probably due to tubercular meningitis. Asked about the conditions of life in his family, he told me that his parents were poor peasants and that very often their meal consisted in sitting round a string, suspended from the ceiling, at the end of which hung a grilled sardine. Each of them had a piece of bread which they ate while rubbing their lips against the sardine, without biting it, so as to give some flavour to the bread. Apart from the meagre nutritive value of this diet, the infection which one tubercular child passed to another was obvious. In the comfort of Barcelona, notwithstanding the disorders of the times, it seemed to me incomprehensible how a few miles south of Valencia, where people ate well—and often too much—there could be those who starved to death unnoticed.

The other case history concerns a corporal in the Civil Guard who had a stomach ulcer on which Corachan was to operate on the following day. I was told the evening before by one of the housemen that the corporal wanted to see me before I went home. When I visited him in his room he asked me to close the door and, with a shifty shamefaced look, he told me he wanted to confess as he felt he might die as a result of the operation and asked me to bring him a priest. He said the matter was urgent as he did not want to die with a guilty conscience. It appeared that for much of his life he had been leader of a Civil Guard platoon stationed on the immense estate of an aristocratic landowner in western Andalusia and had been obliged to beat women whom they caught on winter nights looking for firewood in the woods. In self-justification he told me: "I was only obeying orders from my superiors, but it was clear that if we had not stopped them from taking wood, which did not belong to them, there would have been no end to their wanting more important things, such as the house itself and the land." Before the priest came, he added: "I do not want to die without being pardoned for the pain I caused so many poor and cold women." I am happy to say he survived the operation.

These two anecdotes of life in southern Spain will show why I came to understand the reason that so many Andalusian peasants came to Catalonia as soon as they could and never wished to return to their birthplace.

It seems to me that I have dedicated more space to the disturbing factors of the life of my city than to the manifestations of the vigour which abounded there. There were plays, in both Catalan and Castilian, books in both languages, concerts, opera, exhibitions, academic and professional courses and in 1929 the International Exhibition which the Spanish royal family came to visit. It was a symbolic appearance which was in effect the farewell to Barcelona of Alfonso XIII, that monarch of faulty judgment, who had all the makings of a good king but who brought down the monarchy because of his obstinate determination to play the great statesman, antagonizing all the able politicians he had at his disposal, and whose policies he often blatantly obstructed. Meanwhile, the city expanded inexorably in open competition with Madrid which was certainly not disdaining the challenge.

While I was still studying, my time was occupied by too many things. My medical studies which took up most of my time eventually had to give way to my passion for sport, to the extent that I not only took part in swimming, football, athletics, tennis and skiing but also helped to organize some of these sports. In 1922 I was made vice-president of the Catalan Athletics Federation. I also wrote a regular column on swimming in a sports weekly. We had started some years before the Athletic Club of Catalonia, which had facilities for a full range of track and field events. I excelled in none of these sports being rather a jack of all trades, master of none, but they enabled me to lay the foundations for the good health which has never failed me in seventy-five years. Eventually I have come to limit my activities to swimming and tennis, the latter only intermittently.

With the passage of time and as a result of my studies I have learnt that one of the great dangers accompanying the improvement of living standards in modern life is the growing disuse of our legs: by using lifts instead of stairs and riding in cars when we could just as well walk, modern man denies his heart the help of the muscular contractions of his limbs. The consequent formation of varicose veins and resultant venous dilatation directly cause overloading and eventual failure of the heart. Walking has almost entirely replaced sport for me, and I must say that despite long periods of worry and stress in my life I have always been able to sleep without sleeping pills and to enjoy meals without digestive aids. Once again I am grateful to my father for stimulating in me a love of sport. Among other things it developed in me a competitive spirit and at the same time taught me to be a good loser, qualities which I found very much alive years later in Britain.

I remember with great pleasure the swimming races Lord Selwyn-Lloyd and I had, much later, when we used to spend our summer holidays from the middle Fifties onwards at the Costa Brava Hotel and later at the beautiful Hostal de la Gavina at S'Agaró. The course we took depended upon wind and currents, and we were always accompanied by my beloved niece Carmona who used to follow us in a boat manned by a tough fisherman and with a bottle of cognac aboard, just in case we had to be fished out of the water. Carmona used to tell me that everyone knew what we were doing when either of us stopped swimming, now and then. . . . We always finished the races without any help, the last being I think in 1958, when I was already over sixty years old. I have always maintained the closest friendship with Selwyn, for whom I have a sincere admiration as being a great British statesman who held the highest posts in his country except that of prime minister.

Chapter 7

FAMILY LIFE—POLITICS IN CATALONIA

WHEN WE MOVED to a new home in 1926, we thought that we would never wish to move from there as, apart from its splendid situation, the flat could accommodate my consulting rooms as well as house children and domestic staff comfortably. In 1924 we bought our first car—a two seater Peugeot in which the gear change was like that of a motorcycle. This may explain how I managed to drive it to Barcelona from the French frontier although I had never driven a car before; I had however done a lot of miles sitting next to my brother-in-law Lluis, a great expert at the wheel. We were managing quite comfortably on my income from insurance and private patients. Our first daughter, Meli, who was born in our first home nine months after our wedding, was followed by a boy, whom we christened Rafel after my father; he was fair-haired and soon proved himself to be bright and intelligent. We considered ourselves very lucky.

In 1929 the old Hospital de la Sta Creu was moved to new buildings and became known as the Hospital de la Sta Creu i de St Pau. The old hospital, originally built in 1401 as the General Hospital of Catalonia, was then turned into a national monument in which were lodged the Biblioteca (Library) de Catalunya and the Institut d'Estudis Catalans. In that old hospital I had carried out my first scientific research when in 1926 Corachan instructed me to study the artificial production of joints in dogs—for instance half way up the thigh bone. Although this investigation was interesting, it never got published except as a small note in the hospital's own magazine. For me it was like a revelation as it enabled me to experience the excitement which the finding of new data in the scientific world produces.

I still worked at the Accident Insurance Company, and the

most common complaint I came across at the time of the building of the International Exhibition was lumbago or, as patients called it, kidney ache. The majority of the workers were new arrivals from Murcia. Working with pick-axes and shovels soon gave them back aches and they sought medical attention and sick pay. The number of those on sick leave rose to such heights that the insurance company was faced with ruin. It is not easy to make a diagnosis of a disorder in which only pain is present; for the most part, unjustly, it was believed in many cases that workers preferred living on two-thirds of their wages, i.e. on standard sick pay, rather than earning the full amount by working.

Shortly after the closure of the International Exhibition came the economic collapse on Wall Street, sweeping away in its train the remnants of the optimism that the great nations had felt on the defeat of the Austro-German empire. The king soon sent Primo de Rivera packing.

As a result of an amnesty granted by the new government which followed, the news spread that the great Catalan patriot Francesc Macià, then in exile, was coming back to Catalonia. A friend of mine who knew of my family's friendship with Macià in my youth, asked me to join the caravan of cars that would meet the train bringing Macià to a station some miles outside Barcelona. He was coming back a famous man partly due to his having been tried by the French authorities following a frustrated attempt at "invading" Catalonia from the French side. I gave a lift in my car to Josep Tarradellas, then the president of a Catalanist society in Barcelona.

About 200 cars must have gathered at the station where Macià, who was to become the first President of the Generali-tat, or Catalan Autonomous Government, set foot in Catalonia again. I was given his suitcase to carry to the car, and we started off towards Barcelona by the coast road, along which we witnessed unforgettable scenes. Whole villages en masse, with the elders at the head, stopped Macià's car, kissed his hands and freely gave vent to their emotions, laughing and crying at the same time. All the way to Barcelona we saw the most spontaneous, touching manifestations of support that any political machine could ever dream of. I had no doubt then that this old man, who years before had torn off his military badges as an officer of the Spanish army, was from this moment the head of Catalonia.

On 13 April 1931, municipal elections were held and throughout Spain, and particularly in the larger cities, the republican parties won. These were the first elections held in the country after eight years of authoritarian rule under Primo de Rivera. At 11 am on 14 April, the head of the Catalan party Esquerra Republicana,* Lluis Companys, appeared on the balcony of the Barcelona Town Hall and, unopposed, proclaimed the republic. The news spread like wildfire through the city. My father and I went to the Town Hall Square, which was already full of excited people. At around 3 pm Macià appeared and from the building opposite the Town Hall, the Generalitat proclaimed the Catalan republic, raising the Catalan flag on the balcony to the accompaniment of a storm of cheering from all those in the square.

In Madrid, meanwhile, the Republicans were still in doubt as to what to do, and it was not until 7 pm that Macià heard that the king was leaving.

It has always seemed to me that one of the factors which motivated the king's decision to leave Spain was the proclaiming of the Basque and Catalan republics. Thereafter, the main thing for him was to restore the political unity of Spain. Once this was accomplished the restoration of the monarchy would follow. If there is any doubt on this point, one only has to remember General Sanjurjo's anti-Republican rising in 1932 in Andalusia—at the very moment when the Catalan Statute of Autonomy was about to be debated in parliament.

Apart from the proclamation of the republic and the fact that, eight years after being appointed his assistant by Corachan, I was nominated consultant at the hospital, the year 1931 was also significant for me because of other personal experiences. The post of Director of Surgery at the Hospital de St Pau became vacant and Corachan insisted that I apply, even though it was a general surgery appointment. I was not elected, the post very rightly going to an older, more experienced surgeon. I was *proxime accessit* though, which obviously enhanced my chances of appointment to a future directorship. My father was terribly disappointed, as if he had a

* Literally, Republican Left.

premonition that he was not to see me elected to the post which he had always dreamt I would one day occupy.

A blow of incalculably greater impact on me in that year was the loss of our little son Rafel, who died from acute pneumonia, developed from a cold caught while playing in some woods near Barcelona. After nearly half a century the memory of the death of our son is for Amelia and myself still like a wound which will not heal. This tragedy did not come alone since my father, for whom his grandson was the apple of his eye, died of a heart attack three months later.

In the space of a few months, then, I lost my son and my father. The possibility of passing on those things which every young father dreams of for his son had disappeared forever. I firmly believe that my later efforts to promote and guide the professional formation of the young in Barcelona, Oxford and elsewhere have largely been due to the effect my son's death had on me.

My father's death united the family more firmly around my mother, with whom my brother Rafel lived. He was well on the way then to becoming an ear-nose-and-throat specialist. I missed the wise counsel of my father even though, thanks to him, I was now capable of making decisions for myself which fortunately were generally on the right lines. I had inherited from him a passion for reading and work, and also a great love of family life. Like him, I supported that which appeared to me to be noble and generous and I tended to be inflexible when I thought, sometimes wrongly, that justice was not being served—not always an easy thing to assess— an emotion which has too often upset my life. Perhaps with the years I have learned to control myself and not give rein to my instinct to speak out in protest, even though, in my old age, in my innermost self I still heed the cry which in my father's case would have led to an open manifestation of dissent. It is to my mother that I owe this restraint; she was so unlike my father in this respect.

I remember on one occasion my father was called out by a family he had known for many years to a case of acute appendicitis requiring an immediate operation. With the agreement of the patient's relatives, he sent a note to the surgeon whose services he used in those days pointing out the urgency of the case. The next day my father was surprised to find out that the operation had been performed by another surgeon. On enquiring what had happened, he was told that a neighbour had insisted on calling her own surgeon, who, when he came, was told that my father, the patient's physician, had summoned another surgeon of his choice. The newly arrived surgeon nevertheless insisted that not a minute must be lost and abducted the patient to his own nursing home. A few days later, having received no excuse or explanation from this surgeon, my father sent him a note saying: "My distinguished colleague: to be hungry is physiological, but even the most elementary rules of politeness teach one how to behave at table." Years later, when he was already a distinguished surgeon and working, like me, at the Hospital de St Pau, the surgeon in question showed me my father's card saying: "A pity he was so intransigent, because your father was a great man."

In March 1932 we had a second daughter to whom we gave the name Montserrat and in July 1934 a third, whom we named Júlia, after my Secchi grandmother and my sister Júlia, whom we asked to be godmother. The hoped for boy did not come and the Civil War two years later finished forever my hopes of having a son to follow after me.

Following the International Society of Surgery's Congress in Madrid in 1932, which I went to with Corachan, who had two of us pupils made members of the society, several of those attending from abroad returned home via Barcelona to watch a demonstration of a gastrectomy by Corachan who, as a result, was invited to perform the operation in several European cities, starting with Turin and Milan and ending in Prague. I was invited to attend as his assistant, and we were accompanied by Sra Corachan and an anaesthetist for general anaesthesia. For the operation in Milan I gave a local anaesthetic known as splanchnic, much in vogue at the time. On the journey to Prague we read a report of the historic speech in the Spanish parliament by the President of the Republic, Azaña, defending the Catalan Statute of Autonomy which of course gave us great pleasure. At the end of the operation in Prague the fifty or sixty surgeons watching broke into spontaneous and very moving applause as Corachan finished suturing the incision.

3*

Through the kindness of the famous Professor Jirasek, we were introduced to the head of the Czech government, Edouard Benes, who in 1937 was to take over from Masaryk, the famous Czech patriot and first president of the newly born republic. How could I have imagined then that Benes and I were later to be for some years members of the same senior common room at Oxford? Amelia unfortunately could not come on this trip as she had recently given birth to Montserrat.

We also went to Vienna, to visit the famous Unfall Kranken Haus of Lorenz Böhler, who was then in full creative activity and who impressed us greatly, despite his excessive dogmatism. The journey back to Milan, where we had left the car, was made by plane; for most of us it was the first time we had flown.

In 1933 I was admitted as a member of the Société Française de hirurgie, and Amelia and I attended the congress in Paris in the summer. I arranged to go to Bochum as well, where there was an internationally famous surgeon, Dr Koch, who had published interesting papers on industrial traumatology, Bochum being in the heart of the German heavy industry region. I particularly wanted to see his organization, so after the congress in Paris we flew to Cologne. On the same aircraft was a young Italian engineer who was going to Germany to attend acceptance tests of some railway locomotives being built for the Italians in Bochum. This man, no doubt well connected with the high circles of the Mussolini régime, told us that the plane in which we were flying was, in fact, a new type of German bomber, built in such a way that in a few hours it could be converted for war service. Hitler had been elected a few months before, and had taken over the power which he was not to relinquish until his death in a Berlin bunker in May 1945.

In Cologne we managed to get seats to go to the opera where we saw a beautiful production of *Tannhäuser*. At the end of the first act we were surprised to notice that no one got up to stretch their legs or smoke. It appeared that during the first interval there was to be some special spectacle, and, sure enough, a few moments later the curtain went up again to reveal a great mass of uniformed men on the stage, arms raised in the Nazi salute, and ringed by swastika-ed flags. From their midst a small man limped forward and through a microphone declaimed a speech which we did not understand but which, judging from the clamour it raised from the audience, was obviously aimed at their patriotic feelings. We all had to stand up to listen to this diatribe which ended with a concerted shout of Heil Hitler! We were later told that the little man with the limp was Dr Goebbels, so soon to be internationally infamous.

While I was visiting the hospital at Bochum next morning, Amelia—already thinking of what to buy for her girls—went sight-seeing and shopping. When I returned to the hotel I found her almost hysterical and barely able to speak. The director of the hotel, who spoke Spanish, told me that she had been a witness of the terrifying and degrading sight of five uniformed thugs, with swastika brassards, beating a young man senseless in the street. This all happened within a few feet of Amelia, who was horrified, especially when one of the five youths suddenly looked at her and cried out: "Juden! Juden!" Although Amelia certainly did not look Jewish, her dark hair and Mediterranean eyes made them suspect her. She reacted quickly and said, "Ich bin Spanier, ich bin Spanier," but only with great reluctance had they decided to be on their way.

The hotel director told us this was the first time that he had heard of personal aggression, but that he was not surprised as the atmosphere had daily got increasingly tense since the Nazis had taken over. He even said he was afraid that unless they were stopped it would end in disaster, adding incidentally that this sort of thing would do tourism no good.

I do not have to stress how worried we were by our first brief sight of nazism: first the Italian engineer who had more than hinted at German rearmament in defiance of the Treaty of Versailles; secondly, our personal experience of the Nazi take-over in Germany presaging what would later happen throughout most of Europe.

The visit I had paid to Dr Koch's hospital had been useful. I had seen the most modern equipment in a hospital specially devoted to the treatment of accidents in the heart of Germany's main industrial zone. Koch was a good technician, having made himself independent of the Viennese school of Lorenz Böhler, who had had such an extraordinary influence following World War I.

In April 1935 Amelia and I, together with a colleague of

mine and his wife, were invited to Turin by the famous Italian
surgeon Dogliotti, who was then busy founding the Italian
Anaesthetics Society of which my colleague and I were both
made founder members. I remember this trip with pleasure as
we were able to relax after the strain of events at home. The
Italy we saw however was already influenced by Mussolini's
dreams of a new Roman empire; though whether Nazi Germany, with similar imperial aspirations, would have let these
be realized is doubtful. Our Italian colleagues did not seem too
happy at what was going on.

Back home, my life followed the established routine of one
preparing to play a responsible part in limb surgery. From 1929
onwards I had started to have papers published on matters
with which I was well conversant—among them one on
primitive malignant bone tumours and another on hydatoid
bone. By 1935 a fair number of these had been published, some
on traumatic subjects, but most of them on bone diseases and
malformations.

All this time political and social matters were going from
bad to worse. After a plebiscite in which more than ninety per
cent of Catalans had voted in favour of an autonomous system
of government for Catalonia, this was finally granted by the
Spanish parliament, although in a modified form and only
after the suppression of the military revolt of General Sanjurjo
which took place in the summer of 1932. The reasons for the
uprising were, quite openly, to stop the granting of autonomy
to Catalonia and, less obviously, to thwart agrarian reform,
by then already three centuries overdue in Andalusia. Sanjurjo was condemned to death, reprieved and finally pardoned
less than two years later, when the forces which had blocked all
moves towards progress for so long were elected to power again.
Sanjurjo was not the first to take up arms against the republic—
the anarchists of the FAI (Federation of Iberian Anarchists)
preceded him. The focal point of their activities was the potash
mines in Catalonia, where most of the miners were non-
Catalans. People of little or no education, leading hard lives, they
were easy prey for anarchist ideas and especially "libertarian
communism", a sort of Utopia which its advocates believed
would be achieved by doing away with laws and authority.

In 1933 the Autonomous University of Catalonia was

established. This had little in common with the old university and was truly a step forward in education. With the new statutes, the university authorities were empowered to select the professors and in this way the heads of department of the Hospital de St Pau became eligible for chairs. Corachan was among those appointed and I, as one of his first assistants, became auxiliary professor and took part in the organization of the new teaching programme. For the first time a comfortable residence was built for the students and everything was done with such enthusiasm and dedication that the prospects of concrete achievements seemed bright. The Catalan language was officially put on an equal footing with Castilian in Catalonia. It never caused any language difficulty in my lectures or classes, although many students were non-Catalan. Before starting the class I would ask if there was anyone who did not understand Catalan; if there was, then we had the class in Castilian. This attitude of tolerance and understanding meant that I was rarely asked to speak Castilian; it usually only occurred when we had a newly arrived South American. Conversation and discussion were normally bilingual, without anyone taking too much notice of which language was being spoken. As some of the most distinguished specialists in the country were appointed to chairs, the teaching of medicine at the "Autonoma" soon exceeded in prestige that of the State-controlled university.

Unfortunately, President Macià died on Christmas Day 1933, when everything seemed set for the establishment of self-government. Catalonia was orphaned just as the work of reconstruction had begun. It was a day Catalans will never forget. Although everyone knew he was ill, the "Avi" (or grandfather), as he was affectionately known, died suddenly before there was time under his guidance to consolidate the new statute, or even to select the personnel to ensure its implementation. His elected successor, Lluis Companys, was a lawyer from Lleida who had defended many political detainees in the past. He was a Republican and an experienced politician, but not particularly known for his Catalanism.

The Generalitat government in 1934 was moderately left and had no programme of nationalization or expropriation of industry. Elections were held in Spain and in Madrid, Gil

Robles, purporting to head a centre-right party in fact conducted a typically fascist election campaign of which one of
the corner stones was the abolition of Catalan autonomy—this
to gain votes in the interior. This campaign was witnessed with
great sorrow by Catalans and all our optimism drained away
when he won the elections. If Gil Robles' party could not get
the autonomy statute actually rescinded, it was obviously
going to make sure the statute allowed Catalans as little freedom as possible.

This right-wing triumph in Spain gave rise to agitation in
the whole country, particularly in Asturias. The coal miners
there have always been inclined towards violent dissent, and
now, probably because they were misinformed, they rose in
insurrection in the belief that this would coincide with a general
strike throughout the country.

At this point, Companys, under pressure from Catalan
extremists, proclaimed an independent Catalan State. This
created a furore all over Spain, especially among the army.
The rebellion in Catalonia was not martial in character due to
its onesidedness. The Generalitat only had about 400 special
police at their disposal, whereas the military could draw from
barracks all over Catalonia. The captain-general was a Catalan
and a man of excellent qualities. Acting with great moderation
following a short skirmish which resulted in only a few
casualties, he entered the palace of the Generalitat and took
Companys prisoner without resistance.

The consequence of this military action meant in effect the
suspension of the Catalan statute of autonomy. The very thing
which Catalans had wanted to avoid was actually provoked
by a psychological error of Companys. The whole Catalan
government, as well as some of the university sponsors and
many others, were imprisoned outside Catalonia, mainly in
Huelva in Andalusia.

At the trial before a military tribunal, Companys was found
guilty of treason against the State and sentenced to death. This
was commuted to life imprisonment due to the unceasing efforts
of his competent defence counsel, and when new elections
returned the centre-left to power in most of Spain, Companys
and his colleagues were set free and the Generalitat was re-
established as before.

All this time I was looking at events as they happened around me simply as an ordinary citizen busy with my medical work. In October 1935 one of the leading Barcelona surgeons died and his post at the hospital and his university chair became vacant. The appointments committee seems to have placed most importance on the fact that I had been runner-up for the post in 1931 and I was unanimously invited to fill the vacancies.

This particular department needed a great deal of re-organizing as it had fallen into a lethargic routine which so often happens with the aging of a professor. In order to modernize it, I planned a tour of Great Britain and the United States lasting about four to five months, designed to bring me up to date on the latest techniques and equipment. So when I was officially invited to accept the chair and to take over the department at the hospital, I asked the committee to await my return from the overseas tour. I could not foresee then that my eventual absence would last not a few months but three decades.

I was particularly proud of the fact that at the age of thirty-eight I was becoming the colleague of Corachan, my teacher. An enormous responsibility was placed on me not only to maintain the tradition of his teaching but, if possible, to improve on it. This was the main reason I wanted to go abroad and glean all the benefits of Anglo-Saxon experience which could be assimilated in a Latin country. Unfortunately, events were not to permit it.

When new elections in 1936 gave the majority to the left-wing parties, Azaña became president of the republic. From this moment Spain was sharply divided in two. On one side, a united Catalonia with its regained autonomous government and a police force, which was efficient and well organized without exceeding its powers, directly under the president of the Generalitat. On the other, the rest of Spain with a great division between right and left wings. This part of Spain was principally maintained by the landowners of Andalusia and Extremadura who refused to accept any form of land reform— overdue since the fifteenth century. When violent reactions broke out in Andalusia and Madrid, the Falangists were particularly active, the Socialists responded by organizing their own shock troops and Spain fell into a period of utter chaos and disorder which discredited the republic, governed as it was by liberals and impractical idealists. It must be admitted that the starving peasants took the law into their hands in taking over the lands of their "señores", most of whom they had never even seen. In these conditions it became virtually impossible to stem the tide of violence, and rival factions shot at each other from speeding cars, churches were burned in Andalusia and grave social disorders and public unrest were rife; all very similar to the terrorist acts of IRA and ETA activists today.

In Catalonia, however, with the exception of the murder of the Badia* brothers by members of the FAI, conditions were totally different from those in the rest of Spain. I remember a titled Madrid lady whose son I was called on to treat for a broken arm, begging me to make her out a certificate testifying to the fact that an operation would be necessary—in fact it was not—so that her husband could obtain permission to come to Barcelona from Madrid. He was able to come, and when later he thanked me he said: "How lucky you are in Catalonia—this is a real oasis of peace." It was an expression I heard used often right up to the outbreak of the Civil War.

If one looks for the root cause of these disorders, the facts behind the murder of the leading right-wing politician Calvo Sotelo, which provoked a widespread reaction throughout Spain only days before the outbreak of the Civil War itself, are truly illuminating.

In May a Socialist army officer, Faraudo, was assassinated in Madrid by Falangists while out for a walk with his wife. Two months later, Lieutenant Castillo, a police officer of moderate political views and one of the pall-bearers of Faraudo's funeral, was murdered either by or at the instigation of Falangists. His men, with whom he was very popular, lost their self control and in a deplorable act of irresponsibility took Calvo Sotelo from his home and killed him. I have no doubt that had Faraudo and Castillo not been murdered, Calvo Sotelo would have gone unharmed.

The left wing must undoubtedly bear its share of responsibility for the chaotic social situation; equally, there is no doubt that the right wing actively planned disorder and breakdown. While it is true that elements of the population, illiterate and

* They were two extremist separatist brothers.

starving, were driven to excesses by the possibility of being able to enjoy a well-being beyond their dreams, one only needs to note how victims fell in regular order, day by day, first on one side then on the other, to realize that what on the popular side was disorder, on the other side was a well conceived plan. Those on the right wing had had a lot of experience.

Calvo Sotelo had said a short while before in parliament, in regard to Catalan autonomy, that he "preferred a red Spain to a broken Spain." In other words he preferred a Spain united under communism to a partitioned Spain, even though the latter only comprised the granting of modest concessions such as the statute of autonomy for Catalonia.

This ties in with my contention that when Alfonso XIII left Spain there was already a tacit agreement to achieve a united Spain, even though it were republican, to revert later to the traditional monarchy once more. This eventually necessitated the Civil War but Franco refused to relinquish power until he died.

On 9 July 1936, my colleagues and teachers gave a banquet in my honour at the Ritz Hotel to celebrate my having been elected to fill the vacancy at the Hospital de St Pau as head of a department. It must have been one of the last social occasions at the Ritz before the "Alzamiento".

PART II

The Spanish Civil War

(1936–1939)

Chapter 1

THE BEGINNING OF THE CIVIL WAR

ON THE EVENING of 18 July 1936, my wife and I went to a nearby cinema. We were startled on our way back home to see police carrying carbines, which were normally not used in cities; obviously something was very much amiss. They were armed because, as I learned later, President Companys had been warned in advance of the revolt, by officers loyal to the Spanish Republic. This warning was the explanation of the subsequent failure of the uprising in Barcelona and the rest of Catalonia.

About 5 o'clock next morning, Amelia and I were woken up by the sound of firing near the house. It came from soldiers who, after the declaration of a state of war, were on their way down from the Pedralbes barracks to the administrative centre of the city to seize the Generalitat, the Telephone Company building, the building of the civil government and other government offices. These soldiers, according to what some of their wounded told me later, had been persuaded by rebel officers that they were rising in defence of an imperilled republic. Some had even shouted "Long live the republic!" as they blindly followed the disaffected officers. When I started to treat the wounded I found that many soldiers were reeking of alcohol and one of them told me that before leaving their barracks, they had been issued with tots of some strong liquor.

The shooting turned into a real battle between two armies: on one side, two blocks away from our house, the police, under the command of officers loyal to the Spanish Republic, were firing from the roof tops at the rebels on the other side who seemed to be a disorganized rabble. At that moment, watching from our balcony, we could see no civilians because there was as yet no popular participation. It was simply a confrontation between two bodies of the regular forces. I went inside for a moment, but Amelia called me back: "Come quick, they are throwing down their arms and the soldiers are picking them up!" I said, "That's the end of us." However, on going out on to the balcony I saw that it was an entirely different state of affairs; the soldiers were throwing away their rifles, which were being picked up by civilians who were just beginning to come out into the streets. From then on a popular element became involved, taking up arms abandoned by the soldiers and putting them to immediate use.

At about 7 am the hospital rang to ask me to go there immediately as it was beginning to fill up with wounded. As I was already dressed, I said good-bye to Amelia and ran to the garage behind the house where I kept my car. My problem was how to cross the Diagonal avenue, which was under cross-fire. With one hand on the steering wheel and the other trailing a white handkerchief out of the window, and with the disregard which comes from knowing that one has to carry out a duty at all costs, I took advantage of a lull in the firing, pressed the accelerator of my new Mercedes-Benz hard down and careered across the fifty or so metres of the Diagonal in a flash. I had the feeling I had gone faster than sound as I arrived on the other side unharmed.

At the hospital I found my department already full of wounded, mostly soldiers and policemen—especially the latter. I remember a sad case which typifies the callousness and stupidity of civil war. A certain police lieutenant was brought to me with a serious abdomen wound. While I was performing an emergency operation on him, I was told that his brother, a rebel officer, had just been brought in, also badly wounded. One of them did not survive; I cannot now remember which.

The battle for the city has been described many times, and besides I had no first-hand experience of it as from then on I was unable to leave the hospital. For three days we were on continuous duty, fortified by cups of strong coffee. Our only news was over the radio and from the wounded or their visitors. By the second day of the rebellion though, it had already become obvious that the coup d'état had failed.

Around noon of the third day, taking advantage of a few minutes of relative quiet, I borrowed a car (mine had already been stolen) to make a quick visit to my family. Just after leaving the hospital machine-gun bullets spattered across the road a few feet ahead of the car. The firing came from one of the two finished steeples of the Church of the Sagrada Familia. I needed no further urging to put the car into reverse and retire hastily into the hospital. I later learnt that it was anarchists of the FAI, starting up a revolution on their own.

General Goded, who was in charge of the rebel forces in Catalonia, arrived too late from Mallorca; when he landed, the issue was already practically decided. He was arrested and had the good sense to accept the advice of President Companys and tell the insurgents in so many words: enough bloodshed; the rising has failed therefore stop fighting. Goded was court-martialled and shot for having taken up arms against the legally constituted government.

Meanwhile, the news from the rest of Spain was very confused. All we knew was that fighting was still going on in Madrid; that the army had locked themselves inside the Montaña barracks. Unlike the rebels in Barcelona, where they came out into the streets to fight, they stayed inside their barracks and were besieged until they surrendered. With Barcelona and Madrid in the hands of the republic, the issue was half resolved. Valencia followed suit and by the end of the second or third day, Bilbao, Malaga, San Sebastian and most of the industrial cities had also proved themselves loyal to the republic.

In Barcelona, as the fighting continued, more and more civilians took up arms. Under the guiding control of the predominant trades union in Catalonia, the CNT,* brigades were organized when it was decided that Zaragoza, where fighting still went on, must be won over for the republic. This would have made a bridge between the Cantabrian regions—all solidly Republican—and Catalonia. The area conquered by Franco would thus have been effectively cut off from France. Some columns were formed immediately but were infiltrated by many escapers from the Model prison in Barcelona. This is one of the factors which, it seems to me, had most bearing on the atrocities which occurred. The prison was stormed on the first day of the uprising and its occupants streamed out into the streets. In effect this meant the liberation of large numbers of

* National Confederation of Workers.

hardened criminals, along with political detainees, not all of whom can have been of extreme left tendencies since a left-wing government was in office at the time. These dissolute elements, together with a group of FAI anarchists, gradually took over control from the CNT and it is they on whom the responsibility must be placed for the course the war took and for preventing Spain from becoming one of the most advanced democracies in Europe. To illustrate this I need only describe what happened to me personally.

I was considered by my colleagues and patients to be a friend of the people, belonging to no party, but with the same distaste for Francoism as I had for Italian fascism or German naziism. At the Hospital de St Pau we had a porter, not long arrived from southern Spain, who was a self-confessed member of the FAI. Two days after the uprising, this man appeared at the bed of one of my patients flourishing an outsize revolver, which he pointed at me saying: "If he dies, I am going to shoot you for being a Fascist." He was accompanied by a friend of his who, luckily, knew me well, and who winked at me as if to say "It's just a lot of talk." However, it was not a question of braggadocio because, shortly after, the porter came back and I could tell he was undoubtedly in earnest. I let Corachan know about this and because of the influence he had with the workers' authorities the violent impulses of the aggressive porter were restrained.

A few days later, Sister Carme Gurnés got word to me that a group of FAI anarchists had been to the Remei Clinic, accused one of the male nurses of being a Fascist, and taken him away. All that we knew was that the group was from the Barcelona suburb of St Andreu. The man was well known to me, and I knew the charge was totally unjust. I asked Corachan to lend me the official car he used with the two policemen who acted as his guards, and we drove to St Andreu. After going through several check points, we arrived at a garage where the local committee of the CNT had installed itself. I had purposely left on my doctor's white jacket, and after repeatedly identifying myself I was allowed to enter a crowded room where, huddled up in a corner, was our male nurse looking more dead than alive from fear. A man with an immense black beard came towards me and said: "Aren't you Dr Trueta? What the hell are you doing here? I am the brother of . . . whom you operated on recently for a spinal defect." I told him about the male nurse and that he was innocent of what he was accused. Meanwhile, my protégé had been moved to a room above the garage reached by a wooden stairway. The bearded man told me to go up and as I followed him up the stairs my brain was working away trying to remember his sister's case history. I was sure my future would probably depend on the result of the operation I had performed on her.

Five men were sitting in the room behind a long table, each with a revolver in front of him. The one who appeared to be presiding asked me what I wanted. I said: "I have come to take this young male nurse away with me as I cannot operate without him. I can guarantee that he is not a Fascist." The presiding member of the group then said to me: "And who can guarantee that you are not a Fascist yourself?" At this moment, my friend with the beard spoke up saying: "I can; I know him well." That was good enough for the others and I was told I could leave, taking the nurse with me. I had no doubt as of that moment that the operation on our saviour's sister had been successful.

An even more significant event took place at the Remei Clinic, where I had my private patients. The clinic was looked after by eighteen or nineteen nuns, all of whom had been awarded nursing diplomas as we had made a point of seeing that they studied hard and passed their exams. The insurrection had no sooner started than it took on a very marked anti-clerical nature, partly due to the fact that both during and after the electoral campaign, the Church hierarchy had shown itself as being hostile to the republic. We were soon aware of the danger our nuns were in. My wife took over at this point, dressed them in nurses' uniforms, insisted that they wear make-up (most of them were young and pretty anyway) and converted them overnight into attractive nurses. We hid all the holy relics we could find and, despite their loud protests, burnt their habits and thought we had solved the problem.

However, one day I was called urgently to the clinic where a grave crisis had seemingly arisen: one of our nurses was accused of having killed the brother of a FAI leader by injecting him with a toxic substance. I rushed to the clinic and was faced with a "committee" of eleven members of the FAI, all armed with rifles, who wanted to take away the nurse, Sister Herreros. In the course of the discussion it emerged that I had given the instructions for the injection to be administered. Accusations were then levelled against me for having been the instigator and against Sister Herreros for having carried out my orders. We were to face immediate trial and, if found guilty, summarily shot.

The leader of the group appeared to be an educated man and it seemed to me that I had seen him before. He looked as shabby and dirty as the others, with a red and black (the anarchists' colours) kerchief round his neck. Suddenly it came to me: he was a doctor who, years before, had asked me for a job in the Caixa de Previsió i Socors (the workers' medical insurance society where I worked). He had come from Italy and had told me at the time that he was a Fascist. I was not able to give him a job because at that moment there was no vacancy. Quite calmly, he had then suggested that I should dismiss one of the doctors and give him his place. I told him this was out of the question and he had replied menacingly that we would see whether it could or could not be done. This was the same man who was now heading the FAI committee.

Fortunately, the mother superior of the clinic, Carme Gurnés, a woman of exceptional quality, had the presence of mind to send a male nurse immediately to the rival union, the Socialist UGT, to inform them that I was being accused of having murdered a FAI member. Apparently, the UGT asked how many men were at the clinic and immediately sent along an equivalent number of UGT members, suitably armed and led by a man I had known as a male nurse at a hospital where I had been a student years before. He pretended not to know me and after discussing the case with the other leader said: "Justice must be done. If it is true that a fatal injection was given, then they must both be shot. What we must do first of all is to examine the material used. Bring the box of ampoules." A box of camphorated oil ampoules was produced, appropriated by a representative of each of the two unions and then taken to the municipal laboratory for analysis. The two doctors in charge of the laboratory, Pere Domingo and Francesc González, had been confidentially advised of what was going on and reported back that the ampoules contained the purest camphorated oil either of them had ever seen. The disreputable doctor disappeared. I never saw or heard of him again. Although I remember his name very well indeed, it does not appear in the register of the Barcelona Medical College. Far better just to record that the nun and I were set free—with apologies all round—without anyone finding out that the nurses were in fact all nuns. When someone on one occasion chanced to say: "I've been told they are nuns," I rose to my feet in indignation and told him that we only used fully qualified nurses. On seeing their diplomas he left fully convinced; it probably seemed impossible to him that anyone could be a nun and a nurse at the same time.

Chapter 2

THE HEALTH MINISTRY—
DR CORACHAN AND HIS SONS' EXILE

As soon as the Generalitat—the autonomous Catalan government—was re-established shortly after the elections in February
1936, Dr Corachan was invited by President Companys to
take over the Ministry of Health in Catalonia. It was rather a
surprising suggestion as Corachan had never before been
involved in politics. Nevertheless, although not fired with
enthusiasm by the offer, Corachan accepted, despite his
wife's objections. She had discussed the matter with me and
we had both agreed it would be a mistake for her husband to
get mixed up in politics, even though the Health Ministry was
more a technical than a political appointment. I had a long
talk with Dr Corachan, pointing out to him the difficulties
he would face at a time when reaction throughout the country
to the leftist victory was becoming increasingly apparent.
However, his reasoning left me with no words. He said: "I
came to Catalonia from Valencia in my childhood to live with
my uncles in their barber shop in Sants.* By shaving customers
I was able to earn enough to be able to study medicine.
Everything that I have achieved in reaching the position I
hold today I owe to Catalonia. Now that I am fifty years old,
it is only right that I make some sacrifice, however small, for
the country which has welcomed me as a son." I could not
argue against such a fundamentally ethical decision. Corachan
immediately got down to the task of organizing the many
reforms of which Catalonia stood in need.

But before he had had time to complete this work the
increasing disorders in Spain finally provoked civil war, in
which Catalonia became involved on 19 July. Corachan
realized then that there was nothing more that he could do

* A workers' suburb of Barcelona.

and, not being fitted to cope with the in-fighting of national politics, a few months later submitted his resignation, which was rightly accepted by President Companys.

Soon after he returned to being just an ordinary private citizen, Corachan was threatened by a group of anarchists whose leader asserted that Corachan had operated on him and left him incapacitated as a result of a surgical error for which he claimed Corachan should pay him substantial compensation in cash. My mentor sought advice from a doctor friend who, recognizing the danger in which Corachan found himself now that, as a result of the Francoist uprising, total anarchy had taken over and the FAI ruled the streets, advised him to go to France and himself arranged the necessary authorization from President Companys.

Before leaving, Corachan summoned me and his two sons—the elder, Manuel, already a distinguished neurosurgeon, the younger, Ricard, still a student and suffering from acute asthma—and told them in my presence that they were to consider me as being *in loco parentis* while he was away. I accepted this responsibility with certain misgivings, but nevertheless felt proud to be thus trusted. Manuel was in army captain's uniform and I had the feeling that this would be a protective shield against any threatening moves on the part of extremists.

Unfortunately, not long after Dr Corachan left for France, Manuel told me that he had been tracked down by the persons who had threatened his father and that, because of the supposed injury caused to one of them by his father, they were threatening to kill him unless he paid them the sum of Ptas 30,000, not an easy sum to raise at that time.

With contributions from two or three of Corachan's friends and a small one from myself, we got together the necessary amount and I personally took it to the Palace of Justice and handed it over to a person in authority who could vouch that the payment had been made. I was assured that Manuel would not be bothered any more after that. This was not the case though, for shortly afterwards Manuel informed me that his persecutors were claiming that they had only received Ptas 20,000, a third apparently having vanished after I had paid over the money. The moral standard of the individuals was certainly not such that we could be certain whether or not they were telling the truth. One thing though was quite plain: they would eventually bleed Corachan's sons white.

I went to see Dr Jaume Aguadé, brother of the Security minister, who had arranged Dr Corachan's journey to France and who, now wearing a worried expression, was told by me of the plan concocted with Manuel and his brother. This consisted simply in getting an ambulance to take them to a village in the Pyrenees, Boltaña, where there was a sanatorium for tubercular patients. Ricard would pretend to be the patient and Manuel would go as his doctor. We duly arranged this with Aguadé's help and when they were ready to go they were joined by a third person—a Dr Ruiz from Andalusia who was also in danger as he had the "misfortune" to own land in the south of Spain and thus feared for his life.

Once in Boltaña, which was very close to France, Manuel tried unsuccessfully to find a guide to take them across the border. After several preliminary reconnaissances by Manuel, they decided on the seventh day to make the attempt unassisted. They started off just before midnight one November night and were already within sight of the French frontier when Dr Ruiz (who was wearing patent leather shoes!) slipped and broke his ankle. They sheltered in a wooden hut while Manuel went for help. He and his brother could no doubt have gone on, but Dr Ruiz would probably have frozen to death. As it was quite obvious to their rescuers that they had been attempting to escape, they were arraigned before the local FAI committee and sent under escort to Barcelona.

I was told about all this by a mutual doctor friend who had seen them by chance on the road. We immediately made every effort to find out where they had been taken. Fortunately, as it was Barcelona Aguadé could use his influence to get the three of them released. Their faces lit up when they saw me. That night I took them to the civil government where Aguadé took them into protective custody for a few days until we could find a safe hide-out inside the city. After they had spent several weeks in hiding, we laid plans for them to try again—this time properly shod!

We later learnt that they were driven in a car belonging to the CNT to Vic, and there were transferred to a FAI [*sic*] car which took them to a point near the frontier. This was towards the end of December. They then walked all through the night, with a guide, and although, due to Ricard's asthma, they had to rest up during the day, they finally arrived in France the next night.

I shall always remember advising Manuel not to let himself be persuaded to join the Nationalists by going into Franco Spain, as the fact that his father had been Health Minister of the Catalan Generalitat could be dangerous for him. However, once in France and re-united with his young wife, whose family were in territory occupied by Franco's forces, the pressures on him to ignore my advice were too great and he went. Although he was, as I have mentioned before, a very good neurologist, he was not allowed to join up as a surgeon because of the opposition of some military doctor. He volunteered as a stretcher-bearer and while in no-man's-land rescuing a wounded soldier in the Basque country he was hit in the elbow and the thigh by fragments from an ill-directed German bomb. Neither wound was in itself of any apparent importance it seems, but at the hospital in Vitoria they sutured the wounds without having previously excised them adequately, thereby committing the surgical error which I later tried to convince my British colleagues to avoid. Three days after the suturing, gas gangrene developed and Manuel died soon afterwards. Ricard stayed in St Jean de Luz until he heard that his brother had been wounded, when he also crossed into Francoist Spain. Unfortunately, when he arrived at the hospital, his brother had already died.

Chapter 3

THE FIRST BOMBARDMENT—
MY MARXIST EXPERIENCE

EARLY IN SEPTEMBER 1936, towards evening, the air
suddenly vibrated with the passage of shells from a warship
out at sea. This was the first time we really became conscious
that we were at war. The city was being shelled by an Italian
ship, whose target was the centrally situated Elizalde car
factory—or so it seemed. It had a great effect on us. Amelia
and the three girls were with me, an all too infrequent
occurrence as I was practically living in the hospital, and I
told them: "I am going to send you to France—bombing has
begun." This was possible—I had enough friends to help me
with their passports and exit visas, and even had a place to send
them to—at least the two elder girls.

When the Civil War started, my eldest niece Mercè was
learning English at a school run by an American in Mallorca.
The whole school was evacuated to Marseilles in the British
battleship *Repulse* to be out of all danger. A suitable house was
found—La Loggia in Bordighera—and the children were
moved into this provisional school until they could return to
Mallorca. All we had to do, therefore, was to send Meli and
Montse and their cousin, Carmona, to La Loggia, which we did
at the beginning of November 1936.

At that time, anyone with jewellery was officially required
to hand it over to help pay for armaments and the war effort,
although in fact it may have benefited less patriotic causes. On
leaving Spain therefore, people were searched and even
stripped at the frontier to make sure they were not taking out
any valuables. We knew this, and Amelia even took off her
wedding-ring. She had a fair collection of jewellery, much of it
inherited from her mother, and we did not know what the
future might hold in store for us, or whether one day we might

have to sell it to buy food. In fact we were later often on the verge of having to do so.

Through the good offices of a kind English friend, my wife before going through Customs and being searched, gave a small parcel to a man who identified himself to her. When the British ship on which they sailed was well out to sea, a sailor came up to her and returned the parcel, to her great relief. Throughout the Civil War and later the Second World War, the jewels stayed in the care of distant relatives in Perpignan who were thereby often involved in great personal risk, and they were finally returned to us in 1947, for which we were most grateful.

I heard later that the voyage to Marseilles was most unpleasant—with the sea as rough as it can be in the Gulf of Lyons. However, with luck and the help of a British sailor who made them all go below—the girls had already nearly gone overboard—all ended happily. One must remember that Meli and Carmona were twelve, Montse four and Julie two years old. The warship, although it was peacetime for Britain, was not exactly designed to cater for children, as my wife found out when she went to the galley for some warm milk for Julie. Asked by Amelia, in her bad English, whether it might not perhaps be too hot, the cook, certainly one of the most kind-hearted if not hygienic of men, tested it by dipping in the milk the dirtiest finger that my wife swore she had ever seen.

They arrived in Bordighera by train from Marseilles, and after a few days' rest, having left Carmona and our two elder children there, Amelia returned to Barcelona with Julie, who was too small to be left at the school.

Meanwhile, things in Barcelona were going from bad to worse. Towards evening of Thursday, 1 October 1936, a doctor friend of mine telephoned to ask me to go straight to the Hotel Majestic where there was a foreigner with a fractured foot. When I asked him for the patient's name he excused himself in an odd way and said I would be advised of the room by the hotel receptionist. I went as soon as I could to the hotel and was informed that the patient's name was Vladimir Ovseenko, of the USSR Embassy in Paris. A box had fallen on his foot while waiting for the train to leave Paris for Barcelona and he had fractured a metatarsal but without any bone

4

displacement. I immobilized the toe with sticking plaster and went to see him two or three times until he was cured. On 7 November I received a very official-looking invitation from the Consul-General of the USSR, the very same Mr Ovseenko, to attend a reception in the house they then occupied.

He was a distinguished looking man, who spoke several languages, including French in which he was fluent, and always dressed very smartly in the West European style. His elegant pure silk shirts had early on caught my attention.

Ovseenko soon made several friends in Barcelona, and at my suggestion he appointed Pepa Barba, daughter of neighbours of my parents, to be his translator and interpreter in Russian, which she knew well. On Wednesday 14 October the first Russian vessel, the *Zirianin*, arrived in Barcelona harbour with food and supplies, and Pepa was requested by Ovseenko to be at his side at the berthing of the vessel, which had been widely publicized by the press.

A great mass of people, including my brother-in-law Lluis, went to see the spectacle at the port, and when I saw Pepa later she told me she had overheard the captain of the vessel, who thought no one would understand him, say: "And these are the people who are to carry out the Bolshevik revolution?" Ovseenko had merely smiled sardonically.

My contacts with him slowly lapsed, until one day he asked my advice about bringing his wife to Barcelona from Paris. She suffered from a chronic heart condition and he wanted to have a good heart specialist ready before she arrived. I decided to put this request to good use. My friend Lluis Trias de Bes, a renowned heart specialist, was trying to get to France as he considered himself increasingly in danger under the rule of the FAI. I therefore recommended him to Ovseenko. Trias de Bes treated Mme Ovseenko and some time later I heard that he had crossed into France with the necessary permit. Ovseenko reacted as I thought he would—in other words, although he had been responsible with Trotsky for the formation of the Red Army, and must therefore have been a hard man, he was nevertheless humane.

Some time later I was again called to the USSR consulate, this time to visit Mr Marcel Rosenberg, diplomat and first ambassador of the USSR to Spain, who required a specialist in my field. I was driven to see him by a well-known Barcelona boxer, Sáez, who told me that Ovseenko was insistently being recalled to the USSR with his wife, on the pretext that he was going to be made commissar. This, Sáez told me, was a very bad sign, and Ovseenko ignored the appeals as long as he was able. When he did return Sáez was proved right as news came some time later that Ovseenko, together with others of his entourage, had been liquidated in one of Stalin's purges, as indeed was Rosenberg himself afterwards.

With the exception of the wounded who naturally came under my care as head of a department at the Hospital de St Pau, I can say that this was my only connection with the Soviet elements which slowly but increasingly put in an appearance on the Spanish Republican side. The first Communist patient of any importance whom I treated was the Yugoslav Ilitch. He was brought to me from the front with an infected open wound of the forearm caused about ten days before by a land mine. The illustrations of this case, published in my book *Treatment of War Wounds and Fractures* show how, in less than four months, complete healing was achieved with the exception of an incapacity caused by an irreparable lesion of the median nerve. This man, although a Yugoslav, was an ex-Red Army officer, trained at the Frunze Military Academy, and was one of the first foreigners of the International Brigades to arrive in Barcelona. He was the head of the Yugoslav units and in charge of the shock troops which crossed the Ebro river the night the last big battle of the Civil War started, when he was again wounded. Years after my arrival in Britain, I was pleased to hear from him from the Yugoslav Embassy in Norway where he had been appointed ambassador. Later on I saw him personally when he was still a diplomat, and it was he who told me that it was untrue that Tito had ever fought in Spain and that he had only served on the recruiting committee for the International Brigades in Paris.

Although the International Brigades were mainly commanded by Communists, their ranks were filled with idealists of other beliefs, from anarchists to simple liberal bourgeoisie. I remember, for instance, a professor of Greek from Oxford University who was brought to me with a fractured leg and who told me he had no sympathy with marxism.

Another of the men I met through my work as a surgeon was the Italian, Vittorio Vidali, or Carlos Contreras,* with any number of other aliases, whom I treated for an open wound of the hand caused by a shell splinter. He was an out-and-out Communist and the leading organizer of the so-called Fifth Regiment in Madrid.

I must have treated quite a few dozen of these International Brigade members in the course of more than two and a half years of the war. For the most part they were men of stoic self-control who had come to fight for a cause worthy of the utmost sacrifice. Many had the misfortune to die in Spain; others, like George Orwell, went back home disillusioned. On his return to Great Britain he wrote *Homage to Catalonia* in which he despairs of seeing a new world born; a book which was a souvenir of, rather than a homage to, my country. André Malraux, whom I met many years later, wrote *L'Espoir*, a truly great book about the Spanish Civil War. He lived to be a hero of World War II and later Minister of Culture under de Gaulle. He refused to come to Spain while Franco lived, although this must have created difficulties while he was a minister. And many others also . . .

* An Italian professional revolutionary. A very efficient organizer, with the reputation of being utterly ruthless.

Chapter 4

MONTSERRAT—FROM REST CENTRE TO
WAR HOSPITAL

IMMEDIATELY AFTER THE insurrection started, the monks
of Montserrat, under the protection of the Generalitat police,
were evacuated from the monastery and a friend of mine, Carles
Gerhard (brother of Robert the famous composer who went to
live in England), a Social Democrat member of parliament,
was appointed administrator of the monastery; a sort of secular
abbot, as it were.

When later Amelia was ill with pleurisy, and rest and
adequate food were recommended, it was suggested to me that
the monastery might provide these facilities. So Amelia, with
Julie, our youngest daughter, was moved to Montserrat in
February 1938, accompanied by the mother superior of the
Remei Clinic, Carme Gurnés, to look after them. I used to take
advantage of any free time I had to go and see them and others
who were living there. One day Gerhard telephoned me in a
very worried state asking me to come at once as one of the
inmates, the eight or nine years old daughter of Comorera, the
head of the Catalan Communist Party, was complaining of
violent abdominal pains which had been diagnosed by the
local doctor as acute appendicitis. I confirmed this upon
arrival, and asked for permission from the mother, whose
husband was at that time on a visit to Moscow, to operate at
once. The mother gave her consent, and that same night I took
out the inflamed appendix. The post-operative period was
happily quite normal, and the child went back to Montserrat
to convalesce.

Some days after I had discharged Comorera's daughter, he
turned up at my home to thank me and to explain his absence
which, he said, had been due to "important national interests".
He told me how pleased he had been that I had performed the

operation on his daughter, and added that he had already had undeniable evidence of my ability since in 1926, while he was in exile in Buenos Aires during the dictatorship of Primo de Rivera, I had operated on his mother for breast cancer and on coming out of the operating theatre had told his wife that the patient had only six months to live. "Do you know that my mother died six months to the day after your performing the operation? You could not have been nearer the truth." Try as I might, I could not convince him that all I had done had merely been to express my pessimism regarding his mother's prospects, without attempting to predict the time she had left to live.

Not many months later I was required to attend his wife, also for appendicitis. I remember the effect it had on me going into the well-known Gaudí-designed house, La Pedrera, escorted by two "comrades" who had taken over from the servants of the former owner of the house, Count Montseny, with the exception that instead of livery and breeches these men wore leather jackets with guns in their belts. I operated on Sra Comorera at the Remei Clinic to which her husband accompanied her. I offered to let him be present at the operation, in view of his importance—but he answered me in a low voice: "I am sorry to have to tell you that I could not bear it as the sight of blood makes me faint"—a surprising admission coming from a man with a reputation of being a hardened leader of the newly founded Catalan Communist Party. It seemed to me that this weakness was indicative of the marked sensibility of a man who, years later, having returned to Spain after the war, died in prison there in order to escape death at the hands of Stalin's executioners, as happened to Andreu Nin.

On another occasion too he gave me proof of his humaneness. I was visited one day by a pretty, tremulous lady from the textile town of Sabadell who, knowing of my acquaintance with Comorera, had come to ask if I could arrange for a pass for her husband to go to France. Although my relationship with the Catalan communist was slight, I did write to him and received the reply that if the person for whom I was interceding could produce a "certificate of good conduct" signed by at least five workers from his factory, he would issue the permit. I handed this personally to the lady, who did not seem too pleased with the answer. After a few moment's thought she said: "It is possible that my husband may find the required five workers. If instead of him though the permit were required for his father, there would not be a chance! The count has never replied even with a nod to any worker's friendly 'Buenos dias, Don Juan', when they pass one another in the factory. My husband, on the other hand, usually returns their greetings."

The excellent nursing of Mother Gurnés and the rest and good food at Montserrat soon improved Amelia's health. Nuns of the same order worked at the nursing home in Perpignan of Dr Pierre Nicolau who, on learning through the nuns of our problems (Montserrat was having to be evacuated) offered to have Amelia at his home, an offer which we gratefully accepted.

Another anecdote connected with Montserrat relates to Colonel Escobar, of the Civil Guard, who was sent to Montserrat after being wounded in the spine by anarchists during the revolt in May 1937. He was one of the most unusual military commanders I had ever met. I had looked after him once before when he had been wounded in the hand at the Madrid front. But on this occasion, Escobar had been shot by FAI machine guns while driving in his car in Barcelona and was lucky not to be paralysed for life as one of the bullets penetrated a vertebra, fortunately without seriously affecting the nerve.

Colonel Escobar was a remarkable man. Brought up in the old tradition of the Civil Guard, he told me he could not understand how this body could ever take up arms against the legally constituted state resulting from the last elections held in Spain. That was why, despite his profound religious feelings—one of his daughters was a nun—and though politically he was a conservative, he never doubted for a moment where his duty lay when practically the whole of the army rose in Catalonia. He often told me how the very deep feeling against the Civil Guard worried him. He thought it unjust and probably provoked by those who feared that the Civil Guard might oppose the social revolution which was being planned.

Unfortunately, Escobar was proved right, and notwithstanding everything that was done on the Republican side to save the Civil Guard as an institution, the body went on declining. When the war was well advanced and Escobar was already a general, he was put in charge of the Republican army in Extremadura. After the fall of Madrid he was taken prisoner and shortly afterwards shot by his former colleagues.

I remember him as a noble man, with an implacable sense of destiny. His religious faith and the knowledge that he had done his duty must have comforted him in his very last moments.

Later, when the time came to evacuate Montserrat because the battle front was getting close, Camarasa, the famous Catalan painter who was living there, made me a present of a painting he had done at the monastery saying: "If you have to leave Catalonia, you can get $800 for this in the United States." I duly took it out with me and later gave it to my brother Rafel who in turn took it to Mexico with him.

Chapter 5

A TRAUMATOLOGIST IN MODERN WARFARE

My INTERVENTION IN the Civil War was that of an active surgeon, depressed by the magnitude of the tragedy but firmly resolved to play my part in helping to mitigate it. It went on for nearly three years, and I spent them working with my hands and my heart rather than with my head. My one attempt as an organizer failed when my proposals were not accepted.

On the third day of the rebellion, Dr Lluis Trias de Bes, a good friend of mine although our political beliefs and convictions differed, and whom I later helped to get to France, arrived at our hospital, still wearing his doctor's coat, enquiring anxiously for Dr Corachan. He said the anarchists wanted to take away a Dr Garcia Tornel, ostensibly to serve at the front as a medical officer but in fact to have him assassinated. Corachan, who was still Health Minister of the Generalitat, said to me: "As soon as it gets light, go to Aguadé's home and ask him to have Garcia Tornel called up at once and ordered to remain in Barcelona." Dr Corachan's eldest son, Manuel, and I did so, and it was after he had issued the necessary orders that Aguadé said to me: "As a surgeon, what would you suggest be done to organize the medical services at the front?" "I have it all thought out," I replied. "I would divide Catalonia and Barcelona into two zones, north and south, and would allocate two hospitals to the southern zone, which would mean about 2,500 beds, and two to the north, with an equal number of beds. I would mobilize the doctors and surgeons of the four hospitals and would commission them as officers, according to their medical status, thus protecting them from any attack by terrorists and agents provocateurs." On a marble-top table at Aguadé's home I pencilled a sketch-map of Catalonia dividing it horizontally south of Lleida.

Aguadé said he thought the idea interesting, and that they

4*

would study it, but I never had any reply on the subject. All I know is that some time later Dr Corachan and I were asked to go to inspect the hospital of an industrial complex near Casp, at Flix, which had a well-equipped building with beds and operating theatre. This was on the river Ebro, at a strategic point on the route of the motorized columns' advance on Zaragoza.

On the way we had an unnerving experience. Although the train was full, we found ourselves alone in a first-class compartment—egalitarianism did not yet apply to the railways!—when suddenly a man walked in and sat down opposite us, obviously very sure of himself. Speaking in Catalan he announced: "Last night I executed three, the day before five; now I am going to Casp where I have to execute so and so . . ." I could not resist saying to him: "You seem to do away with people very easily. We have studied for years in order to try and save a finger. You kill as if life did not matter!" "Life is of no importance," he answered, "the only thing that matters is that where an enemy exists he should be eliminated." Corachan and I spent the rest of the journey in some trepidation.

We stayed two or three days at Casp and it was decided that young Manuel Corachan and I, together with a surgical team, would settle at Flix and work as civilian surgeons, as there were as yet no war casualties. So, after a brief return to Barcelona to make all necessary arrangements, we went back to Flix. It was at Flix that I witnessed the rebirth of the coin. . . . We had returned to prehistoric times when trade was by the interchange of food and clothes. The first act of the local committee ruling the village had been to abolish money. Consequently, people came to one and asked: "There is a girl with appendicitis. If she has to be operated on, how many and what kind of fowl will it cost?" "What is worth more, to remove an appendix or operate on a stomach?" For instance: "If a stomach operation costs one chicken, is an appendix only worth a rabbit?" And so on.

It was not long before one of the committee members, very politely, suggested an idea which was discussed and thought to be interesting: that instead of giving us a goose, a hen, a chicken, twelve eggs, etc., they would give us paper or cardboard vouchers which we could collect and then we would settle, for example, that a hen was worth six vouchers, a chicken eight, etc. It was decided that this was a great advance; this way we would not walk out of the operating theatre laden with baskets like farmers returning from market!

This worked fine for a few days, but soon there were protests. Some said their vouchers had torn, that they were too soft; too fragile; they disintegrated; they got lost and the holders were then refused the rabbits or the bread they asked for. Finally, someone had the bright idea of making the vouchers metallic and round! Thus we were present at the renaissance of the peseta in the course of the three weeks we spent in that village.

The drive back to Barcelona after finishing our job at Flix, where incidentally we hardly treated any war casualties, was a depressing experience. We were with a Socialist doctor, Tussó, whose car, driven by a militiaman with a large revolver at his hip, probably belonged to his party. Also in the car was another doctor, Dr Mir. When we left Flix it was getting dark. Our aim was to reach Barcelona between one and two am. Suddenly, on a long stretch of road we were surprised to see ahead of us the lights of a stationary vehicle, cars being rare in those days. We approached slowly and I noticed that both Tussó and the chauffeur were getting their guns out. It was a two-seater car, with a dickie or rumble seat at the back, and two men were standing by it with drawn guns. At the side of the road were the bodies of two men. Sitting inside the car was a terrified lad of between ten and twelve years of age. We were later told that he was one of the boys being trained at an early age to get used to sudden death.

The assassins were members of the FAI. We had some anxious moments, especially I who was sitting in the seat nearest them. They asked us: "Who are you and where are you going?" Tussó identified himself as a member of the Socialist Union. Mir, who was in the army, had by then also brought out a gun. I was the only defenceless one and found myself sitting in the middle of a possible cross-fire. Presumably, as they were only two with guns and we were three, they dared not open fire; but, according to Tussó, they might well have done as they were unmasked and could therefore have been identified later. Finally they said to us: "Go on, we all belong

to the same cause. Off you go. We have just wiped out two
Fascists, so there are two less. Good-bye." At this we drove off
at high speed—Tussó repeatedly telling the chauffeur to drive
faster, but the car had its limitations. Tussó was sure the two
FAI men would follow us, and he was right—we soon saw their
lights behind us. Eventually we arrived in Tarragona, where,
luckily for us, Tussó's party were in charge and he was able to
tell them about our adventure. His friends put out guards and
our pursuers were not allowed through. We decided to spend
the night in Tarragona on the understanding that some of
Tussó's men would accompany us next morning, in case the
FAI men might be waiting for us further up the road.
Understandably we did not sleep too well that night. At dawn
we drove off under escort to Barcelona. On arriving home I can
truthfully say my personal military intervention in the war
came to an end. The rest of the war I merely dedicated to
trying to alleviate the havoc wreaked on my countrymen,
spiritually as well as physically.

The mention of Tussó's party reminds me of Andreu Nin,
one of its leaders, and of the only occasion I had of speaking to
him. Some neighbours of my parents came in tears to see me a
few days after the rebellion broke out. They told me that their
son, a soldier, had been captured after joining the rebels on the
day of the uprising. He and five others had been arrested,
although, according to his parents, he had only gone to his
barracks in compliance with orders from an officer. Through a
friend of mine I managed to see Andreu Nin, then Minister of
Justice of the Generalitat. I told him that this boy's parents
were afraid he might be shot. They were equally sure that some
of the others might not be shot simply because they had
influence in the right quarters. Nin listened carefully, made
some notes and said: "There is nothing I can do about the
officer who ordered these boys back to barracks; but I
promise you that even if just one of them is pardoned, your
neighbours' son will not be shot." And so it happened. It is
many years now since Andreu Nin was himself murdered for
being a Trotskyist on the orders of Stalin, but I often see the
son of my parents' neighbours walking around the streets of
Barcelona even now. Had it not been for Nin he would have
died forty years ago.

Chapter 6

THE COMMITTEE OF NON-INTERVENTION

THE FACT THAT Amelia was convalescing in southern France gave me more than one opportunity to visit the Nicolaus' home, and thus we laid the foundations of a truly fraternal friendship with them. They treated Amelia as if she were a member of their own family, and thanks to them she made a complete recovery from her illness.

Pierre Nicolau was an exceptional man. He was a person of liberal ideas, very cultured and a genuine connoisseur. He had married Yvonne, daughter of the l'Héritier-Guyot wine family of Burgundy. He was a skilled surgeon of great repute, a very hard worker and an expert in modern art with, among his large collection, some forty paintings by Dufy, with whom he was on very friendly terms. Pierre was a stimulating conversationalist and we spent many agreeable hours chatting in his home. After the Second World War he was decorated for his services to the Resistance.

In his home I met most of the "observers" of the Committee for Non-Intervention in Spain, whose base was at Perpignan. I remember a Mr A. F. Procopé, a Finn, who was the leader of the observers. There was a Mr Knud Broch, a young Danish army officer (who later helped me with the Spanish refugees) and others besides, and of course whenever I arrived from Spain they squeezed all the information they could out of me on the situation in the country.

By then it was already obvious that, precisely due to Non-Intervention, the war was lost for the Republic, while slowly the Communist party was taking over all the powers. How long the Republic held out finally depended on the USSR, and when the Russians decided that they had had enough, the war came to its inevitable end.

I am convinced that the pact between Germany and Russia

was conceived while the war in Spain was still going on. I have good reasons for this belief: a friend of mine, who was a recently converted Communist, came to see me in despair one day saying: "The Russians are betraying us! Now that Franco's troops are nearing Tarragona, they have instructed all the construction unions in Barcelona to have their members build fortifications on the river Llobregat.* Eighty thousand construction workers have come forward only to be told that they must produce five photographs to guard against Fascist infiltration. Five photographs! There isn't a single photographer left in Barcelona! Where are they going to get five photographs from? Obviously they do not want us to carry on resisting. As they are not sending supplies any more, this means that the war is over." And so it was.

The war really ended at the Battle of the Ebro, from which front we received so many wounded that once again I could not move from the hospital. It was really the only battle in the Civil War between two modern armies in direct confrontation. If not on complete parity, they were for at least a week on roughly equal terms; that is to say, until Franco received the extra help, just sufficient to be superior to that received by the Republic, with which he was always provided at critical junctures. In the Battle of the Ebro Republican casualties totalled almost 50,000. It is an interesting fact that although the majority of Republican soldiers in this battle were Catalans, the Spanish government took good care to see that not one of them should rise above the rank of major. This was an army which was defending its own homeland. . . .

If I go back now to the first month of the Civil War it is because it was for me of the greatest consequence. The day after the Francoist rebellion broke out I was visited at the hospital by a newspaperman, the Paris director of a Czech news agency. He asked me what kind of wounded we had, and how many. Fighting was then going on in the streets. I told him all I knew, and also that I was very worried because the conflict was taking on the air of a destructive social revolt, which I did not like. That same morning the bodies of five assassinated

---

* The three major entry routes to Barcelona from the west and southwest had to cross this river on the outskirts of the city. It therefore constituted a natural strategic defence line.

citizens had been found just behind the hospital. No construc-
tive legislation was being enacted—killings and disorder were
rampant. He told me not to worry—that the same thing had
occurred in Prague, when Czechoslovakia became independent, but that it had only lasted a few days. Masaryk put a
radical end to it in the only way, he said, that these things can
be ended. "You will see how it will also end here," he
concluded. In fact, it did not end radically until May 1937,
when the Communists of Castilian Spain, organized into a
body of police carabineers, came to Catalonia to take over, and
nearly succeeded in seizing control of the Generalitat.

All this made a great impression on me. I could do no more
than put into practice and perfect the details of my treatment
of war wounds, certain that the surgeons of the Western
democracies would hear of it soon enough. I was sure they did
not realize the danger they were heading for.

The results of my method were commented on in Barcelona.
The British consulate heard of it and, so I was told, in turn sent
a message to the Foreign Office advising them that there was a
surgeon in Barcelona with continuous experience of treating
wounds resulting from bombing, which was a new development. MacLeod, director of His Master's Voice in Barcelona,
also helped in making this known. No modern city built of
stone, bricks and concrete, which Barcelona was, had been
bombed from the air before on this scale. The Italians had used
bomber aircraft in Abyssinia, but had only destroyed sheds and
fields. Guernica was gutted by incendiary bombs since wooden
structures predominated there. "Here," one imagines the
Englishman saying, "there is a man with an efficacious method
of treating casualties caused by falling houses." Be that as it
may, two English women doctors turned up: one, a Catholic
ear-nose-and-throat surgeon of great experience and authority,
Miss D. Josephine Collier; the other, Dr Audrey Russell. They
arrived together in a car bulging with medical equipment to
help the Republicans. These women belonged to an interesting
and certainly overlooked sector—English Catholics who remained faithful to the Republican cause, principally because
of their sympathy towards Catalonia and the Basque country.
Their visit lasted the whole morning. They wanted to see the
patients and to know what I would do if there were a world

war. They were very charming and when they left it was as if I were taking leave of friends of long standing.

About three or four months later—this was already in 1938—I was telephoned from the Generalitat to say that an English surgeon, Mr E. M. Cowell, would like to see me personally if I could spare him a few minutes. He told me he was a civil surgeon, but that during the First World War he had been a colonel in the RAMC, that he had heard about my method in England and wanted to see it for himself as he and a colleague of his, Mr P. H. Mitchiner, also an ex-colonel, were preparing a book on modern warfare and, in particular, on wounds incurred in air raids. This book was later published under the title of *Medical Organization and Surgical Practice in Air Raids*. He told me the only place with the necessary concentration of experience was Barcelona.

Mr Cowell spent almost a whole day with me. I had just published my first small book, in Catalan, on war wounds (*Tractament de les Fractures de Guerra*), setting out the basic points of my technique, and Cowell bought one. He asked me if they might reproduce in their book certain of the photographs which interested him, with an acknowledgment of their source. Naturally, I made no objection. He went back to England, but the war in Catalonia went on until February 1939.

PART III

My First Ten Years of Exile in Oxford

(1939–1949)

Chapter 1

I LEAVE CATALONIA

As the end of the Spanish Civil War approached its inevitable conclusion, I had to decide what to do. Amelia and my daughters were in France. I was in doubt as to whether to stay or to leave. I was not a politician, nor had I ever been one. I had never been a Communist, militant or sympathizer, nor a freemason. I was simply a Catalan liberal of a political conviction which in Britain would have lain somewhere between the Liberal and the Conservative parties. Needless to say, I had never held any political post. I had the impression I could safely stay. There was, however, one consideration which would not allow me to do so. I knew that with the arrival of Franco's armies, Catalonia would be crushed until spiritually there would be nothing Catalan left larger than a grain of birdseed. I was convinced that one of the reasons for the Civil War had been to stop the progress of Catalonia and to destroy her autonomous status. I would be incapable of watching in silence this persecution so, unless I wanted to fall foul of the new authority, I must leave.

Besides, I had had a warning. In 1938, at the International Congress of Surgery in Brussels, I was advised not to return to Catalonia as it might cost me my life. The congress, incidentally, was due to have been held in Vienna but because of the invasion of Austria by Hitler, the reaction of the intellectual world was such as to insist on the convening of the congress somewhere else, and Brussels was chosen. Six or seven of us surgeons went from the Republican side, with the necessary government-issued passports. Amelia and I arranged to attend with our friends the Nicolaus of Perpignan, so both couples travelled in their car.

In Brussels I met several of my Italian friends, amongst them Dogliotti, and they all said: "But you are still in Barcelona?

And you are going back? That is impossible!" I answered: "No, it is not impossible. Life there would not be too bad now were it not for your aircraft. The murders have long since ceased. There reigns a certain order—though on a Communist basis, which I personally utterly dislike." Although no laws had actually been passed doing away with capitalism, we all knew that control was in the hands of the Communists. Meanwhile, the "Peace of Munich" was being hatched, incubated by Chamberlain, who went to Germany with his umbrella and succeeded in getting Hitler to sign a worthless piece of paper for him.

While in Paris on our way back I saw a Spanish writer, an acquaintance of mine who had passed over to Franco's side, and he also stressed that I should not return to Barcelona. "Ask permission to go to Franco's Spain. They wouldn't do anything to you because they need surgeons so badly. Otherwise, stay here. But if you return to Barcelona do not be there when Franco arrives—and he will, make no mistake about it— or you will be shot if they find you."

This advice was more valuable than I could imagine since I later learned that only a few hours after the "liberation" of Barcelona five individuals had come looking for me at my home with the intention of "paying off old scores". It is certain that if they had found me I would not be writing this now. One must remember that, at the time, the ranks of Franco's supporters were filled with men who shared the views and ideology of the Nazis.

Finally, therefore, I did decide to leave and I joined Amelia to rest, eat white bread again and try to put on some weight. My normal weight was just under twelve stone; by the time I left Barcelona I had lost two. After many difficulties I reached the frontier at Le Perthus on 3 February 1939, in the company of many thousands of refugees heading for France. At Figueres, where I spent one night, we were subjected to heavy bombing which stopped us from sleeping. My last night in Catalonia before going on to France was spent in Vilafaié. The next day Vilafaié was destroyed in an air raid.

I recently found a letter I wrote shortly after arriving in Perpignan in which I said: "The last part of my stay in Catalonia was characterized by the determination of the

German pilots that we should not arrive in one piece. Between their good aim and our agility, a relentless battle was waged, won by those of us who arrived unharmed."

Once across the frontier at Le Perthus, I went straight to the first restaurant I saw and asked for a two-egg omelette, with white bread, which seemed to me like manna from heaven. When I tried to pay with pesetas they were not accepted; the waiter insisted on receiving francs and I had none. In the face of the owner's inflexibility I offered him my gold watch, which he accepted straight away. Exhausted, but no longer famished, I walked towards the French customs and to my great joy who should be there waiting for me but my smiling friend Pierre Nicolau. Accompanied by him I went through the various police barriers while Pierre was saluted by one and all as though he were a high-ranking officer.

He told me that Amelia and the girls were at Amélie-les-Bains, in the Pyrenees, where they had stood at the door of the hotel with other helpers dishing out soup to passing soldiers and civilian refugees who, with the despair of final defeat written on their faces, were flooding into France, being disarmed and sent to improvised camps at Argelès, Bacarès and other localities. I must mention that my kind friend, Pierre Nicclau, on learning how I had had to pay for my omelette, retrieved my watch and returned it to me.

The emotional scene of my reunion with my four womenfolk —Amelia and the three girls—can be imagined. Meli told me that her mother had spent the previous night crying, when it looked as if no one else was crossing into France and after she and her mother had spent the day asking everyone arriving from Spain if they had seen me. Everyone said no until someone told them that he had seen me at Figueres, which was unfortunate since that town was known to have been razed to the ground by bombing. My sudden appearance was therefore, in the eyes of my sweet wife, nothing less than a miracle.

Next day we moved to the Hotel de la Paix in Perpignan. On our second day there an English newspaperman, Donald Darling, who had lived for many years in Barcelona, came to tell me that the two English women doctors who had visited me at the hospital some months before, Miss Josephine Collier and Dr Audrey Russell, were enquiring whether I had left

Catalonia. "I told them you were here at the hotel and they are coming to see you."

The two doctors made me the same proposition they had already made to Amelia in writing some days before: that I should go to England, all expenses paid, simply to have a private conversation with members of the organization responsible, in case of war, for the civil defence of the country. The visit would last between ten and fifteen days. I told them that what I needed was sleep, food and quiet. "I am in no condition to go and start any form of campaign. Besides, my knowledge of English is so rudimentary that it would be of no help to me." "Oh," they said, "do not worry about that. The persons you would be dealing with all speak French as they are ex-officers who were in the army in France during the 1914 war."

Dr Frederic Duran, head of the Blood Transfusion Service in Catalonia, a friend of the English women doctors who had accompanied them around Barcelona, was also invited, as was Gaspar Alcoverro, an excellent person and great Catalan, whom I got to know very well in London where he lived until his death not long ago.

Finally, after three weeks, they convinced us; it was to be only a short visit which could however be of great benefit to Great Britain, as war was obviously inevitable. So, guided by Miss Collier, we were all put into the train bound for Paris.

It was a remarkable adventure. We had no papers, no money, and we were going to a country where no one was allowed in without going through an exhaustive check beforehand, for fear that spies might easily slip into the flood of fugitives from Europe wanting to cross the Channel. Finally, we were leaving the three girls alone in France in the care of a committee for Spanish refugees.

At Calais we boarded the crowded vessel for Dover, where Miss Collier drew us apart from the hundreds of people queueing, many of whom must have been Jewish doctors, and left us in a corner. After a while she came back with an officer who stared at us fixedly; they spoke awhile and finally the officer said "Follow me". We did so, to the curiosity of the crowd pressing against the barrier; we went through customs (we hardly had any luggage) and so found ourselves in

England. In London we split up. Duran was invited by Dr Newfield, a left-wing doctor; Alcoverro went to Miss Collier's and we were driven to a small hotel, the Lincoln Hall, now long bombed out of existence, near Russell Square.

It was a quiet place, clean, with good food and all essential services, occupied for the most part by retired civil servants. We were there on "demi-pension" which meant we had an abundant English breakfast and dinner. At midday I was usually busy with people who would invite me to a light lunch, sometimes a sandwich. Amelia however had no means of getting lunch, so she would secrete part of the breakfast in a cupboard and eat it later, cold and none too appetizing, when she was hungry. Sometimes—as I found out years later—she would not go out for a walk as it only made her hungrier.

As I have said, we had no money. However, the hotel director had a mysterious store of envelopes each containing a couple of pound notes and, from time to time, when I apologetically approached him in my poor English, I would be given one.

This then is how we entered England at the end of February 1939. I was allowed to rest a few days and then Batista i Roca, the representative of the Generalitat in Britain, accompanied me to the headquarters of the Civil Defence on the Embankment near the Houses of Parliament. There I met Dr (later Sir) Francis Fraser and four other doctors, all of whom spoke French. They welcomed me very courteously and started to fire questions at me, finally asking me what I would do if I were in charge of the civil defence of London. Where would I situate the ambulances? How would I distribute the hospitals? Where would I place the most active doctors? And the nurses? etc. I told them that I could not answer their questions as I did not know the topography of London: I did not even know how many bridges there were across the river. I said I thought the first thing the Germans would do would be to try to destroy the bridges, as they had done at home. I did not know how many hospital beds they had on each side of the river, nor how many doctors, nor how many nurses they had available.

They explained to me that nurses were no problem. They had been running courses lasting three months and already had 40,000 provisional nurses. Half-trained girls, who would be in

charge of First Aid Posts for the initial treatment of the injured.
I was horrified when I heard this. I tried to make them understand that the seriously hurt would arrive dead at the
hospital if they were first taken to First Aid Posts; that they
would only be extracted with difficulty from the bombed site,
because the building would probably have collapsed and the
street have been destroyed; that they would be placed on
stretchers, and transferred from stretchers to ambulances,
from which they were proposing to remove them to be treated
by young girls, as it was impossible that they would have on
call 40,000 doctors most of whom would be with the armed
forces. I advised them to eliminate these posts which they had
planned: to send the wounded direct and as fast as possible to
hospital where there would be a ward for selection and someone to decide who was to go home, who to be taken immediately into the operating theatre, to be put to bed, etc.
They told me this was impossible. That they had only started
the recruiting campaign for nurses six months before and its
success had been heartwarming. If what they had planned
proved a failure, there was always time to modify the
organization as I was proposing.

They then asked me if I would like to prepare a project for
London, and that they would be glad to give me any details I
might require. I prepared a project in French, of which I still
have a copy (as also of the English translation), in which I
explained that, given the construction of London, I thought
the Germans would primarily use incendiary bombs. I reminded them that these bombs had not given the enemy good
enough results in Barcelona, where houses are built of bricks
and stone, but had been very successful in the Basque
country and in villages where wood was largely used in
buildings.

In outline, my scheme was divided into sections correspond-
ing to such diverse matters as the types of ambulances, picking
up of the wounded, etc., but always on the premise that
casualties should be taken straight to the nearest hospital,
without going through the First Aid Posts which, I insisted,
would not only be useless but potentially harmful to the
injured.

The second part related to hospitals inside the city area, with the conclusion that the nearer the hospital to the bombed zone, the quicker casualties could be treated, always assuming the hospital itself was intact. I stressed again that the hospital had to have a ward for immediate inspection of patients. In this way the injured who needed urgent surgical intervention would be treated without delay and without incurring the shock caused by the various successive moves: from the ruins of a building, into and out of ambulances, without having received the essential attention they really required such as blood transfusions or surgical treatment in the operating theatre, and with a surgeon on stand-by.

I also emphasized the importance of the adequate disposition of ambulance stations and a sufficient availability of hospital beds especially in or near industrial zones at which one could assume the air raids would be directed, rather than residential areas.

Based upon my own experience, I made an approximate calculation of the number of doctors, nurses, ambulances, etc., which might be required in a period of twenty-four hours in London, assuming that the number of casualties would not be over 10,000 in any one day. My calculation was based on the statistics of Barcelona. Assuming an attack by 1,000 bombers which equalled, amply, the total number of aircraft which bombed Barcelona during the whole of the war, we could expect some 5,500 serious stretcher casualties requiring removal to hospital; some 2,500 could be expected to arrive more or less conscious, or slightly injured, also on stretchers. Around 2,000, I thought, would be sitting or walking wounded. I calculated the number and types of ambulances which I considered indispensable to cope with around a maximum of 10,000 such casualties a day.

I took into account that in the most severe air raids which we suffered in Barcelona, between 17 and 19 March 1938, 670 persons were killed, 1,200 were wounded, 48 buildings were destroyed and 71 badly damaged.

Less than a month after the beginning of World War II, a letter appeared in the *News Chronicle* in London suggesting that if the experience of the war in Spain were valid, it would seem that treatment of air-raid casualties in First Aid Posts was not only inadvisable but actually prejudicial to the healing of the injured. It was written by a newspaperman who, without realizing it, was confirming my views. Barely three months after the air raids started on the large industrial cities of Britain, the First Aid Posts, on which so many hopes had been laid, were closed.

The fact that on the first day we met I was told by the Civil Defence heads that they were expecting 100,000 casualties a day, as opposed to the 10,000 foreseen in my calculations, makes my failure to convince them understandable. Horrified rather than merely surprised, I concluded that it was best that we leave matters to run their course.

In fact, statistics of the air raids on London show that the maximum number of casualties in any twenty-four hours when London Docks and the City were "blitzed" totalled some 9,250. This proves the wisdom of Leonardo da Vinci's observation that progress is not due to the acceptance of the criterion of any credible authority, but to the general acknowledgment of its accuracy over the passage of time.

This thought brings me to the consideration of a number of axiomatic beliefs, as regards the treatment of war wounds, with which I was faced from the moment of my arrival in England. Conscious of approaching international conflict, the leading medical and surgical authorities of the country expounded their knowledge in a series of articles which appeared in *The Lancet* and *The British Medical Journal* during 1939. For example, my acquaintance, Mr E. M. Cowell, together with P. H. Mitchiner, said in *The Lancet* at the beginning of 1939 that in order to treat a war wound it was essential to resect the "channel" caused by the shrapnel and suture the skin immediately, if the suture could be performed without tension. In another article, also in *The Lancet*, the author insisted that the injured should be transported to places where they could be treated and bandaged, but never directly to the hospital. In 1940 another article, also in *The Lancet*, repeated that resection of the damaged tissue must not be carried out if the first hours had been lost, because by then infection would have set in and excision of the tissues could kill the patient through septic dissemination. My authority, in accordance with da Vinci's dictum, was relatively of little use; but by the beginning of 1943 experience had proved me right, when enough blood had been shed to correct the errors. More recently, in the Vietnam war, the surgical head of the Australian Expeditionary Forces wrote in *The Journal of Bone and Joint Surgery* that, contrary to what had been believed before, excision had to be performed on wounds, no matter how much time had elapsed since the wound was sustained, "as Trueta said".

Famous surgeons, like Reginald Watson-Jones, opposed me early on because at the beginning they advocated the suturing of wounds immediately after the operation. Others, following the example of Winnett Orr, placed all their hopes on the drainage of the wound—giving no importance to the excision or resection of the damaged tissue—by packing the wound with gauze spread with vaseline ("to avoid the gauze becoming soaked with pus"), as if it were a case of chronic bone infection.

My presence in London obviously aroused a certain amount of interest as I kept receiving letters asking me to clear up doubtful points of my method. On the advice of Miss Collier and Dr Cecil Flemming, I wrote a letter to *The Lancet* in answer to distorted information in that distinguished medical journal which our acquaintances Mr Mitchiner and Mr Cowell had quoted from their book in which illustrations of mine appeared. They stated that the danger of my method was that it could induce gas gangrene, a frequently lethal complication. In my letter I said that when he came to visit us in Barcelona, Mr Cowell had not seen a single case of gas gangrene, and that therefore one wondered where he had got the information from. Later he confessed to me that he himself had not wanted to connect my method with gas gangrene, but that Mitchiner, his senior, had insisted on saying that my method, so different from the conventional method which Mitchener had consistently recommended in his articles, could not be dissociated from this dangerous complication.

My report to the Civil Defence authorities was not received with any enthusiasm. Possibly because it did not predict the daily casualty rate of 100,000 which they expected, it was considered of little, if any, value. That is why when Dr Fraser told me, very politely, that in some ways I had disappointed them, reacting with Mediterranean heat—I had only been in London about a month—I replied in French: "Donnez-moi mon chapeau, s'il vous plaît." Fraser asked me why. "I'm going home since I believe that, with a casualty rate of 100,000 a day, the war will be over in three days." With some irony, I added: "Maybe it would last three days in Barcelona. In London, as you are English and therefore more stoical, it will probably last four." I never found out if they understood me. What is sure though is that it was the last time I saw them. I went back to the hotel and told Amelia to start packing as my mission was accomplished—and not very brilliantly at that.

Next day Miss Collier came to see me again and to my great surprise told me that as a result of my conversations with Fraser and his colleagues, there was now a very special interest in hearing me speak on my treatment of war wounds before I returned to France. She had come to tell me that I would be visited at our hotel by Sir Cuthbert Wallace, surgeon to His Majesty the King. The purpose of the visit by my most distinguished colleague was to ask me to give a private lecture to a select group of surgeons, many of them university professors, who, in time of war, would be in charge of the military surgical services. Sir Cuthbert said they wanted to discuss with me the possible advantages of the treatment of war wounds I had used in Catalonia.

I do not have to say how pleased I was to hear that my colleagues wanted to know about and discuss my work as a surgeon. I accepted the flattering proposal at once. If they wished, I answered, I could have the lecture ready in a couple of days as it was a subject with which I was fully conversant. With the calmness characteristic of his countrymen, Sir Cuthbert said I did not have to rush things, since a meeting attended by the highest surgical authorities in the country would not be a mere improvisation, bearing in mind that many of them lived in places as far from London as Belfast, Edinburgh, Glasgow, Cardiff, etc.

What with one thing and another, here we were in April with Amelia and I in London and the girls in France. My wife and I lost no opportunity of insisting on their being allowed to join us, otherwise we would leave. When it was proposed that I should stay to lecture on my treatment of war and air raid wounds, and that the actual lecture would not take place for some time, I again insisted that the girls should join us.

We kept receiving letters from Meli, by then fourteen and in charge of her two sisters of four and six years of age, complaining that we seemed to have abandoned them.

Before we had left for England, intending only to spend a few days there, one of the English ladies taking care of Spanish refugees, a Miss Esme, had taken the girls by car to Bayonne, having told us that they would be going to a house specially leased to take care of the children of intellectual refugees. Amelia and I were assured, before we set off for London and left them for what we thought was to be a short while, that they would be well looked after.

Meli told us later that the place they were taken to was frightful: straw palliasses on the floor, dirt, lack of services, etc. They were the only children with any luggage at all and the others shared anything that they received from the Spanish refugee committees. They were all utterly miserable.

As we were still in Perpignan, which we were leaving that evening, Meli left her sisters and sought the nearest public telephone to tell us of their predicament. We remembered a Mme Durand who had a hotel in Bayonne; I had operated on her son and she had offered to help us in any way she could. Meli telephoned her explaining their situation, and she offered to have them at once. The same afternoon Meli moved into the hotel with her two small sisters and their luggage. All went well until a few days later when it seems Mme Durand panicked, perhaps at the prospect of finding herself landed with three penniless children although she had been promised that she would be paid as soon as this could be arranged. Whatever the reason, she threw them out, accusing Meli of lying since, according to her, she had discovered that we had no money. Miss Esme appeared again and this time took the girls to a farm house they had rented near the small Basque village of Itxassou, in the French Pyrenees, from where Meli frequently wrote to us. Her letters spoke of cold, hunger and scabies ("Is it contagious? What do I do if the girls get it?"), and so on.

On 10 May, having spent nearly three months at Itxassou, we finally succeeded in getting the girls to England and when they arrived from Paris at Victoria Station they looked so fat and healthy that we hardly recognized them. We had been expecting three skeletons, and here they were like balloons, bloated from a diet of potatoes, bread and milk.

One of the things which helped in finally getting our children from France was our insistence that, if it was a question of finance then the five of us should be found somewhere to live for the same price they had been paying to keep the two of us at the Lincoln Hall Hotel. We never did discover who paid for our lodging, incidentally. A boarding house at 67 Eaton Avenue, Swiss Cottage was found where not only did we have accommodation but also, on the ground floor, there was a kindergarten, the Lyndel School, which Montse and Julie attended from the first day of our arrival. Julie learnt English with the ease of a child of four which I should like to have been able to emulate.

Meli, who knew English passably well thanks to her two years at the Anglo-American school in Bordighera during the Civil War, was required to do a grown-up job. We could find no one in London speaking Catalan and English with the time to translate my book *El Tractament de les Fractures de Guerra*, which I had originally written in Catalan and of which I only possessed one copy. Therefore no sooner had Meli arrived in London than she was put in front of a typewriter to translate my book.

I do not have the original of what she wrote at fourteen years of age and with no knowledge of medicine. I remember with pleasure that Dr Cecil Flemming put her translation into good English and I have a letter from him dated 14 June 1939, asking that Meli should translate the captions which were to accompany the photographs of my book.

Having thus solved the problem of our reunion with our three daughters, I was able to accept the proposal to lecture on war wounds.

Escorted by Dr Cecil Flemming and Sir Cuthbert Wallace, I walked to the magnificent building of the Royal Society of Medicine at 1 Wimpole Street, with certain misgivings. I was fully aware of what was at stake; it was not so much a question of my staying in the United Kingdom, which at that time was not of any decisive importance for me, but of my reputation as a surgeon. I kept saying to myself—If I do not convince them of the sincerity of the report and of the efficacy of my treatment, it is going to be very difficult for anyone else to believe me.

The meeting was held on 14 July, in the lecture room with a

horseshoe-shaped table, seating about fifty people. At the centre
of the curve of the horseshoe, on a high rostrum, sat Sir Cuthbert, with me on his left and Flemming next to me. Around
the table sat about forty-five senior surgeons, some of them
professors and others high-ranking service officers who, according to Sir Cuthbert, represented not only the army, navy and
air force, but also the newly created emergency medical
service. Little did I realize looking round the table that, two
months later, nearly all those present would be among the
surgical heads of the armed forces of Great Britain at war.

After a short, cordial introduction from Sir Cuthbert, I
started off, as previously agreed, in French. Not five minutes
had gone by when I noticed a rumble of protest coming from
one of the ends of the table. The most outspoken objector,
addressing himself to Sir Cuthbert, said he did not understand
one word of my French and requested that I be asked to make
an effort and speak in English as, no matter how weak my
English was it would be better than his practically non-existent
French. Looking slightly guilty, Sir Cuthbert said he and
Flemming would help me. My morale at that moment hit
rock-bottom. Mainly with the help of my hands, I tried to
explain the characteristics of the wounds caused by the various
types of bombs. It makes me smile now to remember that, years
later when I no longer had difficulty in expressing myself in
English, Flemming told me of the great impression my description of the disturbing effect of delayed action and armour-
piercing bombs had made on them all, with my imitation of
the whistle of the falling bomb and the thunder produced
when it exploded inside its objective. According to Flemming,
many of them were on the point of diving under the table. . . .

My lecture came to an end and, to my great relief, the
discussion which followed it was brief. I felt as if I had been set
free. I was sure I had convinced no one and notwithstanding
the fact that they had brought us the girls from France, I was
quite certain we should all be back there very soon. With his
usual kindness, Sir Cuthbert told me not to rush away as some
of those present wanted to greet me personally. By the door,
standing on the right of Sir Cuthbert, I shook hands with the
departing medical heads all of whom murmured a few words
which I took to be a sign of polite English upbringing rather

than any form of acceptance of my contentions. The queue shortened and finally there was just one gentleman left, about sixty years old, with a splendid physique. This gentleman, while shaking my hand with manifest cordiality, let rip a flood of words so unintelligible to me that they might have been Shakespearean verse for all I knew. Once again, Sir Cuthbert spread his protective mantle over me and explained what our distinguished colleague was saying. He was excusing himself for having been the one who complained that I was speaking in French. His name was that of a figure of international repute in orthopaedics—Gathorne Robert Girdlestone, the first professor of orthopaedics in the United Kingdom and head of the famous Wingfield Morris Orthopaedic Hospital at Oxford. I little knew then that fate was to decree that I should one day follow after him in his chair at Oxford.

When I got back home, I said to Amelia: "Today I have met a number of very important gentlemen, amongst them the Professor of Orthopaedics at Oxford, who is a very famous man due to his surgical treatment of tuberculosis. Our troubles are now all over. Let us go straight back to France as they did not understand one half of what I told them."

However, shortly after that I received an invitation from Professor Girdlestone to join a collective visit being made to Oxford by delegates of the World Conference of Workers for Cripples, which was then being held in London. He had added a personal note on the invitation—insisting I should go; he said it would only take one morning and I would be back in London by the evening. Amelia said she thought I should go—if only to see Oxford.

We were to meet at a certain London square on 19 July. I arrived too early at the meeting place. After a while someone started calling out people's names: "Trueta, bus number nine." I made for the bus, which was empty. The others were filling up but no one seemed to be coming to this one. After a while a small gentleman, with a Panama hat and a fancy waistcoat got in, made straight for me, gave the Fascist salute and asked me, in Italian, if I spoke his language. Heavens above! So that was it. This man was Mussolini's delegate. I answered yes, I did speak Italian, which pleased him greatly as he said he did not speak a word of anything else.

A few minutes later the bus suddenly filled with very tall, Nordic gentlemen, led by a giant. "Heil Hitler!" they all said to me. It seems that those responsible for the transport arrangements, on seeing the name of an unknown who came from Spain thought I must be Franco's delegate; and so I was placed with Hitler's and Mussolini's. After we had talked awhile, they soon realized that I did not share their ideology. One German said to me that all we could see would soon be "ours". I said no, not "ours", perhaps yours but not ours. I told him I was sure Spain would not enter the war which was coming. But the German insisted she would; that everything was arranged. I tried to make him see that Spain was utterly devastated, after nearly three years of civil war. That there were no bridges, roads, railways, nothing. How could she get involved in another war? The German had a ready answer. He said they would look after all the details. That Spain would come into the war with the Italians and that the great courage of the Spaniards together with German technique would make us masters of the whole world. He insisted so much that finally I told him that I for one was not going to come into the war. He gave me a nasty look and left me alone. No one said another word to me for the rest of the journey.

A little while later we arrived at Oxford where, for the first time, Professor Girdlestone welcomed me with open arms, a welcome he maintained until his death ten years later. But not without first seating me in his professorial chair.

Chapter 2

MY THOUGHTS AND FEELINGS ON
LEAVING CATALONIA

THE INFLUENCE OF the conditions under which we were living—public disorder, deplorable State administration (which, incidentally, must have been similar to what the former Spanish colonies in America had had to bear), made us Catalans think that, if left alone, we would be able to establish a social system in which the individual could prosper commensurately with his own capabilities and inclinations in fraternal collaboration with the rest of Spain so that, in a few decades, we might get Spain to make up the ground achieved by Western Europe in the course of the last 300 years. We felt that the mission of Castile, and therefore the Spanish State, was misconceived in that it sought to suppress us because this desire on the part of the majority of my generation was not understood by the Spanish leaders. Consequently, not only Catalanism but merely being Catalan was considered a violation against what they called "the unity of the fatherland", which in fact meant nothing more nor less than subjection to Castile. This is how it was then and still is, fifty years later.

Many of us, future scientists, artists, craftsmen and the like, felt deeply the need to achieve something personal which should at the same time have a social impact. Although we were considered citizens of a different category, with customs differing from those of other Spaniards, we believed that through our efforts we would be able to win recognition of the fact that we still existed as a people and that the characteristics described by the best Spanish writers—Pidal, Madariaga, Sánchez Albornoz, Américo Castro and others—are not applicable to the Catalans. That there are common traits between Castilians and Catalans is the result, on the one hand, of mimicry found in all oppressed peoples where opportunists among the ruled tend to adopt the forms of conduct and expression of those in power in order to gain admission, however superficially, to the dominant society—and on the other hand, of the same civilizing factors which both experienced, such as Christianity, Germanic and Latin miscegenation and the fact that Arab penetration into Catalonia and Old Castile was comparatively slight. The same mixture is to be found, although in varying proportions, in the Italian and French peoples.

The scales of values of Castilian and Catalan peoples also differ slightly. In Catalonia, the source of traditional power stems from the pact between classes, whereas in Castile power runs vertically from top to bottom. We Catalans therefore had a feudal structure as early as France since it was after the battle of Poitiers that the system of feudal dependency began to be established. This system brought order to places where previously only the irresistible will of the strongest prevailed. In Castile, warfare, whether against the Moors or among themselves, constituted the main occupation for centuries, whereas in Catalonia, from the Parliament at Lleida in 1214 until Catalan rights were abolished by the Spanish and French armies in 1714, royal prerogatives never ceased to be debated in accordance with the "Right to Pact", from which system modern constitutional monarchies later evolved. Since 1714, Madrid has tried to make us Catalans feel and think in the same way as they themselves are obliged to, and this is like wanting an adult to continue to think as he did when an adolescent.

This digression is necessary to explain the main motives which led me to act as I did when, already holding a post of certain importance, I decided to stay in England and start a new life in an environment such as I would have wished for my own country as well as for the whole of Spain.

Notwithstanding the instability in which we had lived in Barcelona from my childhood, there was a remarkable flowering of art and in all spheres of human creativity. Not even bombs, assassinations, disorders and strikes could halt the impetus of the artistic renaissance in Barcelona in the midst of which I grew up and matured. It was like a reaction of the Catalans against all the disorders which the Spanish State could not put an end to.

Thus, Barcelona, which had less than half a million inhabitants when I was born, by 1910 officially had a population of 587,411 (only 10,000 less than Madrid)—a rate of growth unequalled by any European city at the time—even though it was known as the "City of Bombs"! Later it was to become famous for possessing one of the finest medieval art museums in the world, for its modernistic "New Century" buildings, for having the first two sports stadiums in Spain, the first concert hall, the first—and, up to now, only—opera house (the Liceu) in Spain, the largest number of art galleries, and so forth. It was also blessed with the popular Catalan Orfeó and the Pau Casals Orchestra of international repute. One can add that all this burgeoning of artistic and creative activity occurred without any State aid, unless we consider that lack of official support can paradoxically in itself create a stimulus. I have myself always thought it to be a stimulant rather than a depressant, as is evidenced by the Jews who, despite 2,000 years of persecution have the highest average of capable citizens of all kinds (in particular scientists and musicians) wherever they have settled in the civilized world. Young Jews know that in order to achieve important posts in the society in which they live, they have to make a greater effort than the indigenous Gentiles. For this reason they usually surpass others wherever they establish themselves.

This interpretation of the society in the midst of which I grew up seems borne out by the remarkable absence of Catalans within the Spanish State and para-State services, including the army and the police. It was exceptional for a young Catalan of my time—and later—to join an official body, despite the pensioned retirement which this would have assured him. Personal effort, parental example and the stimulus of contemporary life have always been the most important sources of energy for me and for many of my generation.

From a Spanish viewpoint, this lack of Catalan representation in the administration of the whole country, including Catalonia itself, has been a disaster. Spain failed to take advantage of the statesman-like qualities of Catalans like Prat de la Riba and his companion Francesc Cambó, which were at their disposal. The final result was that the greatest concentration of industry in the whole of Spain occurred in Catalonia

and the Basque country, where socio-psychological developments very similar to those in Catalonia took place, while in
the whole of the rest of the Spanish State—Castilian Spain—
the medieval structure persisted with very little progress to be
seen, if we except increasing officialdom in the armed forces,
the clergy, bureaucracy and state politics; in short, insufficient
to absorb the younger population which increasingly emigrated
to the two great industrial centres, in particular Catalonia,
which gave rise to the phenomena already referred to.

The recent industrial development of Madrid owes as much
to the example of France—the desire to build a new Paris—as
to that of Catalonia, combined with a belated attempt to centre
the uniformity of the Spanish State on the capital, as with
Paris in the case of France since the reign of Blanche of Castile,
during the minority of the boy who was later to become Saint
Louis. The Albigensian crusade, the Inquisition and the dis-
appearance of the Oc-speaking aristocracy were all factors
which permitted France to be forged in the moulds imposed
on it by the North and, from the beginning of the thirteenth
century, by Paris. In Spain this was not possible because the
advances which, under Catalan direction, were made in the
kingdom of Aragon far exceeded in terms of order and progress
those of contemporary Castile.

We had all these thoughts while we were busy studying
medicine. A lot of my friends thought alike, as did most of my
contemporaries. The streets were less dangerous than appeared,
nevertheless the uncertainty of what might happen there
accompanied us all our lives. The Catalan Mancomunitat
(Commonwealth)* gave us an idea of what we could achieve
and we had high hopes that, if with the modest powers it gave
us we could already do so much, Catalonia might become an
efficient country, like other small countries in northern Europe
demographically similar. These thoughts made us all "Cata-
lanists", without wishing for a severance of our ties with the
Spanish State. I well remember the excitement we felt at the
meetings held during the campaign for Catalan autonomy in
1919, when the politicians speaking assured us that we should
have to be granted autonomy because we Catalans wished to
remain Catalan.

* See page 44.

Chapter 3

SPANISH REFUGEES IN FRANCE

DURING MY SHORT stay in Perpignan I managed to get a pet project of mine started—a project which I had been planning since the defeat of the republic became inevitable. In my earlier visits to Perpignan when I went to see Amelia and the girls while the Civil War was still on, I had met several observers of the Non-Intervention Committee. One of them, Knud Broch, a Danish military observer, seemed to be one of the few conscious of the rôle they were being made to play— and he soon gave proofs of his sympathy for the prolonged suffering to which they were contributing. As soon as I crossed the frontier at the end of the war, I met Broch at the home of our friend Dr Nicolau. He was, like everyone else, over-whelmed by the impact of the human flood pouring into France, and particularly worried by the fate awaiting members of the International Brigades. He had been in contact with various people—among them Einstein's nephew, Karl, pro-fessor at the Sorbonne, and Miss Acland Allen, of the Inter-national Peace Campaign in Geneva—advising those members who could not return home, like the Italians and the Germans, where they could go. My project, which I discussed with Broch and Miss Allen, was that the refugees should be grouped according to their origins—such as Catalans and Basques. At that time they were all mixed up in such camps as Barcarès, St Cyprien and Argelès. The general talk was of mass emigration, but those who had the funds to make this possible were doing nothing to foment it. Among the refugees were hundreds of thousands of Catalans, mostly people with a trade or agricultural workers with basic education, whereas the vast majority of the rest were illiterate, a situation which was inevitably bound to give rise to problems. Through Broch we discovered that at Agde a camp was being planned which would be greatly superior to the rest. We therefore aimed at getting all the Catalans together into this particular camp, from whence they could either emigrate, or return home if they could do so without danger. Broch even saw Colonel Touling, who was to be the commandant of the new camp. He then travelled to London, where he had meetings with various persons in authority, including the Canadian High Commissioner. He got in touch with a certain Catalan gentleman in Paris who was supposedly in charge of the refugee problem. He contacted the Bolivian embassy to try and organize mass emigration. Filing cards were filled in and questionnaires answered—everyone seemed optimistic of success.

On 9 March 1939 the group of observers of the Non-Intervention Committee in Perpignan was dissolved, and Broch was able to dedicate more time to my project. I was already in London, but my brother and Eduard Barba were still in Perpignan and they kept me informed of progress. They were preparing a list of some 9,000 Catalans for Broch, listed under professions or trades—however, my brother's letters were imbued with a certain amount of pessimism due to the reaction of the Committee for Refugees in Paris. On 24 March Rafel wrote to me that he had seen Broch who was complaining of non-co-operation by the Catalan exiled authorities and even suspected that they were opposed to the project. Despite all kinds of setbacks, the plan seemed to be going ahead: Eduard and Rafel went on planning—the camp was to have its judge, police, heads of barracks, all elected. There was to be an outside infirmary and sports ground. The dining hall would also be used as a leisure room and for lectures.

However, as progress finally came to a standstill Broch one day got fed up with the whole matter and dropped it. He had even been accused of being an agent of Franco! The project thus came to nought, due in part to internal jealousies among the Catalan authorities and their lack of sympathy with Broch, Eduard, my brother and others. I was not too surprised—I was well aware of the inefficiency of Catalan politicians in power during the Civil War—they had given us plenty of proofs of this while the war lasted. All our aspirations came to nothing, like a passing dream: the ideal of all us Catalans going somewhere together and settling down into a society where we could carry on living as Catalans had proved unrealizable.

My brother Rafel first went to live in Chartres hoping that I would be able to arrange his papers so that he could join me and my family in Britain. This turned out to be just one more nightmare.

My brother had left Catalonia at the end of the Civil War, a bachelor, prepared to help me maintain my young family. He could have returned to Barcelona with our mother as, having belonged to no political party nor having held any official post, his name was on no black list. However, he would not do so: his conscience impelled him to help me since our mother, who had gone to live with my sister in Barcelona, was in no need of assistance.

Until the problem of our daughters coming to Britain, which they did in May 1939, and until such time as my own position in England was resolved, it did not seem reasonable to try to get Rafel permission to join us. However, once Professor Girdlestone had found financial means to keep me and my family in England, originally for six months after the start of World War II, I really moved heaven and earth to get my brother the necessary entrance permit. Both Miss Collier and Professor Girdlestone knew of my anxiety for my brother, and they did their best through their many influential connections. I wrote to Miss Eleanor Rathbone, MP, telling her that three months had elapsed since I had written to the Home Office from whom I had heard nothing. She replied that she thought it unlikely that my brother would be allowed in since the Home Office maintained that no more doctors were required. If, she added, things should change later, they would reconsider the case. Rafel meanwhile had received an offer to go to Mexico—but still refused it in the hope of being able to join us, although his two great friends, with whom he had shared so many joys and sorrows, were leaving for America.

All kinds of friends were now helping me—Mr Geoffrey Edwards, Secretary of the Royal Society of Medicine and a friend of Miss Collier; Elizabeth Montagu-Pollock; Dr J. H. Hebb; Mr Zachary Cope, President of the Surgical Section of the Royal Society of Medicine. But the ministry still replied that, for the moment, the answer was negative. On 23 January 1940, the personal secretary of Sir Alexander Maxwell, Under

Secretary at the Home Office, asked me to let her have all Rafel's details, although the case would not be reconsidered by Mr Peake, of the Home Office, until March. The Joint Committee for Refugees, according to Mr Edwards and Lord Listowel of The British Committee for Refugees from Spain also applied for permission—all to no avail. On 14 May, Miss Collier wrote to tell me that Mr Harry Strauss, MP, had sent her a letter received from the Home Office to the effect that doctors were not needed. The fall of France and the German occupation of Paris compelled Rafel to flee south. Through the good offices of Dr Audrey Russell we heard that Rafel was somewhere near Bordeaux trying to get on a ship to America. I was then told that if he managed to arrive in the United Kingdom somehow, he would be allowed to stay—I was at least pleased to hear that they would not send him back to France. However, in the meantime Rafel was no longer alone: he had married a beautiful exiled Catalan girl by whom he had a baby girl and when he was offered space on a vessel to Mexico he accepted. In Mexico City he became a well-known and highly esteemed ear-nose-and-throat specialist. Later, they had two more children. I have always missed him.

All these many years later I find myself free of any rancour towards British bureaucracy. It makes me half smile to re-read the answer to Mr Geoffrey R. Edwards, dated 3 January 1940, to my request for permission to let my brother join us. It reads:

The Home Secretary regrets, however, that having regard to the policy which he has been obliged to follow in connection with the admission to this country of foreign medical practitioners, with which, of course, you are familiar, he cannot see his way to admit Dr R. Trueta i Raspall at the present time. Should the general situation change, however, in such a way as to make it possible for him to revise his decision, the Home Secretary will be prepared to consider the case again, and it has accordingly been suggested to Mr Peake, who has been approached by Lord Listowel, that the British Committee for Refugees from Spain should draw attention to the case again in, say three months.

After the fearful conquest of Poland and with the massive

5*

attack against France just over the horizon, the British administration still thought they would not need any more doctors.
. . . It was obviously a waste of time to tell them how German
pilots had learnt their tactics of destruction. Guernica and the
Condor Division still smacked of "red" propaganda. By great
good fortune, Churchill, who had been pushed into a corner
by the British Establishment for so long—was not asleep.

I cannot end on this subject without a few words of gratitude
to those noble souls who had enough imagination to continue
to struggle against the lack of understanding and the mental
inflexibility of so many otherwise honest British civil servants.

Chapter 4

WE SETTLE IN OXFORD

AT THE BEGINNING of August 1939, while we were still living in Eaton Avenue, friends of Miss Collier, the Montagu-Pollocks, lent us their beautiful home in Oxford, the Vineyard, for a few days of rest. The house was very near the one we were later to live in for many years. We spent a relaxing time there—the house having a large garden for the children to play in and being near enough for me to visit the Wingfield Morris Orthopaedic Hospital every morning and get to know it well and the surgeons working there.

It was already merely a question of days before war broke out and Professor Girdlestone (GRG) was busy trying to arrange the necessary permits which would enable me to work in Great Britain. Amelia and the girls were evacuated from London as it was feared that immediately upon the outbreak of war air raids would start. Thanks to the generosity of Lord Nuffield, who was a great friend of GRG, I was granted an allowance of £50 per month for six months. GRG was sure that as soon as war was declared, my work permit would come through and I would be able to start operating at the hospital.

On Sunday, 3 September at 11 am Neville Chamberlain broadcast to the nation that Great Britain was at war with Germany. The Germans had invaded Poland the day before, so we all knew what the prime minister was going to say. I heard the broadcast from Miss Collier's home that Sunday morning and clearly remember that no sooner had he finished speaking than the air-raid sirens sounded.

Within a week of the declaration of war, GRG duly obtained the authorization of the Oxford Regional Hospitals Board to invite me to work at the Wingfield. Shortly after, the Minister of Health, Mr Malcolm MacDonald, nominated me "Adviser to the Ministry of Health at the Wingfield Hospital", a stratagem which allowed me to operate without having to revalidate my qualifications.

Exiled Catalan friends of ours in London were looking for somewhere to live in Oxford, like us, and we finally took a large house together at 163 Woodstock Road. It had three floors, which allowed plenty of room for both families. No sooner had we moved in than Meli, just fifteen, developed acute appendicitis and had to have an emergency operation. We visited her the following day in the nursing home and she told us of her amazement when the night before the nurse had brought her a glass of water in which to put her teeth!

At the time I joined the hospital, GRG's staff included Mr Peter Foley, Mr J. C. Scott (a Canadian surgeon), and an Austrian working on a thesis who turned out to be a Nazi and was later interned in Canada. For me it was of great interest to see how GRG ran his hospital on a completely personal basis. He had created it during the First World War, following in the footsteps of the great Robert Jones. He considered himself perfectly at liberty to decide on everything to do with orthopaedics at Oxford. I soon got to know more of his extraordinary personality. He was a very religious man, happily married but with no children. He was a good tennis player and had been awarded a Blue for golf. He had an unequivocal sense of right and wrong which, due to his somewhat impulsive nature, he sometimes carried a bit too far, after which he would immediately be filled with remorse, beg one's pardon and reproach himself for being so bad-tempered, which was being unfair on himself. He was fond of me and I of him. I always took him with a pinch of salt but, although he was aware of this, he never seemed to mind.

GRG, tired of teaching, had planned to leave the Chair of Orthopaedics, of which he was the first occupant, on reaching the age of sixty. He therefore started looking for someone with an academic bent and an interest in research who would leave him free to run the hospital without being tied to teaching.

The candidate selected by GRG was Herbert James Seddon, a brilliant young man who had impressed him greatly at the Congress of Orthopaedics held in the spring of 1939. Seddon was duly appointed and took possession of the Chair on 15 January 1940, when I had already been working a few months at the hospital and had become a member of the Royal Society of Medicine.

Seddon and I soon became good friends. I remember one evening, shortly after his arrival at the hospital, he asked if he could come and see me at home. He looked very worried and told me that he was afraid of not succeeding in his venture as he felt that GRG was difficult to get on with, being a man of impulsive reactions with an imperious bearing. He asked me what I would do to establish my position if I were in his place. I told him I had no difficulty in dealing with GRG; that I was always absolutely sincere with him and told him what I thought, short of offending him. I recognized that he was the creator of the hospital and once this premise was accepted on both sides everything took its natural course. However I did tell Seddon that I thought some things should be changed: for instance, the way the ward rounds were made. GRG would go from bed to bed, accompanied by the hospital team. He would pronounce his opinion first and then ask the others for theirs. If the opinions did not coincide, the differences would be discussed aloud in front of the patient, thus obviously creating doubts which I thought disastrous for the patient's morale and of little benefit to the postgraduate students who were with the team. I thought it would be best to have the patient brought to a lecture room where he could be examined, and then removed prior to discussion of the case. Seddon, I said, should have the final word. This practice was, in fact, successfully adopted without causing any frictions, and although GRG would usually speak at the end, all the discussions were in private with the patient no longer present.

The other change I told Seddon I thought to be essential was the setting up of a photographic department. GRG used to do the rounds with a camera hanging from his neck. When he wanted to take a photograph, an assistant would hold up a blackboard, write the patient's number on it and use it as background. The result was that the case histories were all covered in amateurish pictures, of which only about one in ten could possibly be published; the rest were only fit for the wastepaper basket. I told Seddon that I thought we should have a professional photographer and a fully equipped photographic laboratory. Seddon thanked me for my advice, both my suggestions were adopted and as today, thirty-six years later, they are still in operation, they can be assumed to have been of some practical use.

Around this time another important event took place: the creation of the Accident Service at the Radcliffe Infirmary in Oxford. The Canadian, Jim Scott, who had had some hopes of becoming professor although he was then only thirty-one years old, was in charge and was responsible for organizing it on very efficient lines.

One must bear in mind that accident cases are rarely taken to orthopaedic hospitals. I was asked by GRG my opinion on how the service should be arranged, the original idea being to create a department of fractures only. I said I thought it inadequate—too many cases would escape the orthopaedic surgeon's care. I favoured the creation of a complete Accident Service, under the care of an orthopaedic surgeon. In this way our colleague would be able to centralize its direction, as he would be part of a general hospital. GRG asked me to write a paper on this, which I did, and it came out as an editorial.

Scott, "the father of the child", was put in charge of the new service. At the beginning there were about thirty beds and, with the collaboration of Mr Masina, a very distinguished and able Indian surgeon who had studied at Cambridge, John M. Barnes, with whom I was beginning to do some research work, and two residents, the necessary assistance was assured.

In 1942 Scott joined the RAF and asked me if I would look after his department while he was away at the war.

It must be remembered that I was then still a temporary resident in the United Kingdom. I had decided to stay for the duration of the war, thinking that in this way I could contribute to the Allied war effort because of my experience in Barcelona; but I had no intention of staying on permanently. I was in no doubt that the Allies would win the war, and therefore as soon as it ended we would be able to go home since Franco would inevitably fall with Hitler and Mussolini, as I then believed.

It took me a while to decide on assuming this new responsibility. I little thought that the Accident Service, which began with thirty beds, would eventually end up with one hundred and twenty, and that, unhappily for me, the need for doctors in the services meant that, one after the other, the assistants I had inherited from Scott would leave me.

Eventually, the inevitable happened. The British were going to have to pay for the indifference with which they had contemplated our suffering in the Civil War—notwithstanding the sympathetic smiles, the pretending not to understand and all the other evasions. With the fall of France, and especially with the heartrending evacuation of the British army and elements of the French from Dunkirk, the curtain seemed to be going up on the last act of the drama involving the Western world. I was not surprised, and it was precisely for this reason that I was in England with my young family, in an effort to help.

Notwithstanding the superiority at that time of the German air force, over 300,000 men were miraculously brought back to the United Kingdom, and amongst these were many casualties. A group of wounded Frenchmen was sent to us at the Wingfield for treatment. They kept us very busy but slowly all recovered completely. Being able to converse in French, I used to spend all the free time I could spare with them for human as well as medical reasons. These men were going through a time of terrible anguish unable to forget for a moment their families in France.

Shortly after their arrival at the hospital, a Catholic priest, Father Zulueta, started visiting them. When the time came for their discharge from the hospital, the authorities allowed them to choose between going back to France or joining de Gaulle's Free French forces. One of their officers told me that the Catholic priest was urging them to go back home as "their war was finished". An individual investigation was carried out and we were sad to find that many of them had indeed decided to go back to France. A few stayed in the United Kingdom and some went to North Africa to join the forces of General Leclerc. Fortunately, all the men were able to leave on their own two feet as we did not have to amputate in a single case.

At the Accident Service I slowly lost all my assistants: John Barnes, who helped me a great deal with burns, and finally even Masina himself, that excellent surgeon; until in 1943 I was left alone with Dr Laszlo, a Hungarian refugee, a good surgeon whose English was negligible, and a couple of resident medical students. The clinical case histories left much to be desired. Had it not been for the help of Canadians from the Churchill Hospital, who came more than anything to learn my technique of treating war wounds, I simply could not have managed. All this work was additional to treating wounded at the Wingfield yet somehow I still found time to devote to the Catalan National Council in London.

The reputation of the service was growing, and we had an ever increasing number of visitors from medical services in Great Britain, Canada and especially USA. This pleased and worried me at the same time—I would have preferred more assistants and fewer visitors.

One day Seddon called me. I had already complained several times to him about the lack of help at the Radcliffe. He told me that there was some discontent at the way case histories were being kept at the Accident Service. I lost my temper at this—something which I rarely do. How did they expect case histories to be kept properly when I did not even have time to look after the patients adequately? Some weeks went by and then Seddon saw me again to say that Professor Cairns had found the solution to my problems. The well-known surgeon, Sir Max Page, who had had to retire from the army for health reasons, was going to join me at the Service. The solution surprised me. What would Max Page's position be exactly, I asked? The answer was: co-director, though I was told by Seddon and later Cairns that the operating would be left entirely to me.

I suspected immediately how things were going to be. Because of his prestige and age, Max Page would be the director and I the surgeon working to his orders. I knew Page did not believe in my method and I would be obliged to ask his opinion in severe cases. In any case how could it be expected that a retired major-general was going to write up case histories, which was what was really required? I took a couple of days to reflect and then, with Amelia's agreement, decided to resign from the service which I had helped to develop.

I gave a few days' notice, communicated my decision to Jim Scott and never went back there again after the middle of 1944. Shortly after, Scott came back to Oxford and from then until he retired he was the director of what was virtually the first

First Communion, 1909

The only uniform J. T. ever
wore, 1919

Goal scored—or missed? J. T., in white top, watches with the same
enthusiasm he felt towards all sport

Amelia with Meli, aged 6 and Rafel, aged 4, shortly before he died

Marriage to Amelia, December 1923, Barcelona

At the old Hospital de la Sta Creu, J. T. (4th from left, sitting) with colleagues and Dr Corachan (3rd from left, sitting)

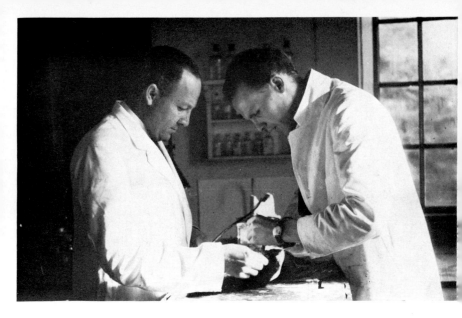

Above: John Barnes and J. T. at the William Dunn School of Pathology Oxford, 1941

Left: Overmead, home for nearly 25 years. Julie holding up the gate

J. T., with G. R. Girdlestone in May 1943, after receiving Hon. D. Sc. of Oxford University

Overmead, 1946.
Left to right: Montse, Amelia, J. T., Julie and Meli. Mickey in
front

Left: J. T. with Pau Casals, Prades, France, 1953

Below: With the Queen Mother, October 1958, when she came to open the new building at the Nuffield Orthopaedic Centre

Official farewell to J. T. as Professor of Orthopaedic Surgery, Oriel College, 1965. Left to right: Julie, Pepe, Meli, J. T., Amelia, Michael and Montse

The five Nuffield Professors (1966). Left to right: L. J. Witts (Clinical Medicine), Allison (Surgery), Chassar-Moir (Obstetrics and Gynaecology), Macintosh (Anaesthetics) and Trueta (Orthopaedics)

Above: Sir Ernst Chain, J. T. and Sir Hans Krebs, Barcelona, 1975

Left: Receiving the Honorary Fellowship of the British Orthopaedic Association from its President, Philip Newman, in London, September 1976

Accident Service of its kind in the United Kingdom. It served as a model for many which were to be set up later all over the country.

While I was at the Accident Service I heard that there was a department being created at the Wingfield to investigate the best method of treating war wounds in which the use of penicillin and surgery would be duly appraised. They appointed an excellent surgeon as head, and the whole thing was carried out in the greatest secrecy. I was not informed of developments, but of course I was aware of the progress they were making. At the end of the war the work of this department was closed with the expected conclusion: that with good surgery excellent results were obtained, but that with insufficient or deficient surgery, penicillin did not rectify the errors. That good surgery is essential I had already stated in my first letter to *The Lancet* in 1939—before penicillin was discovered. Good surgery plus penicillin made the perfect combination.

This period in which I was so very busy, with the Accident Service to look after as well, had a very bad effect on my home life. My poor Amelia was very lonely, and fell into a state of depression which worried me greatly. I used to go home late at night and tired, and worried in case there should be an emergency during the night, which used to happen frequently. The two little girls were at school all day. Meli, who could not go to school at all in our first year at Oxford as we could not afford it, was later accepted free at Rye St Antony in September 1940. When we had the means to pay, the two little ones also went there. So Amelia was alone all day.

In 1943 we left Greycot, the cottage in Headington where we had lived since 1940 in order to be nearer the Wingfield, and moved to Overmead, a larger house, which we bought with help from friends and family. It had a garden of about an acre, a vegetable garden, some forty fruit trees and was in a quiet cul-de-sac. The position was perfect—it had one of the best views of Oxford which we never tired of over the next twenty-five years.

I remember that whenever Amelia went to the butcher, she used to put on what we called her "butcher's eyes"—that is, she would try to look hungry and miserable in the hope that he would add a few ounces more to the ration. She amazed the butcher our very first Christmas in Oxford by ordering a donkey for the Christmas dinner. The butcher could not believe his ears—a donkey? If he had merely suspected before that savages lived on the other side of the English Channel, he must now have had no doubt at all. The misunderstanding was finally cleared up when it became evident that what she wanted was nothing less orthodox than a turkey.

Until 1942, when the hospital bought me a second-hand Austin because of my difficulties in getting about from one hospital to another on a bicycle, and raised my monthly salary very slightly to cover expenses, we had had to rely on public transport or bicycles. This was the first car I had owned since my Mercedes-Benz was stolen on the first day of the Civil War in 1936. Ownership of this new means of locomotion boosted the morale of the whole family although, of course, petrol could not be used for joyriding. However, as I had under my care several clinics within the orbit of the Wingfield in such places as Aylesbury and Reading, Amelia often accompanied me and while I was busy seeing patients she would wander around the local antique or junk shops, frequently coming across nice *objets d'art* at bargain prices. As I look around my cabinets now in Barcelona, I am surprised at the number of things which I have come to value highly and which cost her only a few shillings.

Like so many others we kept hens in the war to boost the egg ration. One winter night there was a commotion in the hen-house and, guessing the reason, I ran downstairs in pyjamas, grabbed the first offensive weapon I saw, which turned out to be an umbrella, and rushed out, shouting at the top of my voice to scare away the intruder. The fox ran away as soon as it heard and saw me, but it had already killed one hen and injured another. I think the dead chicken ended in the pot, as we knew the cause of its death; the other was the victim again in a second drama. The morning after my encounter with the fox, I took the injured hen with me to the Wingfield. It appeared to have only a broken leg and to the amazement of the nursing staff, I took it to the plaster room and proceeded to apply a plaster. Unfortunately, the hen died. The plaster method may have been efficient on people, but it was clear that it did not work on chickens. I cannot remember that we ate this one. If we did, it must have been without the knowledge of

Montse and Julie who would rather have gone hungry than eat any creature adopted by the family, however temporarily. We were considered no better than cannibals if we so much as suggested putting one down.

Some nights we spent in London, and our favourite hotel then was the Mayfair, where for five guineas—it seems incredible today—we could both have bed and breakfast. Despite the air-raid warnings and rushing down to the basement on several occasions, I have nothing but happy memories of our stays there. The only other disturbance perhaps were the shouts of exuberant American GIs calling for taxis at three or four in the morning.

Amelia used to go shopping on a bicycle—she often joked that she had had to learn how to ride one at the age of forty. The girls rode theirs to school and Meli, who went up to Somerville in 1943, found hers indispensable in university life, like every undergraduate. As part of Somerville was taken over by the Radcliffe Infirmary at that time, the girls had to live one year "out" and Meli had the good fortune to be sent to live at the President's Lodgings at Trinity College! Mr and Mrs Weaver looked after her with great kindness—he had a great affection for Spain through his hobby, which was photography. So Meli spent a year in a men's college, and as a result, the two families became very friendly.

For many years the Weavers used to invite us all to spend New Year's Eve in their home, where they always gave a party. They used to see the New Year in with home-made mulberry wine. . . . As it did not seem to us the appropriate sort of drink to celebrate such an important occasion, we used to keep a bottle of something stronger in the car, and now and again a member of the family would disappear to the car for a few minutes! My cousin and god-son, Dionis Montón, who was then studying anaesthetics under the great Robert Macintosh—Nuffield Professor of Anaesthetics and a great friend of the family—came with us once or twice, and having a great sense of humour had us all in fits when he was there. We used to be made to play charades and the Trueta clan always had to sing Catalan Christmas carols. They were great fun altogether, and we were always grateful to the Weavers for inviting us to their home on such memorable occasions.

One day, I remember the postman brought us unexpected pleasure: a parcel arrived from the United States full of tins of food (dried eggs, milk powder, spam, etc.), sheets, blankets and many other comforts. It turned out that we had been adopted by a kind and generous American who had happened to see my name next to Harry Truman's in *Who's Who*. Years later, on one of our trips to the USA, we went to see him and thank him personally and he told us that his reason for adopting us was sympathy for a family which, having suffered one terrible war, was now involved in another in a strange country. The emotion at home every time "the parcel" arrived was indescribable.

All this time, during World War II, we kept in touch with our family in Barcelona by post. Letters in both directions had to be in Castilian (Catalan was forbidden then), but those to us had to be addressed to my wife in her maiden name. My surname could not be mentioned in my country, even on an envelope. However incredible this may seem now, it is the truth.

Chapter 5

RESEARCHER AND LECTURER

As my arrival in Oxford did not coincide with my work permit, I was able to devote time to a subject which had always interested me: to find out the reason why my treatment of war wounds worked.

With GRG's help, we managed to convince Professor (later Lord) Howard Florey to let me work in his magnificently equipped laboratories at the William Dunn School of Pathology, so as to be able to explain scientifically the efficacy of the method I recommended. This enabled me to be in constant touch with professional investigators, biologists, doctors and chemists with no medical responsibilities.

In Florey's team were Professor Gardner, bacteriologist, and Dr (later Sir Ernst) Chain, a Jew of German origin who had fled from Nazi persecution to study in Cambridge, where he met Florey. When Florey moved to Oxford, Chain went with him as head biochemist in the department of experimental pathology. There were also a chemist, Miss Schoental—another German refugee—Dr Abraham, Dr Duthie, Dr Orr-Ewing and others.

This institute has become famous for being the scene where the real revolution took place which led us into the antibiotic age: the putting to practical use of penicillin.

Finding myself among this group of professional researchers enabled me to discover that they worked independently, just as Barnes and I did, but now and then they gathered to discuss something of mutual interest. Tea time was of great importance as this was devoted to general conversation and one learnt of the work of the others. When Barnes and I first joined the group the general interest lay in investigations centred on blood transfusion.

The first time I heard anyone mention the antibacterial

campaign was when Miss Schoental one day brought me my
little book on the treatment of war wounds and fractures, which
had recently been published in English, and drew attention to
where I had mentioned the biological antagonism found under
plaster of Paris casts. I had said that when colonies of B.pyo-
cyaneus develop in certain quantities, the toxic pyogenic
organisms usually disappear.

Miss Schoental asked me for more details, and all I could
tell her was what we had discovered in Barcelona where in
about seventy cases it seemed that the B.pyocyaneus had purged
the wound of other germs. The phrase "biological antagonism"
actually appeared in my book, and the German researcher
asked me if I did not think it worth while studying the problem,
although it had been studied in Germany years before without
any positive results. I naturally thought the investigation would
be interesting, and especially so as so much progress had been
made in biochemistry.

Florey agreed, and about three weeks later Miss Schoental
came to our laboratory with several test tubes containing
liquids of varying shades of green: they were different concentrations of B.pyocyaneus toxins. Even with the weakest mixture,
mice died within a few minutes of having a few drops injected
in the tail. It was not, therefore, of practical use in human
pathology.

Then came the day when Chain, that great German biochemist, remembered the work of Alexander Fleming with
"penicillium notatum". Luckily the laboratory had some of the
original culture available, as Fleming had sent it over ten years
ago: in 1929. A few weeks later Chain brought to the laboratory where Barnes and I were working some samples of a yellow
liquid containing varying concentrations of penicillin. Barnes
took some mice and injected them all with staphylococci and
some with the penicillin serum. Eventually those mice which
had been injected only with staphylococci died, while those
which had also been inoculated with the new drug survived.
A miracle had happened under our very eyes—the antibiotic
era was born.

Someone has said that I was the first person to have given a
penicillin injection. This is not strictly true; I merely held the
mouse while my colleague John Barnes inserted the needle.

In this inspiring atmosphere John Barnes and I tried to discover the value of immobilization in reducing lymphatic circulation, through which the greater part of injected or digested substances are absorbed. Using large, anaesthetized rabbits, we compared the quantity of lymph which we obtained with the leg in total rest with that which we obtained with the leg in movement. This was nothing new. It had been studied many years before, but we wanted to bring the study up to date as it was a nearly forgotten subject and we thought it might be important in explaining the difference in the results of patients treated by immobilization and those who had been allowed unrestricted movement. When we had sufficient data on the great importance movement has in the absorption of substances into the lymphatic system, we went on to study the speed of such absorption during rest and activity. For this study we chose snake venom from cobras, vipers and, most poisonous of all, Australian Black Tigers. We knew the molecular weight of these venoms: the viper's was less than 5,000, the cobra's 10,000 and the Black Tiger's 27,000. The rabbit injected with viper poison died anyway, whether we immobilized it or not, as the absorption was very quick. This meant that, despite immobilization, the poison passed straight into the blood through the capillaries, and not through the lymph. In the case of the cobra venom, immobilization lengthened its life, but the rabbit eventually died. When we used the most lethal venom, that with the highest molecular weight, the rabbits lived during the time that the injected paw was immobilized but when after nine days we took the plaster off, the animals fell ill and in most cases eventually died. This was to me incontestable proof of the importance of immobilizing contaminated war wounds.

We believed that when a limb was immobilized the lymphatic circulation stopped, and thus the bacteria stayed localized where they had penetrated. Thus, if the surgeon uses an adequate technique so that conditions for the reproduction of bacteria are reduced, the general state of the patient improves. This is what I had observed in Barcelona; patients correctly operated on and immobilized were reading the newspaper next day. In fact, the reading of newspapers became a yard-stick for my assistants: when they went into a ward, they noted those who were reading papers and went straight to those who were not.

Barnes and I sent an article to *The Lancet* on our work and the conclusions derived, which was published in 1942. Although we had been working on it throughout 1940 and 1941, its publication was delayed because of the time we had had to devote to our patients. Following this work we went on to study the problem of shock.

During 1940 and 1941, apart from my hospital and research work, I also did a lot of lecturing. I have recently found a list of some of the lectures given from 1939 onwards in cities throughout Great Britain, dealing with my experiences in Barcelona. From 1939 to 1944 we have worked out that I gave some eighty-three lectures, excluding those at the Oxford hospitals.

Three of these stand out in my mind because of their importance to me personally. The first was at the Royal Society of Medicine on 24 October 1939. The president of the surgical section, Mr Rowley Bristow, and Professor Girdlestone first took me out to lunch from which we walked to the Royal Society. Somewhat apprehensively, I saw a large crowd trying to get into the society building. Rowley Bristow and GRG, in authoritative tones and elbowing their way through, opened up a way but the sight of the large lecture room, completely packed, did nothing to allay my nervousness.

Rowley Bristow introduced me, and with a "good luck" from GRG I faced my papers. Reading slowly, it took me about an hour to get through. I had rehearsed time and again to get the emphasis in the right places, but the hall was full and those standing at the back were making a noise that distracted my concentration. Eventually GRG, who was in the front row, got up and said to me "Louder, louder!"; my voice had not been reaching the far corners of the lecture room too clearly; but when it was all over I was touched by the sympathetic applause from the audience.

The press mentioned this lecture, more than anything because of the sensationalism of the bombings in Barcelona, as explained by one who had grasped their import. The lecture was published as a pamphlet and, at the price of sixpence, was quickly sold out. For a long time after this I was known as

"Trueta, the man of the Barcelona air raids". When Churchill made one of his most famous speeches in Parliament, he mentioned the bombings on Barcelona in a paragraph which was reported in the British press. The *Daily Telegraph* of 19 June 1940, quoted him as follows: "I do not at all underrate the severity of the ordeal which lies before us, but I believe our countrymen will show themselves capable of standing up to it like the brave men of Barcelona (cheers)." Probably due to Spanish diplomatic pressures, it was later suggested that Churchill had not been referring to the air raids on Barcelona during the Civil War, but to the siege of Barcelona, the bombardments by artillery in 1714 during the War of Succession; as if on the eve of the systematic destruction of their own cities, our former British allies were recalling the occasion on which they had deserted us just over two and a quarter centuries before!*

The second lecture I particularly recall was also given at the Royal Society of Medicine on 8 December 1939, and probably had an important bearing on my settling down at Oxford. The audience was made up of members of the British Orthopaedic Association, Professor T. P. McMurray, then vice-president of the association, being in the chair, and the theme was purely surgical.

I started with a brief resumé of the main points of my technique and of the results obtained in Barcelona and, as usual, I stressed at the outset the importance of never suturing any war wounds, generally speaking the majority, which involve damaged muscle. A young, dark-haired man with an intense expression stood up and, after apologizing to the chairman for interrupting, informed all present that while what I was saying regarding suturing may have been valid in Spain, such great strides had been made in techniques since the Civil War that suturing was now possible without any fear of gangrene, provided there was enough skin. The young man was Reginald

* Abandoned by England—a bitter issue between Whigs and Tories of the day—and her other allies of the Grand Alliance, Catalonia found herself alone after the Treaty of Utrecht recognized Philip V as King of Spain. After a ten-week siege, preceded by a year-long blockade of the port, the 5,000 defenders of Barcelona, for the most part civilians and outnumbered eight to one, finally succumbed to the Castilian and French infantry and cavalry.

Watson-Jones. I replied that I doubted if any one as know-ledgeable as he would suture more than once in the conditions to which I was referring, for the following reasons: you will not be operating in your own theatre; you may be operating under fire, without your usual assistants or instruments; you will not have had time to study the wound thoroughly, others being in urgent need of your attention; after suturing the wound you may never see the particular patient again, so you cannot keep him under observation. I had not finished when Watson-Jones interrupted me to say I need say no more as I had already con-vinced him that I was right. The ensuing ovation made me realize the popularity of this young surgeon, who was soon to create the Royal Air Force traumatological service, become surgeon to His Majesty and later be knighted.

The third lecture was to the British Medical Association, in London. This was to the biggest audience I had yet faced, the room being large and not even standing room was left. It dealt more with modern warfare and its significance for families, for schools and the man in the street. I suggested that by moving schools to the country and building appropriate shelters, the number of civilian casualties could be reduced. I also stressed the increasingly important rôle of the physician, who was going to have to take on work from those who had joined the medical services of the armed forces; some would have to go back to working in hospitals, for instance. For the same reason it was essential that medical studies be continued so that new doctors could take over these vacancies; the longer the war, the more the problems.

Perhaps I contributed slightly to arousing the country from the insouciance which I found on my arrival. Fortunately, Hitler let slip the opportunity to invade before the tocsin had been fully heeded.

Shortly after the war started, I was asked my opinion on the cause of shock in casualties, especially in those resulting from air raids. I said I thought there was a factor, probably of a nervous vascular origin, which caused a spasm, possibly in the kidney, and that because of this spasm the kidney arteries stopped blood from circulating and urine from forming.

John Barnes and I set out to prove this theory and started by measuring the contraction of the fine abdominal arteries, and especially that of the renal arteries. To do this we moved into the Nuffield Institute for Medical Research, where Kenneth Franklin and Alfred Barclay were doing some interesting research on foetal circulation. They put all their equipment at our disposal, for example fine radiology, which enabled the measuring of vessels previously injected with substances visible by X-ray. We used rabbits, and induced shock by applying a tourniquet at the top of the thigh for about two hours. The animal in this way reached a state of collapse, though it usually revived on removal of the tourniquet. The constriction of the abdominal vessels, and especially of those carrying blood to the kidney, was clearly revealed by radiography. Unfortunately, the techniques available at that time did not permit study of the kidney itself. However we amassed enough findings for a paper to be published in the *British Journal of Surgery*, in which we expressed our belief that the marked vascular spasm visible in most of the abdominal arterioles, or small arteries, probably also occurred in the kidney, and that this was possibly the reason for the diminution of urine. At that point intense pressure of work both at the Accident Service and at the Wingfield temporarily prevented me from continuing with further research.

Towards the end of the war in 1945, although there was still a lot of clinical work, I could already foresee the time when I would have nothing else to do but study the result of extraumatic casualties and the vast number of orthopaedic cases. I wrote a paper then with the agreement of Franklin and Barclay, in which I put the subject of this problem back on the table. Barnes was still away, so Franklin, Barclay and I embarked on a study in depth of renal circulation. Using rabbits again, we started to work with cine-radiography, injecting in such a way that when the opaque substance in the blood was visible inside the kidney we could X-ray it by means of the appropriate equipment. The photographic plates were large enough to enable us to study in detail what went on inside the kidney. As we could take three frames a second, we had ample time to record the coursing of the opaque substance through the vessels.

We repeated the experiment by provoking shock in a rabbit by means of a tourniquet, and observing the kidney radiographically. We injected the opaque substance in the jugular vein at the neck and when it arrived at the kidney we could see it enter, diffuse inside and appear through the renal vein, after following a course which was almost constantly shorter time-wise in all the animals in an induced state of shock. This pre-occupied us. How was it possible that animals in shock had an accelerated renal circulation which enabled the blood to go through the whole of the kidney in a much shorter time than in animals in a normal state? The research immediately became of great interest.

I was in charge of analysing the X-rays and knitting together the various threads of the investigation. I arrived at the con-clusion that there was only one way of explaining the phenomenon: that there were two potential blood circulations in the kidney. One, which in the normal state enabled the blood to circulate throughout the whole kidney—the cortical as well as the medullar parts; another, which in a state of shock took a short cut or by-pass.

I gave a lecture on this with the agreement of my colleagues at the Nuffield Institute for Medical Research, to which some forty experts came. I expounded this disturbing theory, which was until then unsuspected, and a discussion ensued which was satisfying in that no one present could think of any other explanation. At the end of the lecture it was decided that an immediate anatomical investigation must be carried out: we had to find out the exact distribution of the kidney vessels. For this we needed an anatomist—and we were lucky to find Peter Daniel, who seemed pleased to have the opportunity to join a team working on such an original idea; his work was excellent. We had the services of a secretary as well, Miss Marjorie Prichard, highly intelligent with a well co-ordinated scientific mind.

We worked hard to prove this theory and the day came when we had enough material to be able to publish it in book form. A discussion was held as to who should write the book. Franklin and Barclay suggested I should write it, but as I did not feel up to it on my own, it was decided that all five of us should do so, with Daniel, Prichard and I in charge of the actual writing and Blackwells Scientific Publications as publishers. Barclay and Franklin wanted me to appear as the sole author because I had started working on the theory before any of them joined me. They pointed out that I had not only initiated the idea but planned the project and had followed it through to its logical conclusion: i.e. that there was a peripheral or cortical circulation and a central or medullar one; in other words, a major and a minor circulatory system. Finally they pointed out that some of the team had not worked on the subject from the beginning but had joined us after I had already given a lecture on our conviction that there was a short-cut in the kidney.

I was frankly very touched and surprised at this suggestion, but rejected it at once as it was obvious that both Daniel and Miss Prichard were unhappy at the suggestion that their names should not appear on the frontispiece of the book, as they had also played an important part in the work. I was adamant therefore; either we all five signed, or there would be no book. Franklin then suggested that at least my name should be placed first, and that the other four should follow in alphabetical order. This is how the book eventually appeared. One thing that affected me profoundly was that all four of them insisted that I should write the introduction to the book and sign it alone, which I did.

Before the book appeared, we had already published two or three articles, one of them in *The Lancet* which was given priority. As a result of this particular article we received a telegram from Professor John Fulton, the great American physiologist, saying: "Warm congratulations renal discovery most important disclosure since insulin." We also received many letters, including at least two from those who claimed to have already preceded us in this work. In the event the book had a most gratifying reception.

That same summer of 1947, the International Congress of Physiology was held in Oxford and among those attending was my ex-examiner, August Pi i Sunyer, then living in exile in Caracas, Venezuela, who came with some of his pupils. I was showing this group graphically with great pleasure and pride the work we had been doing, when suddenly there appeared a small group of Spanish-speaking gentlemen. Their leader announced he was the Professor of Physiology at Barcelona University. I said to him: "There must be some mistake, the Professor of Physiology is right here—Professor Pi i Sunyer," at which they all hastily about-turned and trooped out. It turned out that this so-called professor was responsible for the attempted destruction of the files at the Physiology Institute in Barcelona, which contained important work by famous Spanish physiologists, most of them either dead or in exile.

I need hardly say how pleased Pi i Sunyer was to see that the young student to whom he had given an undeserved credit in physiology many years before was now presenting an original thesis which was having such an impact on the scientific world.

The fact that I was able to do this work was due in very large measure to the facilities for research which Oxford gave me; but I think that innate curiosity is responsible for my basic interest in investigation. It does not satisfy me to know that a certain treatment works; I have to know why it does. Working with these teams was of great value to me as, once the war ended, I was able to dedicate a great deal of my time to research.

Chapter 6

THE CATALAN NATIONAL COUNCIL

As one Western European country after another came under
the boot of the Third Reich, all the heads of State of the
invaded countries, with the unexpected exception of Leopold,
King of the Belgians, made their way to London, probable
springboard for the crossing of the Atlantic. The last Spanish
Head of State, President Azaña, had died in France—probably from sadness more than physical ailment. The President
of the Generalitat of Catalonia, Lluis Companys, who had
remained in France, was delivered over to the Spanish police
by the Gestapo and the French Militia at the request of Franco,
transported back to Spain and executed in Barcelona. Towards
the end of 1940, José Antonio Aguirre, the President of the
Basque country, managed to escape from the Gestapo by first
hiding in a convent in German-occupied territory rather than
fleeing south. Later he appeared in London, where I had an
opportunity to meet him. The Basque exiles' delegation in
London was also reinforced by the presence of Manuel de
Irujo, born in Navarra and an ex-minister of the republic.

If Azaña had died, Dr Juan Negrín, last head of government
of the Spanish republic, was certainly still alive and in full
possession of his faculties. It is said that when he landed at
Southampton, he had with him such an amount of personal
baggage that the Customs officers were left open mouthed.
From the contents of one of his suitcases alone was born the
Lluis Vives Society, theoretically intended to promote the
education of young Spanish exiles living in England. The
Catalans were the only people who, having had their national
existence recognized by the Republican constitution, and with
a government of their own, now found themselves with no
representation whatsoever in the only European country—
apart from the neutrals—still free from axis domination.

It was not surprising therefore that between them the existing Catalan colony and the constantly arriving Catalans— following the fall of Brest—conceived the idea of organizing a Catalan centre and an executive committee which could speak in the name of Catalans as and when necessary. The first news I had of this was when I was told that a committee had been proposed on which my name had been included. From the start I declined the honour, though pressure was exerted on me to accept.

On 17 July 1940, Batista i Roca wrote to me saying that it was vitally important to form the Catalan National Council immediately, and indeed at the end of the month I received a further letter from him informing me that the council had been formed and that it comprised six members of which I was one, if I would consent.

In October we heard the news of the execution of Companys—the decisive proof of the shortcomings of General Franco. Instead of leaving Companys alone in France, a beaten man with a sick child, Franco perpetrated what no head of the Spanish State before him, however hostile to Catalonia, had dared to do to its supreme authority: have him publicly executed. Even as erudite a Spanish patriot as my friend and neighbour Salvador de Madariaga said to me in disgust when he heard the news: "How dearly we are going to pay for this!" No doubt Madariaga was remembering the shooting of Dr Rizal, which preceded the independence of the Philippines.

As regards my participation in the Catalan National Council, I had made it clear to all that it would be a mistake not only for me to be president, for which I had been proposed, but even to be a member of the council. I felt I could help more in the resuscitation of our country not by taking an active part in politics—which would have been for the first time in my life— but rather by putting to the best use the encouraging welcome which I had been given by distinguished elements of the British government and in particular by certain senior officials of the Foreign Office. We already had a distinguished Catalan politician in our midst, Carles Pi i Sunyer, and it was therefore on him that the onus fell of presiding over the Catalan National Council in London. I wished to remain outside the council in the belief that by so doing I could exert any powers of persuasion that my voice might carry in certain British circles on which I felt our future depended.

My stance was based on a short but intense experience of how the Spanish Civil War was regarded in leading British circles, and on the attitude adopted by the government, and essentially the Foreign Office, towards Spain and her significance in World War II. It was evident that, potentially, Franco's government in Madrid had to be regarded as hostile, but, and this was very grievous to us even to the extent of being considered an injustice, we Republicans could not be considered as *de facto* allies. I do not want to give the impression that this was as clear cut as suggested, but it was sufficiently clear for me to have to steer a course in an ambiguous and difficult situation which could and did result in the most unexpected and surprising accidents of fortune.

In the event, Pi i Sunyer refused to preside over the council unless I agreed to play an active part in it—and without him there was no way of having any kind of Catalan representation alongside that of other oppressed Europeans. It must be remembered that at the time Poles, Czechs, Norwegians, Danes, Dutch and the French (in the figure of General de Gaulle), all had their delegations in London. We were also very much aware of the presence in England of the Socialist, Juan Negrín, politically very active, obviously with considerable financial resources to judge by his way of living and the projects attributed to him, in close contact with the Soviet Ambassador, Maisky, and through him, with all the other countries represented in the capital. All this impelled us to the decision to organize a Catalan Council with the least delay.

My wife, whose innate common sense and conservative criteria have always proved sound, was against my taking any part in politics. She repeatedly insisted that my patriotic duty, as a Catalan, was already being performed in the operating theatre and by the effect of any prestige I might have as a surgeon, and she cited the example of the maestro Pau Casals manifesting his patriotism through his violoncello.

Family opinion apart, there was also that of others like Professor William Atkinson, a great student of Catalan affairs and, until recently, Dean and Head of the Spanish Department

6

of Glasgow University, who during the war lived in Oxford together with experts of Chatham House, advisers to the Foreign Office and presided over by Professor Toynbee. Atkinson, a good friend of mine, advised me to decline to accept the nomination being convinced that I could help much more from outside than inside the council.

Later, on the occasion of the opening of a Catalan Club, Miss Collier wrote me the following letter:

My dear Dr Trueta,

Forgive me if I seem interfering and if you think what I say in this letter is outside my province, please forget it and consider that I am just thinking out loud.

You know we have often said that your value to Catalonia depended primarily on the fact of your surgical position and that when the time came for your country's case to be presented to the world your influence would be significant largely because you had never taken any political position or action. I know that your opinion is regarded with respect in diplomatic circles precisely for this reason. This being so I must say that I am sorry to hear that your name is going out as one of the speakers at the opening of the Catalan Club. This may seem a small matter and the occasion unimportant, but if your name is printed on this invitation it will be inevitably regarded as a political gesture on your part and your position as a surgeon—a Catalan surgeon— . . . will be thereby compromised. Only the other day an Englishman, important in these matters, referred to you as one outside the sordid world of Spanish political life and for that reason respected for yourself, and because of your personal eminence a man whose judgments must be considered.

It would indeed be lamentable if your respected independence should appear diminished.

Yours ever, Josephine.

I was thus being pressed on all sides to refuse. Unfortunately, Pi i Sunyer was adamant: either I came in on the committee, or he would not consent to be President of the Council. In the end there was no alternative, because at the time no other nomination for the presidency was acceptable to the majority. I was therefore forced into accepting, after begging them to put my name, in the smallest possible print, in the remotest corner; and so the council came into existence and the first manifesto was drawn up.

The drafting of the text was laborious in the extreme and despite my efforts and those of my friends in the council, Batista i Roca and Vergés, to try to damp down the declamatory tones in which it was couched, we were not very successful. Re-reading the final text thirty-five years later, it still leaves a bad taste in the mouth and reminds me too much of the style of writing which characterized the manifestos of the ill-fated first independent Catalan government. I was particularly sorry at that moment to have lost contact with an outstandingly honest and intelligent Catalan Socialist, Manuel Serra i Moret, whom I had come across on my arrival in London. Serra, with his excellent political training and wide knowledge of the Anglo-Saxon world would have been a perfect ally. Unfortunately, family affairs had taken him to Argentina, and all our efforts to get him to return to London came to nought because of the ill-health of his wife; and so in him we lost the best connection we had with the British Labour Party headed by Clement Attlee.

It was then that I came to realize the vast gap which culturally separated the Catalan politicians of the Esquerra party (the left) from the group of other Socialists who recognized Marxist doctrines for what they were and who saw in them the danger to the liberty and ultimate well-being of the people. Unfortunately our nation suffered from a total lack of intellectual formation. In the first cultural dawning which had come with the republic, and just at the time when educational standards were beginning to rise, the less well endowed had become aware of the social injustices, seeing themselves surrounded by wealthy people who, while supposedly Christian, were incapable of compassion and charity and who exploited them. Instead of responding to the appeal of men such as Serra i Moret to organize themselves into a national working class, they rallied to the cause of anarchism, as typified by the anarchist party FAI, which was to be principally responsible for the Republicans losing the Civil War and for Catalans being scattered throughout the world, shorn of all prestige and standing, notwithstanding the heroism shown and the sufferings endured by their more humble compatriots, the factory workers and peasants.

The first meeting of the Catalan National Council in London took place on the night of the first air raid on the Port and City of London. I shall never forget the sight of the fires on our way back to the West End from Golders Green after the meeting. Vergés and I had decided to return by bus and we watched the bombing from the top-deck; two and a half years of air raids on Barcelona must have made us insensitive—or reckless!

About this time, many Catalans living in the United Kingdom left for Mexico, where the government was granting entry permits to Spanish refugees on a large scale. Among those who left were the friends with whom we had shared our first home in Oxford, though by now we had already moved to a house in Headington, nearer to my work at the Wingfield Orthopaedic Hospital. We inherited from our Catalan friends Carmen, their maid, whom they could not take to Mexico with them. She remained with us until, some time after the war, she married a Scotsman. We were always grateful to this girl, and it was thanks to her that our three daughters, especially the two smaller ones, learnt Spanish. At home we always spoke Catalan, and of course at school they spoke English—so had it not been for Carmen they would have known no Spanish.

My trips to London for meetings of the Catalan Council were not as frequent as I could have wished, and more than one member complained of this repeatedly in letters to me. Fortunately, despite the fact that he could at any time have been unanimously acclaimed president of the federation of Catalan centres in Central and South America, Carles Pi i Sunyer remained in London for the duration of World War II. As it turned out, for him as for all of us, the triumph of the allies, with which we had linked our ideals, represented no victory for us at all, and therefore those of us who had never given in had to carry on living far from our homes as though the war were still continuing.

In the course of 1941, when the United Kingdom was under greatest pressure from the Germans, the authority of the Catalan Council, not only in Great Britain but in America and inside Catalonia itself, with which we managed to keep in touch by various means, was constantly growing. We ourselves could take no credit for this: it was due to the resistance of Great Britain and the confidence which the democratic world derived from the leadership of Churchill, whose brilliant personality inspired all who found themselves in Britain in those days.

The council had no difficulties other than personality difficulties and these were few. In a group of five people, all of them subject to the same or similar influences, the personality of each one of us influenced the general appreciation of problems, and this, in turn, conditioned our decisions. Despite this, we nearly always agreed on a common course of action. Batista more than anyone did most to keep alive the existence of Catalonia in the public consciousness.

Meanwhile, most of the Catalan politicians in exile in France moved to Mexico and decided that a Catalan Council should be formed there. At first, it seemed that our council in London might predominate. However, internal politics within the numerically superior Catalan community in South and Central America finally prevailed and, by the relegation of the president of the London council to the post of "delegate in England", responsible to the council in Mexico, the Catalan Council in London was virtually doomed to extinction and finally disintegrated in 1945.

Shortly after the war ended, Catalan politics required the presence of Pi i Sunyer in France but the visa he had applied for from the Foreign Office was not forthcoming. I saw Sir Oliver Harvey, having first made it quite clear to Pi i Sunyer that no help could be expected from the British government if there were any Communists either in the Spanish government in exile or in the Catalan. Now that the Nazi danger was over, the western nations wanted Spain kept out of Russia's grasp, which meant keeping Franco in power. Our idealism made us see things differently, but neither Britain nor the USA wanted reasons. The most instructive lesson was that they were right, and one way and another we were all responsible in some measure for Franco's continuance in power until his death.

Pi i Sunyer kept insisting that I should take part in the Catalan government in exile. My reply was irrevocable: "I have never been neutral," I told him, "and I shall carry on fighting with my weapons, which are biological sciences and the lancet." Pi i Sunyer's visa was granted and the Catalan government was finally formed, naturally without me, but with the inclusion of a Catalan Communist. Despite his promises, Pi i Sunyer was forced into this political concession. I wrote to him the day I heard about this:

> Two lines, just to tell you of my disappointment. Everything we did with our heads and hearts, the lost hours, the sufferings, the plans for the future ... everything has vanished like a midsummer night's dream. I hope the memory of what was the Catalan National Council will remain. I must tell you in all sincerity that if selfishness formed part of my nature, I should feel happy at this outcome. Every day I find my true self more in my researches into natural truths ... and I feel further away from the enclosed atmosphere of our national panorama. But despite this feeling of freedom, I am not happy about it ... I am sorry for you ...

The rôle I had played, giving my word that Pi i Sunyer would never form part of any government which included a Communist, left me gravely compromised. From then on I forgot all about the National Council and Catalan politics—though not Catalonia. These sources of preoccupation, which had so darkened my Oxford life during World War II, were thus put out of mind for ever. It certainly had an immediately favourable effect on my ability to concentrate on the affairs of my profession and speciality.

It seems that neither Pi i Sunyer nor his colleagues in France had yet realized that the victors' camp was already divided into two irreconcilable antagonists and that now the threat to Britain and America came from the USSR. Once again the Anglo-Saxon attitude to Russia had reverted to that which prevailed when it was thought that Nazi Germany would be a bastion against communism. America and Britain were now certain that Moscow would not leave one single "liberated" country free, as indeed has largely been the case. The ingenuousness of the Catalan politicians in the euphoria of France's liberation, to which French Communists also contributed, made them commit the same grave error that directly contributed to our downfall in the Spanish Civil War.

Although the allies knew full well that a Fascist régime on France's border was not desirable, they also realized that a régime in Spain directed from Moscow could not be tolerated. All this may not have been too well realized by the Catalans in France, where Communists had formed a high percentage of the Maquis. The advance of Russia, the same imperial Russia as that of the tsars and boyars, had been contained with difficulty within the confines of the Euro-Asiatic steppes. The British leaders whom I knew were sure that the future of Europe depended on the ability of the truly European countries to halt the Russian armies. Taking into account the "fifth column" which preceded the Soviet army and the number of countries already under the Soviet military domination—half of Poland, a third of Germany, Czechoslovakia, Hungary, Rumania, Bulgaria, Lithuania, Estonia and Latvia—other nations had no option but to submit to Moscow's demands. It was thus obvious, at least from the United Kingdom in 1945, that the allied governments would not give support to any element which might allow, albeit involuntarily, freedom of action to Communist agencies within the allies' sphere of control. That was obviously what Sir Oliver Harvey had meant when he expressed worry over the possible presence of Communists in the Catalan government in exile.

One day, in the middle of August, the news came over the wireless of the sensational event which was to change the whole world: the explosion of an atom bomb on the Japanese city of Hiroshima. Although I was aware of the progress being made in nuclear fission—a friend of mine had just returned from America where, for years, he had been working under Albert Einstein and Niels Bohr—the news of the explosion nevertheless had a profound effect on me. By her surrender Japan finally abandoned the Samurai philosophy and entered the twentieth century.

Looking back on it now, it seems to me that the existence of the Catalan National Council in London kept the name of our country alive, at least during the war and, despite Miss Collier's predictions and those of other English friends of mine, my relations with the Foreign Office did not suffer, and my friendship with Sir Oliver and Hector McNeil was unaffected, at least until I gave my word that Pi i Sunyer would not join a government in which Communists were represented. . . .

Some time after the end of the war, Pi i Sunyer, who had a good post in the BBC South American section, decided to move with his family to Caracas where his famous brother was already established as a professor of physiology. He was the second of the two original professional politicians in the council to leave, and he followed many other distinguished Spaniards who had left Britain to live in America, among them Dr Pío del Rio Hortega, the great pupil of the Nobel Prize Winner Ramón y Cajal, and Dr Severo Ochoa, later to win a Nobel Prize himself for his biochemical studies in genetics in the United States.

Chapter 7

"THE SPIRIT OF CATALONIA"
AND THE BBC IN CATALAN

TOWARDS THE END of 1945 I finished the text of a small book
I had worked on during the war, taking advantage of the half
day off I had on Fridays to go to the Bodleian or to the home of
my good Catalan friend Joan* Gili, who put his important
private Catalan library at my disposal.

We had met the Gilis when we arrived in London in 1939.
He was the son of a Barcelona publisher, and had married a
Scots girl, Elizabeth, whom he met while living in London.
Like so many others, when the war started, they moved to
Oxford, where Joan transferred his bookshop which specialized
in books of Hispanic interest.

Throughout the nearly thirty years that we lived in England,
our friendship never wavered and still goes on even now that
we are far apart. Elizabeth speaks and writes Catalan, and has
been a loyal, efficient and charming companion to Joan all his
life. She and Amelia were very great friends and they were
always present at our family celebrations—in many ways
standing in for our absent relatives. I am particularly grateful
to Joan for making available to me his library when I was
writing my little book—and to Elizabeth for the invaluable
help she gave me in correcting my English, particularly in the
case of my book *Studies of the Development and Decay of the Human
Frame*. We miss them continually.

During the first years of the war, I had decided to write a
book about Joan Lluis Vives, the Valencian philosopher who
had been Professor of Humanities at Oxford from 1523 until
1528, when he was forced on orders from Henry VIII to leave
the university, following the help he gave Catherine of Aragon

* "Joan" is the Catalan form of "John" and is not to be confused with
the English female name of the same spelling.
6*

during the legal intricacies of the royal divorce. The collating of
material encouraged me to reply to friends in Oxford interested
in knowing more about the origins of this near genius, who has
on occasions been compared to Erasmus. I started tracing, like
a medical case history, the background of Vives, and in the
process found a chain of thinkers, both before and after the
time of the distinguished Valencian philosopher, going back
to the year AD 1000 and right up to my own contemporaries.
Once the material was in order, I realized I had a small tract
on my hands, with very few pretensions to historical erudition
(although history has always been a hobby of mine). I called it
The Spirit of Catalonia, and it was published by the Oxford
University Press. My only intention was to remind the British
that the Iberian Peninsula had produced other things besides
the Inquisition, intolerance, flamenco singing and bull-fighting.
Although not much was known about Catalonia by Britons in
1945, their great-great-grandfathers had been well enough
informed of its existence at the time of the War of the Spanish
Succession in the early eighteenth century.*

The book lacked critical content, as I was only concerned
with the good that Catalonia had produced, or helped produce,
in the course of a thousand years; on the other hand, I did not
comment on all that Catalans had done to wreck their chances
of developing as a nation. There was no need for it, I thought,
as it was self-evident that, if one of the qualities of the
Catalans was their spirit of enterprise, rooted in an intensive
individualism from which stemmed their faith in democracy,
this excessive individualism was also the reason why Catalan
society disintegrated when it began to be manipulated from
outside.

The book was published in October 1946 and had encouraging reviews in such authoritative publications as *The
Economist, History—The Journal of the Historical Association,
Contemporary Review, The British Medical Journal, New Statesman
and Nation, New York Herald Tribune Literary Supplement*, etc. I
received flattering letters of congratulation from such Catalan
patriots as Pau Casals and Pompeu Fabra (whose Catalan
dictionary is the standard work of its kind). Two adverse
criticisms came from not unexpected quarters: *The Tablet*—

* See note page 153.

mouthpiece in Britain of the Franco régime at the time, and the *Boletin del Instituto Español*—organ in Britain of the partisans of Negrín.

The book had general success among Catalans in South America and those living in France, as was to be expected in the case of a book conceived out of love for Catalonia, although it was not addressed directly to Catalans. It was not long before the suggestion was made that it should be translated into Catalan for the enlightenment of Catalan youth in Latin America. A Catalan edition was therefore published in Mexico in 1950 and proved to be a gratifying success.

I should mention however that the great Catalan historian Ferran Soldevila, for whose comments I asked prior to publication of the translated version, submitted, with the simplicity and humility appropriate to a genius, no less than a hundred observations. Needless to say, they were all incorporated in the Mexican edition.

I was interested that some of the members of the Foreign Office, with whom I had been in contact during the war years, should become acquainted with my small book. One of these was Sir Oliver Harvey, to whom on 1 March 1945 I had written a letter, after the Yalta agreement, in an attempt to make him understand the grave error of giving economic aid to Franco whose régime was tottering as total defeat enveloped the axis powers. Sir Oliver had told me that my letter had been sent to the Foreign Secretary, Ernest Bevin, after passing through the hands of Sir Stafford Cripps, then Minister of Aircraft Production. My grievance subsequently had been over Bevin's words in parliament which were to the effect: Let the Spaniards settle their own problems. How did he suggest, I wondered, that a country totally deprived of its liberty could "settle" the problem of being under a dictatorship?

On 20 October 1946, Josep Manyé (better known by his pseudonym of Jorge Marín), who worked in the Spanish section of the BBC and was principally in charge of programming, wrote to me enclosing a report that was being submitted on the importance of the BBC putting out a programme in Catalan from London. This proposal came at a very opportune moment as my small book had just been published and I had sent copies of it to the majority of the political heads of the country:

Churchill, Cripps, Hector McNeil, Malcolm MacDonald, etc. The suggestion was well received. Manyé organized it and, on 9 November 1946, I spoke from London, in Catalan, to my fellow-countrymen. My talk, called "The cause of hypertension", gave me the opportunity of stressing that if I had achieved any position in the scientific world it had been thanks to the country which had given me refuge, where we lived in an atmosphere of tolerance and freedom which had meant that my years of exile had been the best years of my life—despite nostalgia for my mother and my native country. Afterwards, I repeated the talk in Spanish.

My talk had an enthusiastic reception in Catalonia, to which the British Consulate-General in Barcelona bore witness in a report to the BBC, according to which they had received many letters of congratulation, telephone calls and visits—some 4,000 in all—all enthusiastically supporting the decision, and that from that time more people than ever had been coming to the consulate to ask for propaganda bulletins. The report stated: "This talk has revived Catalan support for the BBC . . . and we are being asked for more talks in Catalan on art, sport, history, music, medicine and literature . . . and this even though the Catalan press, with the exception of two evening newspapers, has not dared to publish any news about the programme in Catalan, despite having been asked to do so."

However, it still required a great deal of effort, especially on the part of Manyé, for programmes in Catalan to become a regular feature of the BBC Spanish Service. Finally, on 7 April 1947, and for the next ten years, a ten-minute programme was broadcast every fortnight in Catalan alternating with Basque and Galician. The Spanish reaction in Britain was unexpectedly explosive. Even my liberal-minded neighbour Salvador de Madariaga pressed the British authorities to suspend the broadcasts on the grounds that "they would only bring about increased military and Francoist intolerance towards Catalonia". It was of no avail to point out that the BBC was broadcasting six and a quarter hours daily in Spanish while the period transmitted in Catalan amounted only to ten minutes once every two weeks. All this sparked off in London a manifestation of Castilian national unity. Successively, Negrín's secretaries and the Falangists in the Spanish embassy in London trooped angrily into the Foreign Office to protest against the insult to the Castilian language constituted by this dedication of even minimal attention to another of the languages in the Iberian peninsula.

As Manyé himself wrote in a recent letter to me, the same British pragmatism which made it possible for Catalan programmes to go on the air, eventually suppressed them ten years later. They have never been resumed.

Chapter 8

MY FIRST VISIT TO THE
USA AND CANADA

THE IMPACT OF articles in *The Lancet* and, later, my book on
renal circulation, resulted in an invitation to visit the United
States and Canada for a tour which lasted nearly three months.
Although the trip was not wholly financed by my sponsors, by
exchanging my first-class ticket for two second-class berths on
the *Queen Mary*, I was able to take Amelia with me.

My first lecture was at Columbia University in New York,
where I was introduced by J. Schullinger, who had worked in
Oxford during the war at the American Hospital (later the
Churchill Hospital) which had been started by Professor
Girdlestone as an annex to the Wingfield Morris Hospital. I
remember that on the day of its inauguration in January 1942,
it snowed heavily and the Duchess of Kent and those of us
present had difficulty in keeping warm. It was shortly before
the duchess lost her husband, when the RAF aircraft in which
he was a passenger flew into a Scottish hillside.

Amelia came with me to the lecture accompanied by a good
friend of ours from Barcelona who could not get over her
surprise at seeing so many Americans listening with obvious
interest to a Barcelona doctor.

From New York we went to Ottawa, where the Canadian
Congress was being held at the Château Laurier, in an isolated
part to which, on account of the deep snow, the only access
was by sleigh.

The Canadians gave us a welcome far exceeding our expec-
tations: receptions, meetings, dinners, banquets. Mr Gallie,
doyen of Canadian surgery at that time, in thanking me at
the close of the congress touched me deeply by referring on
behalf of Canadian mothers to what I had done during the
war. I was also asked to give the Balfour Lecture before 1,500

doctors, among whom were some of my former assistants at the Oxford Accident Service.

The culmination of our visit to Canada came when I was honoured by being elected an honorary member of the Royal College of Surgeons of Canada, the first such body to honour me in this way.

My work in Ottawa over, we went back to a snow-bound New York, with abandoned cars lining the streets. Further lecture engagements followed in Toronto, Montebello and Montreal. We spent Christmas with fellow friends-in-exile, but for us the festivities were marred by the frustration of a plan to visit my brother and his family in Mexico. This was principally because we were still travelling on Nansen documents, like so many other expatriates throughout the world, and had no visas for Mexico. By the time we were finally granted visas I had other lecturing commitments to fulfil and, in any case, our money was fast running out. We had to forget about Mexico therefore, to our great disappointment.

The holidays over, and resigned to the fact that visiting Mexico would have to be on another occasion, we went to stay with Professor John Fulton in New Haven. Conditions were still arctic, and cars were still buried under snow as on the day we had left New York.

After giving lectures at Yale and at the Medical Society, my voice suddenly gave out. The university ear-nose-and-throat specialist told me that, with my throat in such an inflamed state, if I did not give up smoking at once I would end up permanently voiceless. It is true that when I found myself under nervous tension, as I was at that time, I would smoke two packets of cigarettes a day, and the overpowering central heating in the buildings and the sub-zero temperatures outside between them contributed to worsening the inflammation. I was recommended, if I wanted to continue with the lecture tour of America and Canada, to spend a few days in the south. We went by train, watching the scenery change from snow-covered countryside, to green fields and finally to palm trees.

We spent a few days at Miami Beach, and it gave me great pleasure to be able to swim in the sea a few hours after having been in sub-zero temperatures. We found a cheap hotel (this was over thirty years ago), and, money being very short, more than one meal consisted of coconuts which we found under some palm trees near the hotel. Amelia had fun window shopping in the boutiques which were soon to make Miami Beach one of the world's centres of women's fashion goods.

Ten days later, having regained my voice, we entrained for Detroit, Ann Arbor, Chicago and Columbus, then back again to New Haven and New York, always lecturing, which had made the journey financially possible in the first place, as fares and hotels were always paid for and in some cases I even received an honorarium for the lecture.

In New Haven I was delighted to find my compatriot Duran-Reynals, whose research there on the viral origin of cancer was to result in international recognition for its brilliant conclusions.

John Fulton, the great American physiologist, kept insisting that I should travel to Boston, as his Harvard colleagues were anxious to meet me. My trip was coming to an end and I was worn out from meeting people and from ceaseless talking. The fact that some kind people at Harvard wanted to meet me did not seem sufficient motive to extend my travels. Despite Fulton's pressure, therefore, I felt that I could not accept, particularly as our return trip on the *Queen Mary* was only two days off. Finally, somewhat reticently, Fulton revealed that the Moseley Chair of Surgery, attached to the Peter Bent Brigham Hospital and made famous by the great Harvey Cushing, who held it until he retired in 1932, had become vacant on the death of the renowned surgeon Elliot Cutler and that there was general interest in meeting me with a view to considering the possibility of offering me the Chair. Naturally, I was not to disclose that I knew anything about the project. Knowing the real motive behind the invitation, I finally gave in. It was then decided that Amelia would go straight to New York, and I would fly from Boston to meet her there on the day of the *Queen Mary*'s departure for Europe.

At Boston airport I was met by several of the professors and was taken to luncheon. There were some twenty of them, and they submitted me to a veritable cross-examination. Later we took tea and I lectured the students at Harvard on the renal circulation and was driven back to the airport.

The following day Fulton told me I had made a favourable

impression, and asked me whether I would accept the Chair if it were offered to me. My reply had to be negative as Amelia's reaction had been quite specific. Our eldest daughter, Meli, had just married an Englishman. If we settled in Boston, our two other girls, Montse and Julie, would probably end up marrying Americans, and living in places as far from us as Oxford is from Timbuctoo. If I stayed in Boston, Amelia threatened to take the two girls with her and go back to Barcelona. As usual, Amelia was right, so the next day we embarked for Southampton—and a quite uncertain future.

On my return to Oxford in February 1948, it was to find that, in my absence, the Nuffield Institute for Medical Research had nominated as the new director, not my great friend Kenneth Franklin, who had been its initiator and driving force, but a young man recently arrived from the United States. To be sure, Franklin was more of a scholar than a scientist steeped in bio-chemistry, but it was he who had started the studies on foetal circulation which, with the collaboration of Alfred Barclay, were published in the form of a vast tome. In the years that went by, the newly arrived head, perhaps lacking originality, perfected the study of foetal circulation, but I am not aware that he has contributed anything of greater importance.

For Franklin it was a hard blow to bear. Fortunately, shortly afterwards, he was offered the Chair of Physiology at St Bartholomew's Hospital School of Medicine, and, very sorrowfully, left Oxford, where he had studied and lived since he was a young man, and went to work in London.

The new director did not appeal greatly to me. He was a meticulously precise person but seemed to me to be somewhat lacking in human warmth. He was an excellent committee man, always ready with the appropriate detail at the right moment. When I was appointed to the Chair of Orthopaedics at the university, we found ourselves both members of the same college, Worcester, but we were never really on close terms.

My good friend and colleague in research, Alfred Barclay, died in 1949, and so my connection with the Nuffield Institute for Medical Research was limited to my friendship with the excellent technician who had worked there with former heads. Despite these changes, I approached the new director with the

request that I might be allowed to use a corner of the laboratories in order to carry on with my research work. His reply
was that, for the moment, he could not commit himself on this
as he had not yet restructured the future use of the laboratories. I realized that there would never be any room for me in
his laboratories, as I suspected that he would not forgive me
for having supported the candidature of Franklin.

Thus, for the first time since my arrival in Oxford in 1939, I
found myself without facilities for conducting my investigations. A completely unforeseeable event however was to make
available laboratories which were to be not only planned by
me, but freely and completely at my disposal. However, this
was not to be until the 1950–51 academic year.

For the moment, I had the great good fortune to enjoy the
friendship of Franklin and Professor Amoroso of the Royal
Veterinary College in London, as a result of which the college's laboratories were made available to me. I wanted to try
to prove my theory that hypertension is caused by the dilation
of the extracortical vessels. I used to go up to London twice a
week, and Amoroso and his team helped me immensely,
especially since Amoroso had made great advances with the
Spalteholtz technique, which was of tremendous help in the
research we were to undertake in Oxford over the next twenty
years.

In 1946 I received an invitation from my old friend Dr René
Lériche, the famous French surgeon, to attend a dinner in
Paris in honour of our colleague, Merle d'Aubigné, who had
just been appointed to the Chair of Orthopaedics, to fill the
vacancy left by Professor Mathieu. This not only gave me the
opportunity of taking Amelia to Paris, but also of re-
establishing personal contact with Lériche.

My friendship with Lériche, though we met infrequently,
had none the less been intimate, and he had visited us in Oxford
before the war. After the liberation of Paris I got to learn,
through an exiled French doctor with Communist leanings,
that Lériche's life was in danger. When France had capitu-
lated in 1940, Marshal Pétain, a personal friend and patient of
Lériche, invited him to join the French Assembly, an invitation
which Lériche, although I believe he did everything possible
to decline, had finally felt obliged to accept. This, in the eyes

of many, constituted high treason and resulted in his being on the Communists' black list.

My friend and fellow-researcher in the laboratories, John M. Barnes, who had been commissioned as a captain in the RAMC, informed me that British Intelligence, who must have known of my personal relationship with Lériche, were concerned to protect him and wanted my help. I took one of my books on war surgery, wrote in it in French a dedication to a great friend, lover of freedom, etc., and enclosed a copy of the last letter I had received from Lériche, just before the fall of France, in which he had said: "Let us pray the world of liberty will return."

Barnes went to Paris, in uniform, armed with the book and letter, and sought out the house in the Avenue de l'Albonie where the Lériches lived. The house was barred and shuttered and all his knocking and ringing were to no avail until he suddenly became aware that he was being observed through the peephole in the front door. Finally, the door was opened by Lériche's wife, who incidentally was German, who asked him what he wanted. Barnes said he was bringing Dr Lériche a book from Dr Trueta. On hearing my name Lériche himself appeared. The book was handed over, together with assurances from Barnes that they would be under the protection of the British, no doubt to Lériche's intense relief. Shortly afterwards Lériche wrote thanking me for the book, though naturally he did not refer to having been put under British protection. From then on we never lost touch.

In 1947, the Académie Française de Chirurgie awarded me the coveted Prix Laborie, a prize which has been in existence for many years and which I was greatly honoured to receive. Two years later I was invited to lecture at the Académie de Chirurgie, which honoured me by electing me an honorary Associé Étranger. I suspect my friend Lériche had much to do with all this.

PART IV

Nuffield Professor of Orthopædic Surgery at Oxford

(1949–1965)

Chapter 1

THE CHAIR OF ORTHOPAEDICS

WITH THE WAR at an end everyone slowly returned to peace-time work. We were joined at the Wingfield by a new surgeon, Bob Taylor, a very able Anglo-Irishman born in Dublin and a graduate of Trinity College. When he came out of the forces, GRG took him on as his first assistant thereby enabling GRG to dedicate more time to the Wingfield as his wartime job as inspector of hospitals slowly became redundant. GRG came increasingly into contact with Seddon and ended by interfering in his work. It must be admitted that, with GRG practically regarding the hospital as his own child, it was no time before tension built up between them and I found myself caught up in it. As a person, GRG was emotional, sincere and sometimes excessively demanding; but he was also endowed with humility and was capable of acknowledging in public any error of judgment he might have made.

Seddon was quite different. He was a short, slight man, his head slightly inclined to one side, and with a large thin nose; physically he was not an attractive man. He had complete self control, an amazingly retentive memory, and was of a very cold temperament. The two men were bound therefore to come into collision, and each had a fair amount of right on his side.

The regional organization, with which GRG had entrusted the Wingfield, and the academic work of the Chair were more than one man could manage alone, but Seddon was reluctant to relinquish the administrative part of the work which gave him maximum power.

With the help of his colleagues, GRG managed to separate the administrative from the scientific work, the latter of course belonging to the professor. First, Jim Scott was nominated administrative director and Seddon had the regional clinics removed from his hands. A distribution of patients was made so that Seddon looked after hip dislocation, Foley the adult hip, Scott scoliosis, bone infection and later poliomyelitis for me, while Taylor coped with the overflow of GRG's patients. Soon after Amelia and I returned from our long trip to North America in 1948 the tension between Seddon and GRG became explosive. It was then that Seddon confided to me that he had been offered the post of director of his old hospital, the Royal National Orthopaedic Hospital in London, with the probability of a new Chair to be created at London University. He said he was going to bring the matter up at the next meeting of the hospital committee in the form of an ultimatum: either he was given scientific and administrative control or he was presenting his resignation. He resigned and shortly after left for London.

Oxford was a hotbed of rumours. Some said the Orthopaedic Chair was going to be abolished as its occupant could never be expected to hold his own against a man of GRG's personality. Others said the new professor should only be in charge of teaching, leaving all hospital work to GRG. GRG however backed neither of these alternatives. He was in any case very upset that some blamed him for Seddon's departure, and sought the support of Lord Nuffield. Nuffield, a simple man of extreme wealth, had given £2,000,000 to the university in 1936 to create five Chairs which Oxford lacked: surgery, clinical medicine, obstetrics and gynaecology, anaesthetics and orthopaedics, and was not prepared to see any of his Chairs abolished. It was decided to try to fill the vacancy, and in May the university invited applications from candidates to the post. GRG insisted that I send in my application together with a curriculum vitae. The prospect did not really tempt me. I was still virtually a visitor to Britain, albeit with certain privileges, and the idea of remaining there for the remainder of my active life did not appeal to me greatly. It was not that I did not feel at home in Oxford, but staying implied a renunciation of my national identity and my desire to preserve it, which incidentally, and perhaps paradoxically, had been the reason for my coming to Britain in the first place.

After much meditation with Amelia on the subject and taking into account the fact that our eldest daughter Meli had married an Englishman, Michael Strubell, an RAF pilot and ex-prisoner of war whom she met at the university in late 1945, we decided to try for the post. The fact that Michael had no family in England made us think that perhaps one day, when Franco fell, they might come to live in Barcelona with us.

My only argument with GRG was simply on my possibilities of success in an open competition for a Chair which was not only the first in the country but at that time the only one, as McMurray had died and therefore the Chair at Liverpool was also vacant. One fact which GRG thought would strengthen my chances of success was for me to become British. Of course I had no objection to this and so a few days after the competition was opened I applied for British citizenship.

Despite all my doubts, I sent in my curriculum vitae and on 1 July 1949 was fortunate enough to be unanimously elected by the committee consisting of the vice-chancellor of the university, the regius professor, the professors of surgery and anaesthetics, the tutor of medicine at Worcester College, to which the Chair was attached, and the great orthopaedic expert who acted as adviser—Harry Platt, now knighted and undisputed head of British orthopaedics.

I shall always remember the day I was elected to the Chair. I had taken a niece of mine and her husband to the Morris works at Cowley and on the way home we stopped off at the Wingfield and there, at the top of the ramp, was GRG making the "V" sign!

After the family celebrations were over I found myself getting cold feet about the whole thing. How was I going to manage not to offend the natural susceptibilities of my British colleagues, who might feel resentful of the fact that a foreigner was occupying the only Chair of Orthopaedics in the country? GRG however had the answer ready. I would not have to concern myself about anything beyond teaching, research and operating. In a hospital such as the Wingfield, famous for its clinical standards, I could add little if anything to its fame. However, if I was to have laboratories at my disposal, perhaps I could contribute something after all.

The first thing therefore that GRG did as soon as I was appointed was to ask for an appointment with his friend Lord Nuffield whom we went to see in his offices at Cowley. When GRG asked him for £250,000 the reaction was most disappointing.

Lord Nuffield told us regretfully that we were too late as he had recently made a grant of £400,000 to the Royal College of Surgeons which had exhausted his resources.

GRG was even more upset than I. He told Lord Nuffield that his negative reply was a disaster for the Wingfield. Nuffield called his secretary, Mr Carl Kingerlee, and after talking to him in a corner for some time, turned round and asked me if I could manage on £50,000 as a start? GRG was overjoyed and my own spirits rose at this offer, especially as Lord Nuffield added that we could come back for more as soon as this gift was used up. He gave me a post-dated cheque, saying we must not try to cash it until the following January or else it would "bounce"; it was hard to realize this was a millionaire speaking! A few days later Nuffield became my first private patient since my appointment to the Chair.

I spent hours planning how we were going to use the £50,000. The first need was for an animal house, and someone to look after it. I soon found the right person to learn the photography and radiology techniques and how to give vascular injections, and so on.

My appointment meant that I had to stop work on the renal circulation. Someone wrote to me saying that not pursuing this research was like a miner discovering a gold mine and leaving it to be exploited by others. In the years which have passed since our discovery, what we wrote about the existence of the double circulation has been proved to be still valid.

I now had to concentrate on other matters such as experimental bone circulation, and, clinically, on the process of osteoarthritis. The animal house also had a section for microscopic radiography of material injected with opaque substances, an operating theatre and other necessary requisites for laboratory work on animals. Seddon's small department we turned into offices for my secretaries and me, a room in which X-rays could be evaluated and offices for the first assistant and two scholars. We also built on a dining room for doctors, and a lecture room. Postgraduate students soon started coming from all over the United Kingdom, from Greece, Switzerland, Italy, France, Spain and Portugal, and later from the United States, Australia, South Africa, South America and other countries.

In 1950 GRG started feeling unwell and soon became gravely ill. He was just seventy years old and on 29 December he died, comforted no doubt by his great faith. His death, grievous as it was for his wife Ina, was also a terrible blow for our own family. For ten years, day after day, he had watched over us to the extent that one day, seeing us in a very precarious financial position, he and Alfred Barclay, another dear friend, between them gave me a cheque for £900. It was GRG who had made me apply for the Chair and who had surmounted my two objections—the need for funds to ensure laboratories and the guarantee that I would be relieved of all administrative problems. He was able to fulfil the first—but now I was on my own with the second, with all that that implied as regards British bureaucracy and possible rivalry between colleagues. I kept the letter I had received from Seddon in which he prophesied that if I was offered the Chair I would be doomed to failure because, amongst other reasons, I was a foreigner. I had replied to him, also in writing, to the effect that if I was offered the Chair without it being put up for open competition I would not accept it, and that if thereafter I was freely elected I asked him to give me five years' grace before concluding that I had failed.

Luckily I had at my disposal a secretary, Miss Joan Gess, who, despite her youth, was experienced in hospital work. My administrative work for the whole of my many years in Britain centred on her. She is still today the axle on which the academic department revolves. Because of her model efficiency and loyalty, she filled to a great extent the vast void left by Girdlestone. Under her we established a chain of polyglot Catalan sub-secretaries—the last of whom, Flora, I was lucky enough to have as my secretary during my retirement in Barcelona.

There was one thing I had to do therefore: to work tirelessly to ensure that Seddon's prediction did not come true. So we set to work. With Jim Morgan, my first assistant, we studied bone circulation in rats, rabbits and dogs. Clinically, we studied the effect of penicillin on osteomyelitis and collected some two hundred case histories. With my assistant Max Harrison we continued the study of osteoarthritis. We revealed some unsuspected facts, one of them being that osteoarthritis is not due to lack of circulation but, on the contrary, to a surplus of venous blood in the bones. We soon saw that what produces pain in osteoarthritis is this congestion of blood and that the pain is not unlike that of migraine; as we were studying osteoarthritis of the head of the femur we called it "migraine of the second head". With Max Geiser, a Swiss postgraduate, we studied the effect of immobilization on rabbit paws in osteoporosis or decalcification, as it is well known that if a plaster cast is placed on a fracture, the broken bone becomes more and more transparent in X-rays. We found that with complete rest the intra-osseous vessels fill up with static blood, and the bone melts. We cut the tendon of the heel of a rabbit and in fifteen days we found the bone soft like paper. However, if we stitched the tendon, the bone structure was reconstituted within fifteen days. The Catalan post-graduate Antoni Trias studied with us the influence of circulation on growth cartilage, and we found a cause-and-effect relationship between increase in circulation and increase in bone growth. We were then able to use this technique clinically in polio cases. With Gabrielle Stringa from Italy, we studied the mechanism of incorporation and vascularization of bone grafts. With Dr Amato, a Maltese, we completed the study of bone growth and blood circulation.

Mrs Margaret Agerholm assisted our clinical studies on poliomyelitis, of which there were abundant cases at the time. The hospital had two swimming pools built in GRG's time and enjoyed a certain fame in the treatment of polio cases. But we had to develop a section for cases with respiratory paralysis, which was Mrs Agerholm's responsibility.

We had noticed in polio cases that where a lumbar puncture had been performed paralysis was usually more serious. We thought the puncture probably increased circulation at the level of the affected central cells and that the virus filtered through the congested vessels, thus resulting in greater damage. The results of a series of experiments supported this contention.

Towards 1955, the £50,000 from the first donation were coming to an end, so I approached Lord Nuffield, as arranged, to hint at the other £200,000. Without going into all the details of the visits I paid him—I would just say that he eventually gave me a cheque for the balance on one condition: that no architect should be employed. I was to draft the plans and his builders would erect the new building. I prepared a scheme not to exceed £150,000, so as to leave £50,000 for running costs, and it was built just as I planned it. The new building consisted of a large reception room, waiting room, archives, a visiting room which enabled seven patients to be examined at any one time and in privacy. There were also offices for doctors and secretaries. On the first floor there was a lecture room to seat 150, a dining room and small kitchen, more offices and the X-ray department. On the top floor there was the university department—designed for the benefit of all and not merely myself. The most important development was the common room, with comfortable seats, television and other amenities, separated from the dining room by folding doors enabling their conversion into one large room when required. This is where, for years, we held our meetings. On this floor too were the new research laboratories, with an electron-micro-scope, still a rare instrument in 1958. I had a spacious but simple office where the only luxurious furnishing was a Persian carpet bought for a few pounds at an auction sale. The rest were books and a good desk, on which I had a colour photo-graph of Amelia and the girls. I remember one day, when I was receiving Prince Bernhard of the Netherlands prior to a con-sultation, he asked me if the photo was of my family, and if my daughters were married. I said they all were, and very happily. He congratulated me saying: "I have four girls, and I never finish with headaches!"

The building was started in 1956 and opened on 27 October 1958, by Her Majesty Queen Elizabeth the Queen Mother. All the Oxford county authorities accompanied her and I had the honour of showing her around the new building. Amelia, Lady Nuffield (her husband unfortunately was ill), the Duchess of Marlborough, Chairman of the Hospital Management Com-mittee, and my three daughters and my sons-in-law came to give me moral support on such a memorable day. If only GRG had been there. . . .

By sheer chance, the day chosen by Her Majesty to open the new building happened to be my sixty-first birthday. My assistants and pupils who knew this had given me a beautiful autograph album with the idea of asking Her Majesty to sign on the first page. Lady Hammond, the Lady-in-Waiting, whom they approached, apparently told them that members of the royal family never sign in public, but that as they were spending the night at Blenheim Palace with the Duke and Duchess of Marlborough, she would take it with her and ask Her Majesty to sign it privately later. As they were leaving, and the Queen Mother was already getting into her car, she must have noticed the parcel Lady Hammond was carrying and presumably was told what it was and why she was carrying it. To the great surprise of all the retinue, the Queen Mother got out of the car again, made straight for me, took my hands, wished me many happy returns of the day and added a few touching words. I was truly moved.

Next day a limousine arrived from Blenheim Palace with my beautiful album duly signed by Her Majesty. I treasure it above all my other possessions, and I sometimes turn over the pages reliving the many personalities whose signatures are therein and who visited me while I was still living in Oxford.

Chapter 2

TRAVELS AND FAMILY EVENTS

IN 1950 THERE was an International Congress of Surgery in
Buenos Aires which I was invited to attend. I took Amelia and
she witnessed a curious event which might have been
embarrassing. It occurred at the university where several
visitors, among them myself, were to have Honoris Causa
doctorates conferred on them by none other than that Latin-
American hybrid of German nazism, Perón. We were all
gathered in an enormous hall, and as the turn of each came his
name was called out and he walked up to a sort of dais on which
Perón himself sat. Eva Perón was there—looking, as I told
Amelia, very ill indeed, and no wonder, as she died shortly
after. Up the others went, one by one, and Perón shook their
hands and handed them diplomas. Suddenly they announced
"Professor Trueta—Spain". Perón, who obviously was unaware of the presence of a "Spaniard", looked surprised, got
up, and came towards me with raised arms—as if ready to
give me a great big hug! All this under umpteen cameras. I was
flabbergasted—having imagined that I would pass unnoticed—
and the only thing I could think of was to grab his arms tight
as he advanced, pull them down with a shaking movement,
as if in a friendly manner and, taking advantage of his utter
amazement, grab my diploma and retire hastily! When I sat
down beside Amelia I found her with her eyes tight shut, and
when she opened them she said, "Nothing happened—did it?"
My friend and colleague, Robert Macintosh, Nuffield Professor of Anaesthetics at Oxford, who was sitting next to us
said that I had pulled it off passably well, but that he thought
people must have noticed something odd. . . .

That same evening we were told that an English businessman
who had spent a few days in Argentina had made some
statements to the press before leaving, in the expectation that

they would appear after his departure. He had said that the system reminded him of Nazi Germany, with utter lack of freedom, etc. He then proceeded to take off in his private plane for Montevideo, but the plane developed a fault and had to return to Buenos Aires. In the meantime his statements had appeared in the press, and when the police found out that the unfortunate businessman was back in Argentina they sought him out and proceeded to give him a merciless beating up which put him in hospital for a few days.

A day or two after my unceremonious behaviour at the university, Amelia and the other wives were received by Sra Perón. Looking Amelia in the eye, Evita proceeded to deny "rumours" that she said were going round as to her physical condition. "There is nothing wrong with me," she said, "other than exhaustion from serving my country." The spy system, if nothing else, certainly worked efficiently in Buenos Aires. I had commented on the lady's unhealthy appearance only to, as I thought, a very few close friends. . . .

In 1952, taking advantage of an invitation to lecture in Portugal, Amelia and I went back to Catalonia for the first time since the Civil War, crossing France by car, with our British passports. What a depressing experience it was. As I had feared, the anti-Catalan obsession of Franco and the Falange made even that of Philip V insignificant by comparison. My poor country had suffered the most despicable humiliations imaginable. Our flag was not allowed to be flown and was even considered subversive, while the use of our mother tongue was officially prohibited and even privately persecuted.

I learned in detail of the accusations which had been levelled against me; these included being a "separatist-Red". Luckily enough witnesses came forward to give the lie to both accusations. In refutal of the charge of my being a "Red", my nuns came forward forcefully and in great indignation. As to the second charge, this was not so easy to contradict because, although I was not a separatist, as a nationalist not only did I feel separatist *vis-à-vis* the Spanish régime, but I had in fact separated myself from it. With no proofs, and notwithstanding the personal though clandestine accusations made against me by a medical colleague, my case was closed for lack of corro-

borative evidence. Nevertheless, my furniture had been pur-
loined and my library confiscated.

We drove to Lisbon, via Madrid, and were looked after by
two dear pupils—Mineiro and Lima—both later professors of
orthopaedics in Portugal—and I was made an honorary
member of their association. The Spanish Society of Orthopaedics and Traumatology, presided over by an old friend of
mine, did not have, I was told, honorary members,* so I was
asked if I would agree to being made honorary correspondent,
to which I agreed. I was amazed therefore, months later, to
receive a letter from the secretary of this society stating that
my application [sic] must have been mislaid. In my reply I
told them, metaphorically, to go jump into the nearest lake.

As I write these lines, from London in September 1976, where
I have come, among other reasons, to receive an honorary
fellowship of the British Orthopaedic Association, perhaps the
most sincere acknowledgment that my years in Britain were
not in vain, I cannot help recalling the recent annual Spanish
Congress, held this year in Catalonia. I am told that some of
my ex-pupils proposed me for an honorary membership, but
that, not for the first time, the few contrary votes necessary to
veto the proposal were recorded. So I must say with some
sadness that at the end of my life I am an honorary member of
nearly all the orthopaedic societies in the Western world and
America—except that of Spain! I feel only sorrow for the
individuals responsible.

The first time we went to Brazil was in 1953 to attend the
Latin-American Orthopaedic Congress. We were several
European orthopaedic surgeons, among them Sten Friberg of
Stockholm, and we stayed at the famous Copacabana Hotel,
overlooking one of South America's famous beaches. In the
morning, Friberg and I decided to have a swim—he had
played water-polo for his country—to see, without admitting
it to each other, who would get tired first.

Stroke for stroke we swam out to sea until about 200 metres
out we finally stopped for a rest. Friberg asked me what so
many people were doing on the beach and why someone was
frantically waving a red flag. While we puzzled it out, we

* This is not so—there are honorary members.
7

suddenly saw to our horror the reason in the shape of two or three shark fins moving parallel with us halfway between ourselves and the shore. Probably the sharks were not aware of our presence for they never approached us, but our race went unwon as we were intercepted on our way back by a man in a boat with the red flag who proceeded to call us all the names under the sun. It appears that we had unwittingly ignored the danger flags, which were up when we took off for our private race in such carefree fashion. The fact is we were never in any real danger as the sharks kept their distance.

At that time we had already published our studies on osteoarthritis of the hip and Oswald Campos, a colleague of mine in Rio, told me that the son of the then dictator of Brazil, Vargas, would like me to see his father as he was always in acute discomfort from bilateral osteoarthritis of the hips, which prevented his riding except in great pain. We were received by the president in dressing gown and slippers, and it struck me how small he was—although he had the head and face of a tall man. When I told him, after examining him, that an operation would be necessary which would give him freedom of movement to ride horses but would leave him with a limp, Vargas disconsolately declined. Campos told me as we left that whenever possible Vargas rode, for in this way he could disguise his disproportionate physique. He had an ill-starred end, with serious preoccupations, particularly of a political and personal nature. Shortly after our visit he committed suicide. I suspect his physical sufferings and their influence on his personality had something to do with his tragic end. To replace him, normal elections, unknown for many years before, were held, and Dr Juscelino Kubitschek was elected President of Brazil.

The 1953 congress was held in a most beautifully situated hotel, the Quitandinha, a vast building resembling the Grand Casino at Monte Carlo, and capable of housing some one thousand guests. Here we were able to hold meetings and at the same time be with our wives in non-working hours as everything took place in the same building. We used to meet for meals in one of the many restaurants. On the night of the closing banquet, some of us foreigners did a sketch to entertain the large number of those present. Watson-Jones, Amelia and I, the only ones as far as I remember from the United Kingdom, did a parody of Harley Street. Amelia was a patient who came in for consultation, and Watson-Jones wearing red-lined cape, and I in morning coat, pretended to examine her. She lay on an operating table and we proceeded to "operate" on her, extracting from her recumbent body quantities of forks, knives and spoons which clattered to the floor. The patient's recovery was very rapid, and Watson-Jones and I walked up and down, triumphant. Amelia then intimated that she wanted to know our fees, and when Watson-Jones whispered an inaudible sum into her ear, she "fainted", and was removed from the stage in my arms. We had a great success! It was a surprise to those present that people with our responsibilities could make fun of themselves so uninhibitedly.

Family events during this time followed a normal course. The time came for Montserrat to leave Rye St Antony and go to university. She was very fond of animals and decided she would like to read zoology. By studying very hard, she managed to get a place at Somerville, where her elder sister Meli had been before her, had an excellent first term and passed her prelims.

Montse was a very beautiful young lady of eighteen at the time, in full splendour and the centre of attraction for many undergraduates. She had many boyfriends—I remember one especially, who came from Rhodesia—and Amelia and I started to worry about losing her. At this point, the arrival in Oxford of my sister Júlia brought matters rapidly to a head. Coming from Catalonia, she was full of the expectation of seeing the whole family reunited there soon, even though Meli had married an Englishman. My sister Júlia said: "It seems to me you're quite mad! One of these days Montse is going to tell you both: I have fallen in love with a boy who lives on the other side of the world and I want to marry him."

Amelia and I went into a kind of panic. I decided, in true Victorian-parent style, that Montse should forthwith abandon her course and go back to Barcelona with my sister. Montse, who was genuinely interested in taking her degree, protested bitterly against this: nor was the Principal of Somerville, Janet Vaughan, pleased either; she could not understand why I was insisting that Montse should give up her studies and go to Barcelona. How could she understand? The family bond in

Britain is not, nor ever was, as strong as ours. The result was that the friendship between Janet Vaughan and myself was precariously strained—but Montse went back to Barcelona to live with my sister and my mother.

Soon after arriving in Barcelona, suitors were buzzing around her like flies—among them a young man who had been to see us in Oxford some years before, when she was thirteen or fourteen. He was Ramon Trias-Fargas, son of my university and medical colleague and friend, Antoni Trias. After a short engagement, they were married—in Oxford.

The wedding itself took place on a sublime August day in 1954. Many members of both the Trias and Trueta families came over, and we were surrounded by our innumerable friends in England. The reception was in the grounds of Worcester College—to which I had belonged since occupying the Chair of Orthopaedics. Miraculously, after fifteen days of continuous rain, the sun came out and the sky was brilliantly blue such as one finds all too rarely in Britain. We were able to hold the reception down by the lake, with everyone in their elegant best as recorded by the local press. For me, though, it seemed that those who looked more "English" were those who had come from Barcelona complete with their grey top hats! Meli by then had two small sons, who as pages did their best to pull the train off their beloved Aunt Montse's bridal gown. At our request, the organist at St Aloysius played "El Cant dels Ocells", the Catalan song made world famous by Casals, as the couple left the church.

The marriage was a complete success: the bride and groom went to live in Barcelona, where Trias-Fargas has made a fine career for himself, winning an appointment to a Chair at Valencia and Barcelona, working in banking and publishing and now active in Catalan politics. Once they moved to Catalonia we saw them in the summer, here or there, and at Christmas which we all spent together in Oxford.

Christmas 1955 was made particularly exciting by our sitting room chimney catching fire. It was on the evening of Christmas Day itself, as we were all sitting round the fire singing carols, that great pieces of burning soot suddenly started to fall into the fireplace. The scene outside the house was impressive, with flames belching skywards from the chimney stack. Naturally, we had to call the fire-brigade, who came with commendable speed, and, because it was Christmas Day, they waived the statutory £5 charge. It all ended in a very friendly, festive atmosphere with toasts all round in champagne (or was it beer?). I remember that suddenly when the house was swarming with firemen, in full activity, clumping around in their boots and with hose pipes snaking through the house, at the top of the stairs there appeared the sleepy, pyjama-clad figure of my son-in-law Ramon asking what in heaven's name was going on and what was all the noise about! On the job of cleaning up the mess and baling out the flooded ground floor I prefer not to comment. . . .

In 1956, Juscelino Kubitschek sent his thirteen-year-old daughter Marcia to Oxford because of back trouble and after thorough study we put her on an intensive course of exercises under the personal direction of the head of our physiotherapy department. The improvement of Marcia's condition was such that we eventually decided that the treatment could be continued in Rio de Janeiro. Nevertheless, Kubitschek insisted on our head physiotherapist, Miss Margerison, supervising Marcia's treatment in Rio and thereby at the same time helping her to improve her already good English. A few months later complications arose in Marcia's condition and Kubitschek asked me to go over personally to see her.

As Kubitschek's invitation extended to Amelia and one of our daughters, we took our unmarried daughter, Julie, with us, and stopped off in Lisbon to attend the wedding of an ex-patient of mine at which Don Juan de Bourbon was also present. Don Juan told me he would like to have a talk with me and the following day I went to see him at his home in Estoril. I was received by a secretary after first signing the visitors' book and was taken up to the first floor. A door opened and Don Juan greeted me, gripping my hands painfully hard. We had no sooner settled ourselves in his study when, to my astonishment, he suddenly got up, tiptoed to the door and swung it open. After putting his head out and looking to left and right, he came back to his chair assuring me we could talk without fear. In those days the existence of Watergate-type intrigues just did not occur to me. He then started talking about General Franco and Catalonia with a frankness which flattered me. I remember saying to him that we Catalans, who had never before had a king, but only princes or counts, were now the only Spaniards with one, in the person of himself, the Count of Barcelona. The others only had Franco. This seemed to amuse him greatly.

He told me that he did not consider Franco to be a man of great talents, but that he had one gift in which he was unsurpassed: that of always knowing the quarter from which any threat would come to his lifelong occupancy of the position he had usurped. Communists, Anarchists, Separatists, Liberals, Republicans—none of these caused him any disquiet. The only danger which Franco saw to his perpetual continuance in power lay in the Count of Barcelona himself, Don Juan. Don Juan had always seemed to me to be an alert, perceptive person. Now I thought him intelligent as well, since he was absolutely right in what he said and time has shown this to be so. I happened to mention that I was going to Washington shortly, and he asked me to use every opportunity to present the case of Spain there in its true light.

He went on to talk of Prince Juan Carlos' education, which was the subject of a tug-of-war struggle, for Franco was doing all he could to set the son against the father. But knowing his son's character well he regarded the battle as already won beyond all doubt. Before we parted he asked me: "What would you think if I were to send my son to read law at Barcelona University?" "A magnificent idea!" I replied. "That would be the sure way to end once and for all the separatist myth. But would they let you get away with it?"

I have had a sincere respect ever since for this the first Bourbon not to forget that his only rights over my countrymen derive from his direct descent from the counts of Barcelona. He seemed to wish to expunge the tragic image of the Castilian "Conquistador" and to hark back to the dignity of the 900-year-old treaty of Pau i Treva (Peace and Truce), which strove to resist the establishment of the Castilian Inquisition, at a time when Castile and Aragon were still so independent of each other that they maintained separate ambassadors in Italy—in different cities.

We landed in Brazil after refuelling stops, in those days at Dakar and Recife. The Kubitscheks installed us in the presidential palace of Las Laranjeiras and there I was able to put their minds at rest by assuring them that fortunately Marcia did not have to undergo any operation. Donha Sarah and my Amelia had many characteristics in common, even physically, and got on very well together.

One day we were flown from Rio in the presidential plane to the low jungle of the Brazilian plateau. The aircraft—a specially fitted-out Viscount—circled the forested area selected for the birthplace of Brasilia. In a clearing we could see a building under construction, which was to be the president's palace—L'Alvorada. A few kilometres away we could see another building going up, right in the heart of the forest; this Kubitschek told us would be the hotel of Brasilia. We landed on a provisional runway, little more than a stretch of wide roadway, and almost immediately the president, the senior project engineer of Brasilia and I were in the air again in a four-seater aircraft flying low over the trees, setting up flocks of small Brazilian partridges, to be shown, with the aid of a plan, the intended lay-out of the capital, with its diplomatic quarter, its many ministries, its residential area, etc. From the air we saw the small river curving across the plain which, when dammed, would one day provide a lake within Brasilia itself.

From the airstrip we were driven to a wooden hut, supported on stilts some six metres above the ground, to reach which we had to climb up a ladder. The explanation of this extraordinary structure was convincing enough: snakes and the American panther—ounces or jaguars—had to be discouraged from making themselves at home. We had supper there and were entertained by natives and the construction workers playing unorthodox musical instruments to the accompaniment of domestic pots and pans. However, any instrumental shortcomings there may have been in this concert dedicated to their president were more than compensated by their exciting sense of rhythm. Neither Amelia nor I could suspect at the time that, barely four years later, we would be the only non-family guests of the Kubitscheks in the Alvorada palace for the inauguration of Brasilia.

We made a most satisfying journey in 1956 to visit my brother Rafel and his family in Mexico, and finally ended up in

Colombia and Venezuela. In Colombia, where dear friends of ours, parents-in-law of our daughter Montserrat, were living in exile, a trip at first light up one of the tributaries of the River Magdalena was organized for us. We went in two flat-bottomed boats powered by outboard motors. The two natives piloting us (this was in the heart of the Colombian jungle in an oil-drilling area exploited by Shell) obviously regarded the excursion as a race, which was all very exciting no doubt, but with six or seven in each boat we were somewhat overloaded for my peace of mind.

Suddenly our craft collided at full speed with a half-submerged tree trunk drifting down river. The engine stopped and everyone aboard moved aft to see what had happened. Water poured in over the stern and in no time the boat was foundering. The Colombian wife of the oil company's doctor in the other boat began screaming and shrieked: "My God, they're sinking, they're sinking!" I was carrying a heavy twelve-bore shot gun which I had been lent in case I wanted to explore the jungle, so I passed it over to the other boat and helped the ladies with me to clamber across, one by one. Finally, we were all safely aboard the second vessel, her gunwales almost awash on account of her shallow draft, and everyone rapidly jettisoning non-essentials. It was just capable of carrying everyone to the nearest shore. All this time the doctor's wife was continuing to have hysterics. I tried to calm her by telling her, quite untruthfully, that I was a professional swimmer, but she still continued to shriek, constantly repeating a name which meant nothing to me at the time. Proceeding very slowly (fortunately the boy in the second boat must have known what he was about), and towing the damaged boat behind us, we eventually beached on a largish island in mid-river and shipwrecked and rescuers jumped ashore. It seemed that our tribulations were still not at an end, even temporarily, for Amelia suddenly called out: "Look, there are dragons here!" But it was only a magnificent iguana, some two feet long, which with head cocked, was looking with curiosity at its unexpected visitors. The doctor then told me that his wife's desperate anxiety was due to her certainty that one of the species of fish in which that particular tributary abounded was the piraña, small carnivorous fish which, attacking in force, can strip the flesh off the bones of a large mammal in a few minutes. No doubt in order to put our minds at rest—I am not sure he entirely succeeded—he added that he personally did not believe this to be so.

We were meanwhile all left on dry land while the boatman went off in the one navigable boat to fetch help. He appeared half an hour later with a primitive river yacht which had room for us all. The doctor and I were put off on the river bank and, with my gun for self-protection and a small Indian boy as guide, we set off into the forest in search of a banana plantation. After a time the small boy, who spoke Spanish, told me to start watching out carefully and no sooner had he said so than about fifty metres ahead of us a kind of large black dog emerged from a banana grove. The boy cried out that it was "el Tigrito" (small jaguar or ounce) and to kill it. What an idea, I thought: to fire No. 4 pellets at jaguars from a distance of fifty metres seemed to me to verge on the suicidal. At the most, all I could do would be to puncture the animal superficially, almost certainly infuriating it into counterattack. The small Indian boy looked at me in disgust, and promptly lost all respect for me. Was I afraid? was his only comment. We made our way back to the river and the yacht, and eventually returned to civilization.

Before leaving Bogota I lectured there and had the pleasure of being made doctor honoris causa at the university. From Colombia we flew to Venezuela where I lectured at Maracaibo, Merida and Caracas. At the University of Maracaibo, merely as a normal compliment, I congratulated the rector on the magnificent American slide-projector which had been put at my disposal for the lecture, and was the first remote-control one I had ever seen. Three days later, having made the round of several Shell hospitals, we were due to fly back to Caracas. The rector and several doctors came to say goodbye to us at the airport and, noticing that the rector was carrying a suit-case, I asked him if he were perhaps flying to Caracas with us. No, he said, in the suitcase was the slide-projector I had liked so much and which the university was offering me as a gift. I tried to convince him that without due import authorization I would never be allowed to take it into Britain with me but all to no avail; he just would not take no for an answer.

On our return flight our aircraft landed at Prestwick and our baggage had to be cleared through Customs. The Customs officer, half asleep at 5 am, asked me what I was carrying in the large suitcase, and I told him it was a simple slide-projector. When he learned that I was a doctor, he asked to be shown a slide or two. By sheer chance I happened to pick out one of a child with polio. The reaction was immediate and entirely unpredictable. It turned out that he himself had a child suffering from polio, who had just been operated on, and he went on to describe the operation and ask my advice. I told him I had an excellent pupil in Edinburgh whom I suggested he might like to go and see, and I gave him my visiting card, with the surgeon's name written on it. Meanwhile, he was busily chalking crosses on all our cases. . . . We are all human beings, when all is said and done. Looking back, the rector at Maracaibo had been right when he said no one would dare to confiscate medical apparatus from the Professor of Ortho-paedics at Oxford. I am glad I allowed myself to be persuaded.

In 1956 the Jocs Florals (Floral Games), an annual Catalan poetry competition, took place in Cambridge, organized by our dear friend Batista i Roca. During Franco's lifetime they were always held in exile. They took place at Christ's College, to which was attached the Chair of Hispanic Studies, held then by Professor Trend, a great friend of Batista—and of Catalonia. Our eldest daughter Meli was queen of the games, and among her eight ladies-in-waiting was her youngest sister, Julie. It was an impressive occasion, and our happiness was all the greater for having with us my brother Rafel and his wife, who were visiting Europe that year.

A year later I lost my mother. She was eighty-six years old, and we had seen each other frequently since our first reunion in Andorra in 1946. She had come to stay with us in Oxford several times. I remember the amazement on her face the first time we took her out for a meal and she was asked if she would like her coffee black or white. "They serve white-coloured coffee in this country?" she asked, in astonishment. She died peacefully but so suddenly that I did not have time to see her before she died though I was able to be present at her funeral. Poor woman, she had suffered so much from having her two sons in exile—although even at the age of eighty, accompanied by my sister Júlia, with whom she lived for so many years, she had flown to Mexico to stay with Rafel.

During this period, due to a combination of circumstances and coincidences, I had several patients from the Establishment with some of whom I later became good friends. One of the first of these was Baron Elie de Rothschild, a great polo player, who had a back complaint. I operated on him at the Wingfield and he went on playing for many years until, when nearly sixty years of age, another accident finally prevented him from carrying on with his favourite sport. Elie had had the good fortune to marry Liliane, incidentally the most charming of hostesses, by whom he had three children. They lived in a luxurious apartment in Paris when we first knew them but later moved to a small palace in the rue Masseran. They furnished it with so many family heirlooms that it was like a veritable museum. I recall among other masterpieces a breathtaking Rembrandt depicting a man with his elbow slightly raised—so realistic that it was an effort to approach it closely for fear of being nudged!—, the portrait of La Fontaine by Goya, and a magnificent Gainsborough.

At the left-hand corner of the building, with an independent outside stairway, they built a small apartment consisting of a double bedroom and bathroom. From its inauguration, this has been "our" apartment in Paris! Once, when Amelia and I installed ourselves in a Paris hotel for a couple of days, we suddenly found ourselves without suitcases: a valet of the Rothschilds had come to the hotel to remove them to, as Elie put it, "where they belonged".

It was in the vast salon of this residence that on 13 May 1963, the French prime minister, Georges Pompidou, with André Malraux, then minister of culture, joined Elie and Alain de Rothschild and their families, and practically the whole Trueta clan (wife, daughters, sons-in-law, sister, nieces and the Nicolaus), in a memorable soirée redolent of the eighteenth century. There, after an exquisite dinner, Pompidou, on behalf of President de Gaulle, removed my red ribbon of a Chevalier of the Légion d'Honneur and replaced it by the rosette of an Officier. I thought back to when, years before, in the name of President Auriol, M. Massigli, the then French ambassador, had draped the chevalier's ribbon on me at the Maison Française in Oxford one 14 July. As all this was going on, and Pompidou was saying some moving words about services to Frenchmen who had served under the emblem of the Cross of Lorraine, I kept saying to myself—what are we all doing here there must be some mistake. . . . The Rothschilds perpetuated the evening for us by giving us two large albums full of photographs of the occasion and when I look at them, now that I am alone, I re-live the hours of happiness shared with Amelia and my family.

In later trips to Paris, I had the privilege of dining *à deux* at the Elysée Palace with Pompidou when he was president, and among the subjects we discussed was invariably the problem of Spain.

Skiing accidents accounted for several calls for assistance and one such was from Switzerland where Tina Livanos, formerly married to Aristotle Onassis, had broken her leg badly by falling over a precipice while skiing. We immobilized her for the trip and brought her back to Oxford in Niarchos' private plane.

The repercussions in the international press were resounding and we were literally besieged by reporters from every quarter, attracted by her name and jet-set fame. She was a very pretty and graceful girl, almost child-like, and daughter of another powerful shipowner, Livanos. During her stay in the hospital her ex-husband, Onassis, arrived from Buenos Aires and, in typically tycoon-style, sought (unsuccessfully) permission to land by helicopter in the hospital grounds themselves. While at the hospital she resumed her friendship with the Marquess of Blandford, whom she married a few months later. The marriage, unfortunately, was not a great success, but her recovery from the accident was total and she was able to ski right up to the time of her tragic death.

This connection, particularly with Niarchos—by then, brother-in-law of Tina—led to my operating on his hand and to my being invited with Amelia to be his guests for a winter holiday at his magnificent house in St Moritz. Here, in January and February, with an outside temperature of minus 10–15°C, one could lie and sun bathe in his swimming-pool.

The central heating, the glass roof and the heated water of the pool made it possible up in the Alps to feel as though one were in a Mediterranean summer resort. If one felt like it, one could ask for a film to be shown, generally one of the latest American or British productions at the touch of a button. This led to automatic blacking-out of the roof and, stretched out in comfort in the dark, one suddenly found oneself in a cinema while drying from a swim.

Another victim of a skiing accident was Hjordis, wife of the film star David Niven, who was brought to Oxford with a broken leg. We remained very good friends of David and Hjordis after the operation, staying at their house at Cap Ferrat and seeing them on various occasions throughout the past few years.

If I mention these wealthy and aristocratic people it is not only because they left me with very happy memories and became firm friends, but because later on, when the time came for me to retire from the Chair of Orthopaedics at Oxford, they came near to solving the problem of where I was to live and work, even though in fact their well-intentioned efforts came to nought.

Although not directly connected with my retirement, I am reminded of a visit from Umberto, ex-King of Italy, which almost turned our house into a scene from a theatrical farce. I had operated on one of his equerries and a day or two later I was informed that ex-King Umberto, with an Italian duke in attendance, would be visiting my patient and that he would be pleased to lunch with us at our home.

The news that a royal personage was coming to luncheon put Amelia into a state of nervous tension and, scarcely knowing where to turn, it occurred to her to telephone Madariaga and consult him on matters of protocol. Don Salvador, ex-ambassador as he was, told her that the king should occupy the most important seat, at the head of the table.

Amelia decided to put the king in the seat she normally occupied, forgetting that under the carpet alongside her chair, was a press-stud which rang a bell in the kitchen. The result was that His Majesty, entirely oblivious of the fact, kept ringing the bell at irregular intervals throughout the entire meal, which meant that our valet-butler spent the whole of luncheon continuously on the run back and forth between dining room and kitchen. When it was a false alarm, Amelia would warn him off with a discreet shake of the head, but by the end of the meal our long-suffering Cristóbal had nearly been reduced to a state of lunacy. I recall that my eldest grandson, Michael, then at the Dragon School, Oxford, came to luncheon and was questioned at length by the king on the subject of British education.

One of the saddest chapters in the whole of this story is the death of my brother in Mexico, of a heart attack, in May 1958. A dedicated swimmer from his earliest youth, he would not give up his regular practice of driving down every weekend to Cuernavaca where he and some friends had constructed a swimming pool near a small cottage. Cuernavaca is some 3,000 feet below Mexico City, which stands some 8,000 feet above sea level. The strain of adapting to the continual change of altitude proved too much and his heart finally gave out shortly after one of his usual spells in the pool.

This was the cause of particular grief to me as my brother, five years my junior, left a widow and three children: an elder daughter of about seventeen years old, a boy of thirteen and a small daughter.

Amelia and I were in Washington when Rafel died, and though we flew to Mexico, unfortunately, because of delays in obtaining an entry visa, we did not arrive in time for the funeral. We did all we could to comfort Pilar, offering her all the help which was within our limited possibilities. It seemed to me that the best thing was for the elder girl to look for a job immediately, so that she could help her mother, who taught painting in a school. As I saw it, the main thing was to concentrate on the boy's education. His father, like me, had had great hopes that he would become a doctor. The smallest child could carry on with her education free at the school in which her mother taught. On returning home to Oxford, I consulted my bank manager, and found that all I could count on were savings of some £2,000 which, despite years of hard work, were all that was left to us after the demands of the income-tax collector had been met. Apart from a small insurance policy, this was the full extent of my assets.

In view of this, I wrote to Pilar saying that I thought the best thing was for us to think first of the boy's studies. I was very upset to hear shortly afterwards from a mutual friend in Mexico that my sister-in-law had circulated my letter throughout the Catalan community and to members of the Communist Party, to which it seems she belonged, condemning me on the grounds that now my brother was dead, I was pretending to have no money in order to be rid of my nieces and nephew. I found this a most unjust insinuation, particularly since the £1,000 or so I managed to send her to eke out her resources were promptly spent on a visit to Europe, instead of on the boy's education as I had intended. It hurt me deeply that a private letter I had written her should have been publicly commented upon, and I told her so in no uncertain terms. To cut a long, sad story short our relationship completely disintegrated, and, as if in an attempt to spite me, it was her eldest daughter who studied medicine, while the boy became a veterinary surgeon.

Family affairs apart—my work went on in Oxford. Since the official opening of the new research building of the Nuffield Orthopaedic Centre in 1958 we had become aware that, while no urgent modification seemed to be required, in certain aspects we were deficient. For instance, we needed a larger gymnasium. This time I did not go to Lord Nuffield for funds, but to a Mr Wallack, an oil magnate who lived in England and whom I knew well as an ex-patient and friend. This kindest of men gave us the £5,000 we required and we were able to enlarge the gym. Another important necessity was a workshop. We had inherited a small one from GRG's time, quite adequate for the making and repairing of the heavy apparatus then worn by polio patients, but not equipped to cope with new developments in electronic and engineering technology. I thought it essential that the hospital should have a centre where first-class technicians could make and maintain the most modern apparatus. For this we needed £40,000, and were fortunate to obtain a grant from the National Fund for Poliomyelitis Research. With this money a truly model workshop was built manned by a few mechanics of a high order of technical ability. This was entirely adequate for our purpose and needs until 1960, when the terrible thalidomide catastrophe took

place. Children were being born without legs or arms because
the mother had taken a particular drug in the first three
months of pregnancy, with fearful consequences for the baby
in the womb. The drug had been developed in Western
Germany, which logically was the first country to suffer its
ghastly effects. When we were faced by the catastrophe, the
Germans were already constructing artificial limbs activated
by compressed air for those children lacking limbs.

While I was away from Oxford during the summer, Lady
Hoare, a Lady Mayoress of London and wife of a banker, who
was keenly aware of the absence in the United Kingdom of
facilities for providing afflicted children with artificial limbs,
contacted the Nuffield Centre. When I returned she had
already had a meeting with my assistant, Mrs Agerholm, and
they had drafted a scheme for sending a team to Heidelberg,
where the Germans were constructing these appliances. Four
of our staff spent a month in Heidelberg, where they were made
very welcome and given the maximum co-operation in an
atmosphere of complete team spirit, so that when they returned
we were immediately able to start building the first British
limbs for thalidomide cases. I would have preferred that this
aid had come directly from a British centre, but in the
circumstances we had no choice. The Nuffield Centre col-
laborated to the utmost and we established a deep friendship
with Lady Hoare, which lasted right up to her death. With the
team of technicians and the financial help at our disposal, we
were able to make limbs for the first thirty or forty children,
whom we watched grow up without arms or legs. Some
modifications were made as time went by, but basically the
appliances were called, inappropriately, "Heidelberg arms and
legs".

While this department was being built and developed, we
employed Dr Philip Nichols, now its director, who dedicated
his time to the perfecting of instruments for paralytics of all
types. This led to the realization of another project—a home
for paralytics: a house where everything that a physically
handicapped man or woman might need in order to live alone
despite his or her disability. For instance, to be able to take a
bath by getting in and out of the bath tub by means of a system
of pulleys and hanging ropes which, with the slightest tug,

even with the mouth, could produce a force fifty or one hundred times greater than that applied. This department at Oxford still carries on very successfully, and was in fact the precursor of several similar centres throughout the country. We named this technical workshop and rehabilitation centre the Mary Marlborough Lodge, after the Duchess of Marlborough, who presided over the hospital committee for so many years, including the first ten years of my professorship and as head of the hospital.

In 1959 a young Spanish doctor came to work for the Accident Service at the Radcliffe Infirmary. He had studied medicine in Madrid and was firmly resolved to specialize in orthopaedics. Although he did not approach me directly when he arrived at Oxford, I assume the fact that I was there may have encouraged him to apply for the post of registrar at the Accident Service. He was a success from the start, winning the support and friendship of my colleagues at the Radcliffe, and shortly afterwards moving to the Nuffield Centre, where he joined my team, first as a scholar and later as one of my assistants.

About a year later our third daughter, Julie, who worked in our laboratories making sections for study under the micro-scope, came to see me with the young man, Pepe Valderrama, to announce that they were in love and wished to get married. This came as no surprise to Amelia and myself and, although I was not too keen on my youngest daughter marry-ing someone who would take her away to live in Madrid, there was nothing I could do about it—the couple quite simply had made up their minds.

On 21 October 1961, Julie, like her two sisters before her, was married in Oxford. We held another Anglo-Spanish reunion, to which the bridegroom's parents, our family and friends came, and this time the reception was held in the garden of our home, Overmead—in a marquee just in case it should rain. The marriage has proved very successful, my son-in-law having built up a thriving practice in Madrid, numbering among his patients the Spanish royal family.

Chapter 3

SALVADOR DE MADARIAGA—
FRIEND AND NEIGHBOUR

FROM THE TIME we moved to Manor Road in Headington in order to be near the then Wingfield Morris Orthopaedic Hospital, we were neighbours of Salvador de Madariaga, whose home was some 200 metres from ours. This, plus the fact that we were both in Oxford for similar reasons, meant that we saw each other often. For many years we used to meet every Sunday morning after I had done the rounds at the hospital and we would go for a walk in the country, whatever the weather might be. We used to cover a couple of miles or so and in that time share the latest news each of us had gathered in the course of the week. Probably this enabled me to get to know Madariaga as few others did, outside his family.

While we chatted, it used to strike me that his years in France and his long stay in England, far from influencing his character and converting him into a hybrid European, had only served to emphasize his Spanish traits which, probably as in no other case today, were so manifest in his written works in any of the principal languages of the Christian world.

While we lived in Oxford we were in contact for over twenty-five years, only interrupted by our respective absences from Oxford on the visits abroad which we were both obliged to make.

Madariaga had been the first professor to hold the Alfonso XIII Chair of Hispanic Studies at Oxford. The confused turn of events in Spain following the fall of the dictatorship of Primo de Rivera and the advent of the Republic in 1931, drew Madariaga towards politics, and he accepted the post of Spanish Ambassador in Washington and later in Paris, which meant renouncing the Chair to which he had been elected barely two years before. The university authorities took exception to this—and, as he himself used to say, they never forgave him until, when he was eighty years old, they conferred upon him a D.Litt. honoris causa. Despite his estrangement from the university, he continued to live in Oxford (until a few years ago when, for climatic reasons, he went to live in Switzerland), and maintained his links with Exeter College, of which he had been a fellow when professor.

Even the scantiest appraisal of his multi-faceted personality would take more time than is at my disposal, and moreover would be out of place in this selection of memoirs. However, I want to dedicate a few lines to one of the foremost contemporary Spanish writers of international repute. Possibly no other Spanish author has been able to make himself understood to English, French and, naturally, Spanish readers without his own works having to be translated. He has the great gift of having been able to write poetry in all three languages and, while it cannot be said that he was a particularly talented poet, I do not believe that he has any equal among his contemporaries as a writer.

This ability became apparent when you knew him. An untiring reader, endowed with an exceptional memory, a hard worker, and profoundly humanitarian, the subjects on which he could converse were innumerable. He was tolerant, except of intolerance; sceptically pro-Franco at the beginning of the world war, he soon became irreconcilably disenchanted with Francoism, an aversion only surpassed by his opposition to communism. Apart from these two factions, Madariaga was rational and inclined towards compromise. To a lesser degree, he felt predisposed against everything connected with Catalans, although at heart I suspect he admired them. When our friendship was well-established, I used to take rather malicious pleasure in pulling his leg about Catalan affairs. Shrewd as he was, he soon caught on, and our walks through the Oxfordshire countryside took the form of intellectual fencing matches which never ended in our parting anything but the best of friends, on our way home to Sunday luncheon.

Madariaga had had the good fortune to marry in his youth a Scottish writer, Constance Archibald, by whom he had two handsome daughters, physically much like their mother. When she died he married Emilia (Mimi) Raumann, Hungarian by birth but educated in Vienna, who lived in exile in England with her family. She was his secretary for many years, and the most excellent of helpmates because, like Madariaga, she has a natural gift for languages. Mimi was a good friend of ours, and Amelia was particularly fond of her.

Madariaga is the archetypal intellectual Spanish Jew. Although I believe his Jewish blood only stemmed from one of his grandmothers, his physical make-up—short in stature and brachycephalic—coupled with his intellectual vitality and faculty for understanding people from other places proclaimed his origins. Despite his separation from Spain from early youth —he studied in Paris and has lived for nearly fifty years abroad—the subject which absorbed him was Spain itself, and the future of the Spanish State caused him grave anxiety. His craving for Spain and for all things Iberian was such that he was not satisfied with the many visits he received in his own home in Oxford from Spaniards: whenever he found out that I had Spanish patients at the hospital he would go along and spend hours with them, chatting and joking—he was a great raconteur—whether it were a young girl, an elder states-man, a bullfighter or what have you, it made no difference.

I recall that when Amelia and I celebrated our silver wedding in 1948, we had a small party at home and Madariaga was asked to propose the toast, which he did in his usual witty fashion.

Nearing the end of our lives, we have had the pleasure of meeting in Madrid, six months after the death of Franco, on the occasion of Madariaga taking up his seat at the Royal Academy of the Spanish Language. Once again I was deeply impressed by his resolution, integrity and above all, his humanism. No other living Spanish writer, in my opinion, has deserved this honour more than he.

We then had the pleasure of a visit from Salvador and Mimi in S'Agaró, on the Costa Brava, where they spent a few weeks resting before going to Corunna where he was to celebrate his ninetieth birthday in his native city. For me personally they were particularly welcome company as it was the first summer I was spending on the Costa Brava without my Amelia. After his journey to Galicia they decided to return to Locarno, where they had been living for some years, as the situation in Spain in the summer of 1976 was still unclear, and besides he was in need of his doctors in Switzerland.

Chapter 4

TEN YEARS AS PROFESSOR OF ORTHOPAEDICS

IN 1959, WHEN I had held the Chair of Orthopaedics for ten years, I thought it would be useful to look back and recapitulate on what we had achieved at the Wingfield, in 1955 renamed the Nuffield Orthopaedic Centre. When GRG and I went to see Lord Nuffield in 1949 to ask for his financial help, GRG insinuated that the name of the hospital would be changed. An attempt after GRG's death to associate his name with Nuffield's did not prosper as it was thought that Lord Nuffield might not like it. Now, the complex was no longer just a hospital, but a medical centre attached to a hospital, together with an experimental research centre on orthopaedic complaints, etc. The change was now imperative, and the idea was well received by Lord Nuffield himself and the Duchess of Marlborough.

We therefore made a study of our ten years' work, and the following are the salient points of a lecture I gave:

The hospital started as an orthopaedic hospital for Great War casualties in 1917. Once the war was over, GRG turned the hospital into a children's home for those suffering from bone deformities, in Oxford and the surrounding areas. Thanks largely to Lord Nuffield's generosity, by 1934 the hospital had one hundred and sixty beds and twenty-two centres under its control in the region.

In 1937 the Chair of Orthopaedics was created, also by Lord Nuffield, and GRG was its first holder, followed by Seddon and myself.

In 1948 the National Health came into being, and some adjustments had to be made.

Laboratories having been constructed as a result of Lord Nuffield's first donation of £50,000 in 1949 and vastly enlarged by means of his second gift of £200,000, the new department was inaugurated in 1958 by Her Majesty Queen Elizabeth the Queen Mother.

In these years we had trained surgeons in orthopaedics from:

Great Britain	37
Commonwealth	36
Europe	20
America	8
Middle East	2
Total:	103

In 1959 ten of these were heads of department in their respective countries.

We had fifty-three cases of polio with severe respiratory paralysis, the results of which were comparable with those of the best centres in the world.

We had contributed new concepts in scoliosis, osteoarthritis, blood circulation in the bone and in Perthes' disease. We were studying the pathology of bone growth, damage to spinal medulla and other conditions and disorders. We had also contributed new systems of operating on congenital hip dislocation, acute osteomyelitis, stimulation of bone growth etc.

We were working in conjunction with the paediatric department at the Oxford Medical School under Dr Victoria Smallpeice. Dr K. Little worked on aspects of bone calcification with the use of the electron microscope. We were formulating new concepts of the mechanism of osteoporosis. Dr W. Rigal was in charge of the study of growth, using the laboratory for the culture of tissue, and its contribution was most promising.

We had had one hundred and seventy papers and eleven books published. The number of operations performed in our hospital in these ten years totalled nearly fifteen thousand. We had two hundred and forty beds, but the number of patients waiting for treatment made it necessary to increase these to three hundred.

During the university terms, we had a lecture every week given by a well-known colleague from Great Britain or abroad.

The success of our insistence that research should be an

integral part of the training of the orthopaedic surgeon had been amply proved by the fact that in 1959 nearly half the publications in the *Journal of Bone and Joint Surgery* were on investigation, whereas in 1940 they only comprised some fifteen per cent of papers published. A great number of these had originated in our centre.

The Mary Marlborough Lodge, as a national centre for the study of problems of resettlement of the permanently disabled was being built with the support of the National Fund for Poliomyelitis Research. This was designed to bridge the gap between the rehabilitation department of the hospital and the patient's home. We had also obtained the help of the same fund to publish a comprehensive encyclopaedia of apparatus and gadgets to assist the paralysed.

In my survey I also mentioned the work we were doing in patronizing an orthopaedic organization in Africa.

Finally I suggested:

That the Nuffield Orthopaedic Centre be placed officially at the disposal of the orthopaedic specialists of the region, from consultants to junior staff. . . . We suggest that these consultants find the necessary facilities from the Ministry of Health to enable them to attend the Nuffield Orthopaedic Centre at regular intervals and to be in charge, if they wish, of a number of beds where they can study their own orthopaedic cases. . . . At the same time the research facilities available here . . . should be placed at the disposal of consultants from the periphery. . . . Being a centre with national and international commitments, we cannot limit our responsibility to the boundaries of the region. We also have national and international duties to fulfil and in these two directions we are at present working.

As will be gathered, my research work never ended. My old suspicion that the vessels of the bone marrow not only form blood but also bone, had become more and more of a certainty in my own mind since 1948 when I had started work on bone tissue. From 1950 to 1960 my suspicion turned into near conviction and I wrote several papers giving details to support my contention. I could not get definite proof until we possessed a means of identifying the origin of the vascular cells—a method which has only been available in the last two years. But by then I no longer had any laboratory at my disposal. When I went back to live in Barcelona in 1967, a project I had for the setting up of a small investigation centre at the Barcelona Zoological Gardens was rejected. I had no doubt that this was because the doctor in charge was a Falangist. I was even asked to give a lecture on my project, but at the end I was told, in so many words: "Don't call us, we'll call you."

The other possibility to have laboratories at my disposal was much more serious but also fizzled out fruitlessly. In 1973 I was visited by some very charming gentlemen from the Fundación General Mediterránea, a body of seemingly modern forward-looking bankers interested in projects designed to promote the future scientific progress of the country. They told me that they were sponsoring an Institute of Investigation in Molecular Biology which they were thinking of setting up in Madrid—in the university city—and which would be named after the Nobel Prize winner Professor Severo Ochoa who had been a colleague of mine for a short while at Oxford.

They had also consulted HRH Prince Juan Carlos on the erection of another institute—for medical research—which the prince had suggested should be in Barcelona and be named after myself. I was most grateful to the prince and also to the princess, who graciously consented to be honorary president.

I immediately set to work on this project, which took up two years of my life. The administration of the Hospital de la Sta Creu i St Pau considered the possibility of ceding space for the building since they needed more beds within easy reach. I had had the experience of planning the research building for the Nuffield Orthopaedic Centre in Oxford, I had visited the laboratories of Dr Andrew Bassett in New York and of Dr Webster Jee, in charge of the isotopes section at the institute in Salt Lake City, both of them close friends of mine. With the suggestions and recommendations of both these experts, coupled with my own ideas, I commissioned a talented young Barcelona architect to draw up the plans of the future Institute.

The total estimate for the project amounted to 160 million pesetas—Ochoa told me himself that the estimate for the Madrid molecular biology institute already exceeded 400 million pesetas—and, barely two years after being invited, I was able to put the whole of the plans before the Fundación General Mediterránea. The result was totally negative: they had no money. Their final suggestion was the splendid idea that I should raise the funds myself.

A few months later the press came out with the news of the creation of an institute for biological investigation under the direction of a distinguished researcher to be built at the cost of—strange coincidence—160 million pesetas.

I now know that I shall never be able to prove or see proved my theory that the bone is in fact an appendage of the blood system with which it is linked by the very blood vessels.

1960 was one of the most interesting years of my life. It began with a visit in January to Padua, the old Italian university of medical sciences at which William Harvey had studied, where I was invited to do a "Visiting Professor" course by an old pupil of mine at Oxford, Caloggero Casuccio, by then Professor of Orthopaedics at Padua. I was enthused by the idea of seeing the place where Galileo had taught and indeed they still preserve the pulpit from which he addressed his pupils.

In April we picked up Meli in Madrid, where she lives, and the three of us travelled to Brazil together, as the guests of the President of the Republic, Juscelino Kubitschek, because a pavilion was to be named after me at the Rehabilitation Centre in Brasilia. We flew to Lisbon and on to Rio where the Kubitschek girls, as sweet as ever, met us at the airport with flowers for Amelia. We were installed magnificently in a beautiful suite at the Copacabana Hotel, and lunched with the president and his charming wife, Donha Sarah, at the presidential palace. After relaxing for a day or two we flew with them to Brasilia in the president's aircraft.

Seen from the air, Brasilia was breathtaking. It seemed incredible to think that so much had been accomplished in such a short time. To me it was an undertaking of such importance as to make it ridiculous that millions of dollars and countless man hours should be spent on putting man into the stratosphere and beyond when there were so many important things to be done on earth. Among these was the historic highway from Brasilia to Belem, on the Amazon, through the jungle: a jungle never crossed before and still peopled by Indians hunting with poisoned arrows. A feat, then, worthy of the greatest accomplishments which had taken place in South America since its discovery.

We stayed with them at the presidential palace there—the Alvorada (the word means dawn)—and attended, as it were, as members of the family, the opening of almost all the buildings in Brasilia—the congress, the senate, the cathedral, the cinema, etc. We met Raymond Cartier, of *Paris Match*, reporting on the historic event, the British ambassador Sir Geoffrey Wallinger and his wife, and attended a reception of over 2,000 people at the Palace of Justice—still uncompleted—the men in white tie and uniforms, with decorations and medals —and the ladies resplendent in their long evening dresses and jewellery. It was as though one had been transported back to the seventeenth-century French court.

It has been said that Kubitschek nearly bankrupted Brazil; it is possible that he put severe strain on the economy by the enormous expense involved in building the new capital. On the other hand, he was only putting into effect a long-standing mandate of the Brazilian constitution which laid down as one of the first duties of the president to transfer the capital from Rio to the interior. Kubitschek, who was in fact not a politician by profession but a gynaecologist, took on the enormous task as if it were a surgical operation. I remember saying to him the night of the inauguration when thousands of lights lit up the capital: "Mr President, I am sure that you have never been present at a more difficult delivery than this!" with which he laughingly agreed.

Possibly he did leave the country slightly unstable economically, but by moving the capital over 560 miles inland, he gave it a territorial constitution and an organic structure which immensely increased its potentiality. As he himself said: "You cannot work in Rio—there are too many distractions!"

The opening of the pavilion named after me was naturally very moving for us. Amelia pulled the cord to uncover the plaque with my name, and the two women of the family present duly behaved emotionally in the traditional Latin manner.

After returning to Rio, where I gave several lectures and

lunched and dined with several colleagues, we flew to Buenos Aires where Amelia had many relatives, all of whom flocked to see us. Again I lectured several times—no language difficulty here—and was honoured to be elected honorary member of the National Academy. We then returned via Lisbon, where all three of us were received in audience in Estoril by Don Juan who seemed very interested to hear all about our trip to South America. We dropped off Meli in Madrid and so back to London.

The other exciting event for me in 1960 was connected with the SICOT (Société Internationale de Chirurgie Ortopédique et Traumatologie) meeting. The meetings or congresses which the Société holds every three years had, of course, been suspended during the Second World War. In 1951 a congress was held in Stockholm, and at this meeting I was appointed second vice-president for the next congress, to be held in Berne under the presidency of the famous Swiss orthopaedic surgeon Dr Scherb. In 1954 José Valls of Buenos Aires was elected president and myself vice-president for the next congress to be held in 1957 in Barcelona, my home town.

At the 1957 congress in Barcelona, Amelia and I were accompanied by our three daughters. The local press duly played up the importance which Spain was acquiring scientifically; a thousand or so surgeons from the whole world having chosen Spain as the meeting place to discuss the latest scientific and medical advances, and many other comments in similar vein. The day came when the committee was to meet to elect the president of the next congress, to be held in New York in 1960. In the middle of the session, Philip Wilson, the great American orthopaedic surgeon, asked me to go outside with him as he had something of great importance to say to me. We went to an adjoining room where he mumbled some quite unimportant details to do with the closure of the congress. After about a quarter of an hour we returned to the congress room and, to my astonishment, our entry was greeted with loud applause. It appeared that during my contrived absence, I had been unanimously chosen to preside over the next congress in 1960, in New York—the first time the SICOT congress would be crossing the Atlantic.

The Catalan and Spanish press were full of references to the congress and reported at length its lectures and meetings, but on the day I was elected president for the next congress they contented themselves with the bald statement: "The next president was also elected," without further comment. Obviously I had not been forgiven for my overt rejection of a régime based on lies and hypocrisy, nor for the fact that I had refused to defer to one who had been referred to as the "Saviour of Spain" (with the help, one must admit, of Mr Chamberlain's umbrella). My name was sufficiently well known internationally by then for me to feel no apprehension. I was simply still showing my rejection of the system invented by Goebbels, even though by now there was less inclination to be seen raising arms in salute.

The organization of the congress in New York was in the hands of a committee of excellent orthopaedic surgeons chosen from among the best in the country under the guidance of Philip Wilson and another excellent American orthopaedic surgeon, Albert Shands Jr. In September, Amelia and I set off once more for the United States, this time accompanied by our youngest daughter, Julie. The day of the opening of the congress was very moving for me because of the reception I received on walking into the vast hall. I remembered with emotion my father and wished that he might have been there; at that moment I leant heavily on the moral support of my wife and daughter.

After the congress we went on a lecture tour of the States and Canada, which included Toronto, Seattle, San Francisco— where I had the honour to be made an honorary member of the American College of Surgeons—Los Angeles and Salt Lake City. I flew back to Oxford leaving Amelia and Julie in New York to enjoy themselves for a few days.

As the culminating event, the Duke and Duchess of Windsor (the Duchess was a patient of mine) invited us to dinner at their home in Paris. It was a happy occasion which rounded off a memorable year.

Chapter 5

MORE TRAVELS

AT THE BEGINNING of 1961, fully recovered from our journeys of the previous year, I had the pleasure of being invited by Elie Rothschild to spend a few days in France for a shoot on an estate where it was usual to bag three or four thousand pheasants in the season. Preceded by a delightful evening, we went out and, still being in those days a passably good shot, I was fortunate to knock down a respectable number of pheasants, hares, rabbits and the odd partridge.

In July of that same year I had to go back once more to the United States to attend the Gordon Conference at which I had been invited to speak. The object of the conference was to discuss for three or four days the research material connected with bone and teeth. They wanted me to explain my new theory on the origin of bone circulation and of bone cells, which I believe originate in the wall of the vessels. Amelia did not accompany me on this trip, as the meeting was to take place in Meriden, New Haven, a small remote town north of Boston where no special programme for ladies could be organized. I met several people whom I knew by name from their scientific papers, and this was to be useful to me in the future.

In September I again went shooting with Elie Rothschild, whom by now I considered to be one of the family, and spent a couple of delightful days in intimate conversation with him. Later that month we received in Oxford the Italian Ortho-paedic Association and, after two days discussing scientific and clinical matters together, wound up the proceedings with between one hundred and fifty and two hundred orthopaedic surgeons dining in hall at Oriel. The Italians, connoisseurs of art, were much impressed by the hall and the British were equally affected by this contact with Italy. It was a return to the past.

In October we went to Munich at the kind invitation of Professor Max Lange of the Deutsche Ortopädische Gesellschaft, which made me an honorary member. Amelia and I much enjoyed ourselves with Professor Lange at the beer festival, where the Bavarians excel in competing for the honour of consuming the greatest quantity of the beverage of which they are so fond. One does not have to look further for the reason why so many Bavarians have an above-average girth!

In 1962 we were visited in Oxford by the Vice-Chancellor of the University of Khartoum. His object in coming to Britain was to try to find an orthopaedic surgeon of standing to take over the teaching of orthopaedics at his university. They wanted a young man, who would be prepared to move with his family at a good salary on a five-year contract, with gratuity—renewable on expiry. My first reaction was to decline with thanks, indicating that this was of no interest to us since it meant virtually disrupting the life of any young assistant or surgeon we sent them. On the other hand, what could be of interest to us was a fluid arrangement permitting the interchange of teachers and pupils which would enable the University of Khartoum to be self-sufficient in ten years from the point of view of instruction in orthopaedic surgery. This suggestion surprised them a bit, but after giving it some thought they accepted the proposal. I arranged for one of the three principal orthopaedic assistants from the Nuffield Orthopaedic Centre to go there. The centre had, and still has as I write this, three senior registrars in charge of the young surgeons—one at the Nuffield Centre, one at the Accident Service at the Radcliffe, and a third whom we would send to Khartoum on a rota basis, for two years, after which he would come back to Oxford and one of the other two would go to the Sudan and so on. They favoured the idea, since it was complementary: they would send us qualified Sudanese Fellows of the Royal College of Surgeons to be trained as orthopaedic surgeons. No more than two would be sent at a time, as well as anaesthetists and nurses, to be trained in modern techniques. The project was initiated with great enthusiasm and success. Two brilliant Sudanese joined us, one from the south and the other an Arab from the north, both different in mentality and personality. We sent them an Australian, Bryan O'Connor, from Brisbane, accustomed to the high temperatures I knew he would encounter in the Sudan. It was a complete success. Some time later they wanted me to go and see for myself the progress which had been achieved, and Amelia and I were invited to go to Khartoum.

We flew to the capital of the Sudan in January 1963, and I was able to visit hospitals and evaluate the organization. The Sudanese government organized a safari in our honour which was scheduled to take place near the Kenya frontier but plans had to be altered due to a violent uprising which ultimately required the intervention of European powers as mediators. In view of the risks involved it was decided that the safari should take place elsewhere, in a very primitive area, north of Abyssinia, where the Blue Nile descends from the heights of Ethiopia to the Sudanese plains. A caravan was organized with an entourage of some twenty-three bearers, soldiers and policemen. Travelling by car, O'Connor, Amelia and I crossed some 300 kms of desert between Khartoum and Abyssinia until we reached a village under the administration of a local sultan. It is a triangular area between the Blue Nile and its great tributary, the Dindar, with Abyssinia as the base. Entry into the whole area was prohibited because it was a zone from which the British had penetrated into Ethiopia during World War II, and was said to be strewn with abandoned rifles which the natives of the area had subsequently retrieved, and with which, before Sudan achieved its independence, they had largely annihilated the abundant primitive wild life. Elephants, white rhinoceros and many types of antelope had been decimated, but the main preoccupation in the zone was the proliferation of lions. These had increased so much that it was said that in an area of 30,000 square kilometres there were no less than some 7,000 lions at large. The Abyssinian lion is an impressive, large-headed species and the game wardens in the prohibited zone had been given orders to shoot all the lions they saw without restriction. It had been calculated that some 300 to 500 had to be killed each year because, since no one interfered with them and the natives were prohibited from entering the area, reproduction was on the rise. If the game wardens, mounted on camels, saw any native in the area they considered him to be a poacher and were within their legal rights to shoot him down.

On arrival at the sultan's "palace", we were regaled with a typical Arab dinner, all squatting on the floor. We were introduced to the sultan's son who, speaking excellent English, told Amelia that his father's wives had heard that there was a Spanish lady guest and that they would like to meet her. She was thrilled at the opportunity of seeing the inside of a harem and was away for well over an hour. When she came back she was in fits of laughter, telling us how she had made herself understood to some of the women there who knew a few words of English, or else by gestures, and that they had asked her, since she was Spanish, to dance "flamenco" for them! Poor Amelia had never before found herself in such a situation, but in view of the extraordinary gala atmosphere, she entered into the spirit of the occasion and performed an improvised "zapateado" (a flamenco tap-dance) to the accompaniment of the rhythmic handclapping of the ladies of the harem. She told me later that they were about twenty in number; four or five of them in obvious stages of pregnancy and children were running around all over the place.

We rested there that night, and next morning went further up towards Abyssinia in jeeps until we arrived in jungle territory, where we started to see animals running around wild. After penetrating into it for a couple of hours or so, in the course of which we passed through a primitive native village, we stopped in a clearing where the lorries had arrived before us and tents had been pitched for the night stop. One of the smaller tents had been allocated to Amelia and myself, and the head of the expedition, the minister in charge of parks and gardens (we would call it ecology today), took me on one side and warned me that, once we had zipped ourselves in for the night, we were on no account to leave our tent. If we heard a noise like a dog, he said, it would be a hyena, which would not attack us if we stayed inside the tent. Naturally enough, I did not want to alarm Amelia so I said nothing to her. We bedded down for the night under mosquito nets and soon fell asleep. Not an hour passed before there came a scratching on the outside of the tent. Hyenas, I thought, and then Amelia woke up and asked me what the noise was. I tried to persuade her that it was the guards' dogs, but she would not be convinced. Worse still, we suddenly heard lions roaring. According to what I had been told, when a lion has made a kill he roars every ten to fifteen minutes to frighten off hyenas and jackals. We did not exactly sleep like logs that night!

The next day we went on a filming expedition. Amelia had a cine camera with her with colour films and we were taken in a jeep into the jungle, where, amid a multitude of antelopes and other species, we saw a dozen or so lions. We had rifles with us and were asked to shoot as many as we could. Unfortunately, I could not get off a single shot as we were in a jeep with a glass windscreen, which meant that when we saw a lion ahead, we had glass between us, and by the time we were side-on the animal had vanished.

With two or three officers, we went out again, leaving Amelia in the camping site with the guards. On our return, I found her in a highly excited state. She was furious with me for having left her alone for so long. I said we had only been gone about ninety minutes, and she had had the protection of the guards. "But it is precisely of them that I am scared!" she said. I asked her if anything untoward had happened, but she said no, not at all, they had been very polite, but they had never left her alone for a second, which had put her in an extremely embarrassing situation when she felt like answering the call of nature! They just would not let her disappear discreetly by herself behind a tree. The officer in charge explained why. The guards had been given strict orders to this effect in order to protect her from the possibility of an attack by a black panther. This animal attacks from the branches of trees, making for the throat of the victim. The only protection against this form of attack is the bayonet—which is why the guards always had theirs fixed. Imagine Amelia's reaction when she heard that she could not relieve herself without being in danger of death! "If only I had a cage," she kept on saying. "What do you want to put into it?" I asked her. "Myself," was the reply.

The whole trip was a unique and truly wonderful experience. On the way back we made a slight detour so that we could see the vast expanse of land which had been irrigated for the cultivation of cotton. I must admit also that I bagged a pair of antelopes, one of them with a particularly magnificent head.

8

They took me bird shooting for a couple of days, one of them on the banks of the White Nile. Around four in the morning several of us were by a watering place, forty or fifty metres apart, waiting in utter silence. We had been told that we would suddenly hear a loud noise like aircraft approaching—which would be birds, rather like partridges, but with longer wings, which came to drink twice a day. We must be ready to shoot— but not till there were eight or nine in a group together, because that way one could bring down five or six at once. No wonder we shot about fifty or sixty in all.

The next day they took me on an expedition to try and bag a great bustard. At one pm, in the heat of the day, in a jeep, we went into the desert where there is no other vegetation but resin-producing trees, shaped like inverted cups. As at that time of day the heat is at its most oppressive, the bustards shelter in their shade. The driver of the jeep suddenly stopped, looked through his field glasses and said: "There's one, under that tree over there!" We approached until, at a distance of some sixty to seventy metres, we were called on to fire. What savagery! The poor wounded beast got up, fell, got up again and started to run towards us, not knowing which way it was going. They shouted at me: "Shoot, shoot." At three metres I shot again, hit it in the middle of the breast and it fell. It had a wing span of some three metres. That evening our cook prepared it in the manner of the country with herbs and leaves—but, to put it mildly, it was not to the taste of Amelia and myself. This was the end of my hunting experiences in Sudan.

Years later, in Britain, a very satisfactory analysis was made of the progress achieved by the setting up of modern ortho-paedics in Sudan. During my fortnight's stay I was able to travel far afield with O'Connor, sometimes by plane, to see out-patient clinics which were being set up for early diagnosis, to observe how they were beginning to construct apparatus for the limbs of poliomyelitis victims, of which there were many; and to note the effects of malaria and numerous other tropical diseases.

In March that same year, 1963, I had to return to the United States again, this time without Amelia as it was for a very intensive and consequently tiring trip. I was invited to assist at the International Symposium on Bone Biodynamics at the Henry Ford Hospital in Detroit. It was a most interesting course where I met many old friends and made new ones, among them Webster Jee, who gave me so much help when I was planning the frustrated Trueta Institute years later in Barcelona. I spoke on "Vascular Dynamics of the Bone" before the élite of the scientific world and my contribution was favourably received.

During my absence from Oxford there occurred the only unpleasantness I ever had with a pupil. It is too painful to speak of; but I can say with pride that in thirty years of teaching, with this one exception, all my pupils have always given me proof of filial affection and loyalty. In this one case, I have erased the doctor's name from my mind; I do not know if he is dead or alive, nor do I care.

The approach of my retirement from the Chair at Oxford resulted not in any diminution of my activities, but in an extraordinary increase. In September Amelia and I attended the International Congress in Vienna of SICOT. Shortly after, I was honoured to hear that the Société Internationale de Chirurgie had awarded me the Robert Danis Prize, for my work on bone research. In November the terrible news of the death of our great friend Pierre Nicolau dealt a painful blow to the whole family. He had been like a brother to Amelia and myself. Such was his sensitivity that on learning of the assassination of John Kennedy he had been stricken by a fatal heart attack while in his bath. It was an irreparable loss to his family and friends.

In January 1964 at Ditchley Park, near Oxford, there was a meeting of the Ditchley Foundation, an Anglo-American body whose aim was to put in touch leading personalities of the two countries in various fields. I had the great honour to be invited and made a modest contribution during the sessions, which lasted four days.

In October 1964 the University of Gothenburg, in the name of King Gustav VI, made me Doctor of Medicine honoris causa for my research work. It is a traditional ceremony, symbolizing the "marriage" of the new doctor to the university. After reading in Latin the duties of the new member, a pleated top hat is placed on his head and the wedding ring on his finger. Afterwards, the new doctor makes a short speech to the students; in my case it was on a medical theme. Meanwhile, during the ceremony, the city fortress fires two salvoes, which resound throughout the city to let the citizens know that they have a new doctor. One of the cartridge cases, engraved with the date of the ceremony, is presented to the recipient of the doctorate. The whole affair is like a happy party where everyone, students and professors alike, enjoys himself tremendously. It all ends naturally, with a banquet where protocol goes by the board, but, just as at Oxford, without the ebullience of youth overstepping the norms of civilized behaviour. Before leaving Sweden I gave two lectures in Stockholm on the origin of bone and on blood circulation.

That same year in November we were invited to attend the joint meeting of the Portuguese and Spanish Orthopaedic Societies in Luanda, Angola, where we spent almost a week in the company of my ex-pupils George Mineiro, professor at Lisbon University, and Carlos Lima, professor at Oporto University. It is an interesting fact that these are the only two Chairs of Orthopaedic Surgery in the whole of the Iberian Peninsula. Angola was overwhelmingly beautiful. Although almost on the Equator, its climate and vegetation are those of temperate lands. We were amazed by the quantity of mulattoes there, and were reminded of Brazil with its blacks and whites—at least in the capital and the cities we visited. I was asked to give a few lectures, and we were received by the governor, the representative of Portugal. Being with George Mineiro, an inveterate hunter, a nocturnal shoot was organized through sparse jungle country through which a jeep could easily pass. With headlights on, we frequently saw the shining eyes of wild animals, but although we fired off a few shots, we bagged no game worth recording.

I must confess in all sincerity that the impression I took with me of Angola was wrong. I thought it was on the way to becoming a second Brazil. Unfortunately, with the advent of independence, Angola seems beset with destructive extremisms unlikely to be conducive to racial and social harmony.

In January of 1965 the Ditchley Foundation met again, this time to discuss world communism. The problem was a theme of extraordinary interest and it intrigued me tremendously to be able to participate actively. In the spring Amelia and I went back to the United States to attend the annual traumatological course in Chicago, which also gave us the opportunity to visit many of our good friends on both coasts.

PART V

Retirement from Oxford and Return to Catalonia

(1965–1976)

Chapter *1*

WHY I DECIDED TO RETURN
TO CATALONIA

WHEN, IN 1965, the time came for me to retire for reasons of age from the Chair of Orthopaedics, my ex-pupils organized a symposium at Oxford, where each read a paper on his particular speciality. I should say that by this time, about ten of them were full-fledged professors of orthopaedics in their various countries.

The session lasted a whole day and culminated in a banquet in the hall at Oriel at which wives were also present. It was all most moving, especially the speech which Rafel Esteve, one of my Catalan ex-pupils at the Nuffield Centre, made on behalf of his colleagues. I shall always treasure the memory of that day—especially as I was surrounded by my wife, my three daughters and their husbands.

The return to Oriel revived many happy memories for me. Although my appointment as Nuffield Professor of Orthopaedics in 1949 automatically carried with it a fellowship at Worcester College, I had had the honour in November 1941 of being elected a member of the senior common room of Oriel College.

By chance, the Czech president, Edouard Benes, also belonged to Oriel during the war years and, having met him some nine years before in Prague, where I had visited him with my teacher, Professor Corachan, I was able to resume acquaintance with him once again.

At least once a term, Benes would dine at Oriel accompanied by a secretary. We had the opportunity of talking about the Spanish Civil War and other affairs. He was a small man on the plump side, with an attractive personality and a pleasant soft voice. He was an excellent conversationalist and when he announced that he was coming to dine at high table, the

8*

provost used to let me know in advance so that I could make a point of being present.

A few days before the inevitable entry of the Russian army into Prague, Sir David Ross, the provost, called me to say that Benes was coming to dine and to say good-bye, and that he hoped I would be there.

It turned out to be a memorable occasion, initially in an atmosphere of joviality. After dinner Sir David asked the president if, in view of the fact that only members of the college were present, he would mind answering a few off-the-record questions. Smilingly, Benes replied that he had no objection, provided it was understood that he would answer as a member of Oriel senior common room, and not as President of Czechoslovakia.

I remember that W. A. Pantin, Lecturer in Modern History at the university, asked the president to explain how it was that whilst Poland and Czechoslovakia were both Slav nations, related to Russia, the Poles had been continually in conflict with the Russians whereas the Czechs had not. Without a moment's hesitation Benes replied that the answer was to be found in geography. The Russian and Polish plains have no definite limit to separate the one from the other, he said, whereas the Carpathian Mountains separated Russia from Czechoslovakia with the result that the area of contact between the two countries was extremely limited.

Another member of the senior common room asked him whether there was not the danger that now that the Russians had crossed the Carpathians they might not want to leave. Benes was in no doubt on the point. He said that the Czechs did not fear Communist propaganda because they had already been given what the Russians were desperately trying to provide their own people with. He added that after Russian shock troops had liberated Czech towns from the Germans, their rearguard forces, Asiatic for the most part, had proceeded to destroy every modern installation they could find, even in workers' houses, smashing with their rifle butts whole bathrooms, taps and all, as being "bourgeois". Consequently, Benes said, "we Czechs have left communism years behind us. We give the people full liberty to change its government when it chooses." They valued freedom above all, he said.

After a long silence, as though we were all thinking along the same lines, Pantin asked, somewhat tentatively, if the president did not fear that this predisposition of the Czechs for electing their governments democratically might not be precisely the greatest danger to Czechoslovakia preserving its freedom, bearing in mind the probable reaction of the Russians. Benes took his time in answering and when he did said: "I pray to God that this is never the case."

The evening continued, but an air of depression had set in. Benes returned almost at once to Prague where he was publicly acclaimed but, inevitably, Russian forces occupied the city and communism infiltrated into the Czech government until finally freedom in the country was totally liquidated. In 1948 Benes died broken-hearted having seen come to pass what he had prayed to God would never happen in his country.

Now, in 1965, I found myself free from university duties and the only task still left for me to do was to finish my book *Studies of the Development and Decay of the Human Frame*, which came out in 1968 and was later translated into Spanish.

When it became known that I was due to retire from the Chair I received several invitations from the United States to work at universities there. The most attractive proposition came from the University of Utah, in Salt Lake City, where I was offered a contract to work primarily in research, with a tempting salary. Nevertheless, Amelia and I decided that to accept at our age would be like starting a new exile, and possibly ending our days in a foreign country, so that although previous experience of Salt Lake City had shown it to be a particularly welcome place, I finally declined the offer.

In July that same year I received another proposal from an old patient of mine, M. Peter Viertel, who knew of my dilemma and offered me the possibility of settling in Monaco. The idea was to build an orthopaedic nursing home which I would direct. This offer was naturally very attractive, especially as the situation in Spain had not altered and we did not feel like staying on at Oxford, divested of university obligations and far from our daughters. The Monaco proposal was promptly supported by David Niven, good friend of mine and husband of an ex-patient, whose friendship with Prince Rainier and Princess Grace of Monaco encouraged the belief that the project might be feasible. The economic question would be no problem, it seemed, as both Elie de Rothschild and Stavros Niarchos had offered their not inconsiderable financial backing, and Prince Rainier would be making the land available. As a result, Amelia and I went to Monte Carlo to take a decision.

The plot of land was superbly sited on the high part of the corniche with all possible natural advantages, although the provision of water, electricity and other services had to be organized from start to finish. The government of Monaco agreed to concern itself with this aspect and promised prompt action. However, after visiting the Hospital of Monaco and the Princess Grace Hospital, which the Americans were then building, I suggested that, instead of constructing a new hospital for orthopaedics and traumatology, a special wing for this purpose should be added to the existing hospital. In this way, the project would be immediately practicable. I would not have to occupy myself with administrative details such as kitchens and the recruitment of nursing staff, etc., which would all come under the already existent hospital organization.

The prince, however, thought that this was too limited and that the project should be on a larger scale. Such an undertaking, at the age of sixty-eight, was too much for me, despite the fact that my ex-pupils offered to help me by coming in turn for three-month spells. I felt I had no alternative but to refuse the offer.

After full reflection, and due to personal and family reasons, explained in a letter which *The Times* published on 1 November 1966, we decided to return to Barcelona in February 1967, when I was already nearly seventy. The letter said:

The fact that I am soon to change my address in Oxford for others in Barcelona and the Costa Brava has caused an unwanted and undeserved turmoil in the press, which, if not clarified, may produce a distorted view of myself.

Early in 1939 I came to this country, through the good agencies of a few English colleagues of mine, to discuss for a fortnight something of my professional experiences in the then new type of warfare, the bombing of cities. A chain of events, and finally the intervention of two great Englishmen, the late Professor **G. R.** Girdlestone and the late Lord Nuffield, offered me the opportunity of settling in our happy home in Oxford, where we were to live for over twenty-seven years.

Since our arrival, Oxford has treated us as its own. In the course of the years it has awarded me an Hon. Doctorate in Science, and the Nuffield Chair of Orthopaedic Surgery, of which I am now an Emeritus holder. Oriel College first, and Worcester since I was promoted to the Chair, have been part of my home, and their fellows are among my dearest friends.

Now as to the real motives for our departure from Oxford. These are so simple that they need no more than to be mentioned. First, all our daughters live now in Spain. Second, in spite of the fact that I have reached the age of retirement, I still feel I can be active for a while, and in Oxford a retired medical professor has little chance of being active. Finally, as the years pass, we have become more sensitive to the rigours of an Oxford winter and prefer the sun of Catalonia.

It is with regret, Sir, that I must conclude this letter with a sad reflection. Twenty-five years ago, Britain was the hope of the tortured continent of Europe. With sacrifices seldom equalled, occupied Europe was freed, and even the enemies of Britain were raised to the moral status of free peoples. What a calamity that Britain was not to be present when the new structure of a United Europe began to crystallize; she, who in the course of a thousand years had shown the way to live under a law of justice equal for all. Let me hope that Britain and Spain may soon find themselves members of a community where the experience, which initially brought me to England, will never again be required.

A last word for our many friends in Great Britain, including my orthopaedic colleagues. We are keeping our Oxford house, and hope that, if God keeps our strength, we shall still have the opportunity of seeing them many times in the future.

Politically, Spain was much the same, and we felt protected by continuing to be naturalized British subjects, although, as has been made clear throughout these memoirs, I never belonged to any political party nor took any part in politics, except for my participation in the ill-starred Catalan National Council, which was more Catalanist than political.

Having taken this important decision then, we slowly started making preparations for our return. Before actually leaving England, I visited the then Spanish ambassador in London, the Marqués de Santa Cruz, himself an Oxonian, to ask for his help in returning to Catalonia. He told me that all I had to do was ask for whatever I wanted. The only condition I put was that under no circumstances would I be given any official state medals or honours* and this was observed, so that in Franco's lifetime I was never faced with what would have been for me an embarrassing and unacceptable situation. I also wanted to stay British; this involved no problem. In Barcelona, since my return, I have indeed had every facility to work privately, but none to teach or to continue in research, which is what I would so dearly have loved to do. I have told elsewhere how my attempts at getting laboratories failed. However, others are continuing to work on my theory of the origin of bone, especially in the United States, and the prospects of its being vindicated one day seem bright. Too late for me, I fear, but I hope future generations will know how to take advantage of the benefits which this theory, if proved right, must mean for humanity.

Our preparations for returning in no way put an end to our travels. On the occasion of the first centenary of the inauguration of the New York Orthopaedic Hospital in March 1966, my good friend Henry Osmond-Clarke, since knighted, and I, were both made guests of honour. Amelia and I took advantage of the trip to New York to combine it with other invitations which I had received to lecture in Miami and New Orleans. We visited Palm Beach and took the opportunity to tour the district by car escorted by George Ford, an American orthopaedic surgeon who had worked during the war in one of the hospitals in the Oxford area. Our commitments in Florida at an end, we flew to New Orleans, where we were the guests of Tulane University.

* In Spain you are not consulted as to whether you wish to accept an honour—it is given as a *fait accompli* and recorded in the State Bulletin.

Tulane University has for me, and many other Catalans, a strong spiritual value, as being a centre developed under the direction of Rodolf Matas, the great Catalan cardio-vascular surgeon who revolutionized surgery in his specific field. His disciples still have the greatest respect for his memory. New Orleans fascinated us because of its curious contrast with modern North America. For example, from Florida where the hotels, office buildings and stores are ultramodern, and characterized by a cold functional architectural style, one came to New Orleans which preserves its old colonial character with extraordinary dignity. Although everyone tells you that everything is of French origin, one has only to stroll through the old streets of New Orleans to see that, although only of a relatively short duration, Spanish colonization also left its mark there. The windows with their iron grilles; the doors, so many of them in the cold, baroque style of Andalusia; the narrowness of the streets, and many of the restaurants, all recall the colonial era. From New Orleans, where I gave two lectures, we went north to Memphis for a short course of three lessons at the Campbell Clinic at the invitation of Professor Harold Boyd. In the Boyds' car we drove to Knoxville, up the Tennessee valley—which called to mind Roosevelt's New Deal.

Following the course of the River Tennessee for some 450 miles, one does not know which way to look as the scenery is so beautiful on all sides. The road climbed on the course of the river, until we came to the large dams which irrigate the immense valleys to be found at that height. We went through the village of Gatlinburg, where there are still Indians who take advantage of tourism to sell objects of their handicraft, and finally the area where the Blue Mountains begin on the Atlantic Coast. There are bears, which one is advised not to feed through the open window of one's car. The bluish-white colour of the mountains is due to irradiation on the mists rising nightly off the forests; the colour effect is of an exquisite delicacy.

On 20 April the Tenth Post-Graduate course on fractures and other traumata was held in Chicago, and I accepted an invitation to attend as a guest of honour. We knew Chicago well by then and were happy to renew contact with friends and colleagues there from former times.

In 1967, already settled back home in Barcelona, I had the great satisfaction of receiving the first honour bestowed on me in my native land since I had left it in 1939: the Barcelona Academy of Surgery made me an honorary member. Two years later, the Barcelona Association of Surgery awarded me one of their two annual prizes—the Premi Virgili—created in commemoration of the great doctor responsible for the introduction of modern surgery not only in Catalonia but the whole of Spain. The other—the Premi Gimbernat, awarded to non-Spaniards—went to the famous Houston heart surgeon, Michael DeBakey.

Catalonia suffered a grievous loss in 1969 when Robert Gerhard, renowned composer and intimate friend in exile, died. Despite the fact that he lived in Cambridge and we in Oxford—a physical rather than a spiritual gulf—he remained a great friend of mine to the end.

I was to give some lectures in Pisa in October 1968 and travelled there from Barcelona with Amelia. At that time, Aureli M. Escarré, the abbot of the famous Catalan monastery of Montserrat, was living in an Italian monastery to which the Madrid government had contrived to have him sent for having had the audacity to criticize the Franco régime in the French press. On learning that I was going to Pisa, a close mutual friend asked me to go and visit the abbot at Cuggiono, some 60 kms from Milan, as he was known to be ill and they wanted my opinion on his state of health. As soon as I saw the abbot, and having exchanged views with his doctor, I was in no doubt as to how seriously ill he was. I got in touch immediately with my friend in Barcelona asking him to tell the acting-abbot that if they wanted Abbot Escarré to die in his native Catalonia his condition was such that they had better transfer him at once. They did so, and he died six days after arriving back home. Amelia and I went to the funeral at Montserrat in utter desolation. Catalonia had lost a great son: we could not know then what a worthy successor was to follow him in the person of the new abbot.

In 1970 the young students of the faculty of medicine at the University of Barcelona, celebrating the third year of their course, invited me as their guest of honour at a banquet in Barcelona. The gesture touched Amelia and me deeply.

Tulane University of New Orleans organized a course in 1971 to be held at sea in the Mediterranean. Seven other of my colleagues had been invited and some 150 orthopaedic surgeons, most of them accompanied by their wives, had put their names down to come as pupils on the course. It was a most interesting experience. A modern German transatlantic liner had been chartered to sail from Genoa. Our first stop was Malta, where Amelia and I were met by an ex-pupil of mine, Amato, who showed us all over the island in his car. The next stop was Piraeus, where Apostoles Cavadias, another ex-pupil, was also awaiting us—it seemed that Amelia and I had reception committees organized all down the line. Then came Istanbul— which we had never visited before. Naturally enough, contact with the East, even when still geographically in Europe, makes an extraordinary impact on one, especially as only a few hours before we had left the serene and classical beauty of Athens. The vessel steamed on into the Black Sea until we arrived at Yalta, where the meeting had taken place at which Churchill, Roosevelt and Stalin had divided up the continent into spheres of influence. We found Yalta, situated as it is on the coast but surrounded by woods, particularly beautiful at that time of year. Some of its vast buildings, private residences at the time of the tsars, now serve as lodgings for trades-union members on holiday. We were told that there were more than five, some of them capable of accommodating as many as five or six hundred persons. The guide explained to us at length how the workers came there to relax with their families, living leisurely and totally devoid of daily worries such as preparing meals. However, we could not help noticing that in the dining rooms, where five hundred and more people ate at one sitting, the tables were regimentally arranged in lines, with chairs crammed close together, and that meals were served strictly at the clanging of a bell. It seemed to us that the relaxation and freedom must have been rather less than our guide was at such pains to emphasize.

From Yalta we sailed to Odessa, an average type of city which by chance, perhaps fortunately, has remained much the same as in tsarist times. The traditional ceremony of the changing of the guard in the port is truly impressive for its discipline and precision, and the city itself is beautiful and clean. The man in the street is quite well dressed but one does not see anyone smiling or even apparently at peace with the world. In the short time we were there we never heard anyone singing or whistling. Odessa gave us the impression of being an attractive place—for not more than a day or two.

At our next port of call, Constanza, in Rumania, it could be clearly sensed that one had left behind Slav-type communism. We were taken to see vast buildings that had been constructed to accommodate tourists from overseas which for the Rumanians is such an important source of revenue. They looked to me just like the typical spas and casinos of the capitalist world.

As we were so many, we were taken sight-seeing in bus-loads, each group with its own guide. We had the good luck to have as our guide a girl who had studied in Oxford for three years and who had a sense of humour. On one of our trips, all the coaches were made to stop one behind the other at the side of the road to give way to a dozen or so black Mercedes-Benz cars which swept by. Our guide told us that this business of clearing the way for the authorities was not a Communist innovation, as it was something already current in the time of King Carol.

On the return voyage I continued to give lectures and in my leisure time enjoyed the views of the Bosphorus. We returned to Athens and Taormina in Sicily, one of the most interesting places I have visited. At Trapani one could note the Catalan influence redolent of the Gothic churches of Barcelona. Thence to Genoa where we said goodbye to our American colleagues. It had been a voyage to remember.

As I had received an invitation to lecture in Rome twelve days after landing in Genoa, we decided to stay on in Italy as mere tourists, quietly and unhurriedly taking in the beauty of the Eternal City, which made a welcome change. By then, Amelia was beginning to tire more easily on our walks through the streets, which was strange for her. She had high blood pressure, that we knew already, but never in fifty years had she turned down the chance to participate in any interesting activity. She certainly did not look her seventy-one years.

In February of 1972, Josephine Collier died. She it was who had introduced me to British life; a firm friend always, we felt her death closely.

That same summer we attended an international rheumatology congress in Aix-les-Bains. Although the visit was short, we were treated royally and enjoyed the natural attractions of Aix.

I was invited in 1973 to take part in the Congress of the Eastern Orthopaedic Association at the Greenbrier Spa at White Sulphur Springs, West Virginia. The organizer, Marvin Steinberg, an old pupil of mine, drove us from his home in Philadelphia through the most beautiful forests whose autumnal colours were a worthy subject for a great painter. To walk through those woods was at once relaxing and exhilarating.

After the congress at Greenbrier Spa, we spent a few days with the Steinbergs in Philadelphia prior to flying to Denver, where I was to give a course on war surgery. Denver is the main military medical centre of the United States, and at that time they were fully occupied with treating Vietnam war casualties. Colonel Burkhalter, the head of military traumatology and recently back himself from the Far East, was gracious enough to pay tribute to me publicly in his inaugural speech for the results obtained in Vietnam by meticulously following my technique. Whereas five out of a thousand died from gas gangrene in World War II, and this was reduced to three per thousand in Korea, where the Winnett Orr method was still partly in use, by applying what he called the "classic Trueta technique" the gas gangrene mortality rate dropped to six per million in Vietnam. It was a touching testimonial from the US armed forces.

We took advantage of our time in Colorado to visit the snow-covered Rocky Mountains and an abandoned village of Gold Rush days. After seeing so many films about the Far West it was interesting to see for oneself concrete proof of a past era.

From Denver we went to Las Vegas, where I had been invited as a guest speaker at the fortieth reunion of the American Academy of Orthopaedic Surgeons, at which the main theme was hip bones. What a fabulous city Las Vegas is—everything there centred on gambling—with immense hotels built in the middle of a desert, and a favourite place for the congresses and conventions to which Americans are so addicted. After Las Vegas we flew on to Miami and to Puerto Rico to see our dear friend Pau Casals.

Chapter 2

MY FRIENDSHIP WITH PAU CASALS

PAU CASALS WAS twenty-one years older than I. Therefore when I was born he had already played before Queen Victoria in the Isle of Wight, and was recognized as a 'cellist of exceptional talent, despite his youth. The first time I ever saw him perform he was conducting his famous orchestra at the opera house in Barcelona during the Civil War.

On 22 March 1939, when I was already in London, he wrote me a letter from his home in exile in Prades, southern France, thanking me for letting him know the documents which were required in order to get an entry permit into the United Kingdom. He was coming to London, he said, and would like my wife and me to visit him at the Piccadilly Hotel. The reason for his journey was a concert he was to give at the Royal Albert Hall in aid of Civil War refugee children. Amelia and I went to the hotel, accompanied by our mutual friend Batista i Roca, and I well remember the afternoon we spent helping Casals prepare 1,000 programmes for the concert—he signing them and we piling them into lots of a hundred. They were all sold at £1 each.

The concert was unforgettable. The great hall was full to overflowing—with people even standing in the corridors—and Casals facing the vast audience with his 'cello. The reception he got was tumultuous. On this occasion he was accompanied by the BBC Symphony Orchestra, conducted by Sir Adrian Boult, and, as usual, he ended the concert with the Catalan folk song he made so famous, "El Cant dels Ocells" (The Song of the Birds). When we went to his dressing-room after the concert we found him pent-up and in a very emotional state, as was always the case after playing to his public. He returned to France soon after.

Casals spent the entire war in Prades, in the French

Pyrenees, and had some difficult times with the Germans, who wanted him to play in Germany. He refused emphatically, even though this put him in some danger. Soon after the liberation of France I was able to write to him at Prades. I told him how happy we were that he had survived the occupation, and that we would soon be visiting him. He answered with such warmth and affection that I still treasure his letter. After some personal comments, he writes:

> We shall soon be able to embrace each other at home. As this wonderful moment approaches, my impatience and longing become so overwhelming that I can think of nothing else. That is why, before making plans to travel around Europe, I feel it absolutely necessary to return to Catalonia. . . . I think with eagerness of my trip to London, and to all the other cities which I love, where so much suffering and devastation has occurred. I envy those Catalans who live in my beloved and admired England. I am one of those who never doubted the outcome for one moment, because I know Britain well. I knew she would make the maximum sacrifice in taking up her responsibilities and protecting other peoples, ever conscious of her true greatness. . . .

By 1946, in a letter dated 17 November acknowledging receipt of a small book, *The Spirit of Catalonia*, which I had dedicated to him, his optimism had given way to utter despair. I asked myself what had happened in the meantime to make him change so? He had come back to England and we had been to his concerts, again at the Royal Albert Hall on 27 June 1945, where he played, I remember, Elgar's violoncello concerto, and a few days later in Reading, with the famous accompanist, Gerald Moore. It was during the interval at this concert in Reading that he told us, in a state of utter despondency: "You know what they have decided? They are going to do nothing to remove Franco, nothing; it is incredible, but true. Nothing—they are even going to help him, and our poor Catalonia will be destroyed! This is the end of everything—I have lost all hope." Gerald Moore was very worried by Casals' excited state, and asked us please to leave, if Casals were to be able to come out for the second half. I doubt if the audience noticed any difference between the first and second parts of the concert—but he was certainly another man. It was at this concert that I first heard him say that he would never play again in any of the countries which contributed to keeping Franco in power, and he kept to his word for many years.

In 1946, Amelia, the girls and I drove to Andorra to see our family from Barcelona, without going into Spain. Some twenty or so relatives and friends came to see us and on our way through Prades we stopped at Casals' home, where we spent a few memorable hours with him.

My eldest daughter, Meli, became engaged in 1947 and I wrote to Casals to invite him to her wedding, although I suspected he would decline. Sure enough, he sent a very kind letter in reply, saying how much he would like to be with us, but that he must keep to his decision, since even though it would be coming to attend a wedding and not to give a concert, he felt in honour bound not to come to Britain.

On 28 April 1948 he wrote:

... Unfortunately, governments and politicians insist on ignoring the feelings of peoples. With the discovery of the word "realist", all ideals have gone overboard; all that is most noble. As regards our particular problem, it is pointless to talk of it any more. . . . Deception, resignation, despair: these are our only reward for having sacrificed everything, for having believed ingenuously in the integrity and moral principles of the USA and England. . . .

Meanwhile, due to representations from famous British musicians, all of them dedicated friends of Casals, Oxford University was proposing to confer on him a doctorate of music honoris causa. We all hoped he would accept—if not rapturously, at least in appreciation of those who had worked so hard for this. But in his reaction was the proof of how little we all knew him. Honours and recognitions did not move him, and he considered that making him a doctor honoris causa was no compensation for the abandonment of Catalonia. Regretfully, and with particular regard to Sir Adrian Boult and other musicians who had proposed him, he declined. I tried to make him change his mind—but all to no avail.

Years later the subject came up again, this time in connection
with the Edinburgh Festival. I was approached once more to
intercede with him to accept an invitation to play; I remember
telling him that Scotland had nothing to do with the mistakes
made by London; that the Scots wanted to pay tribute to him—
a tribute that he could interpret as being dedicated to Catalonia. I thought he hesitated a bit—but in the end the
inevitable happened: he refused again, saying that if he once
weakened he would weaken thereafter, and that therefore he
would not come.

Congratulating me on my appointment to the Nuffield Chair
of Orthopaedics at Oxford in a letter dated 17 July 1949,
Casals wrote:

> What a pity that the government of a country [England],
> where the people are so good and understanding, has done
> us so much harm! With the deepest sorrow, I shall never
> return to England again: I, who so respected and loved this
> nation in which I had blind faith. It saddens me to have to
> admit that it is to her moral debility that we owe the con-
> tinuing tragedy of Catalonia and the whole of Spain. Apart
> from what exile signifies—being far from our families—for
> me personally all this means serious financial difficulties, as I
> am denied access to interest earned over nearly half a
> century of investing in Britain. The last straw is for my funds
> to have been classified as *enemy property*. . . .

At my request, he gave me details of the bank in question,
and I contacted various persons in authority to get the matter
sorted out, which they, rather shamefacedly, promised to do.
On 8 December 1949, Casals wrote again to thank me for my
help and said:

> I am still awaiting a document from the Spanish Consulate
> in Perpignan regarding my blocked monies in England. . . .
> They assured me they have no right to them. On the other
> hand, England put no difficulties in the way of unblocking
> £1,000 which I donated to the fund for RAF widows. I have
> the receipt for the donation, signed by Lord Riverdale, from
> whose accompanying letter I quote the following para-

graph: "Throughout the course of a long and ruthless war the Royal Air Force has without respite, been in action. Cruel losses were bound to follow. There are too many who are so gravely injured that they can never fully recover or who have lost that peace of mind which they will need so much in the difficult times ahead. These are the men you are enabling us to help."

During the Prades Festival in 1950, Casals wrote me: "I have thought of you and even hoped to see you here . . . but I understand your work does not allow you to come. . . . I have never seen anything like the excitement displayed right from the first rehearsal of the orchestra. I saw whole audiences, the orchestra itself, everyone in tears. And this has happened in Prades. Like everyone else here, I have lived a marvellous dream." As always, the festival had been wound up by the playing of "El Cant dels Ocells".

This public reaction was naturally in response to the activity of Casals and his friends, all international musicians and universally recognized as leaders in their own field, who joined with him to create the famous Prades festivals.

Unfortunately, I had only been professor at Oxford for one year and was too busy to take leave to attend what was, in essence, a Catalan patriotic manifestation.

I received a postcard from him in July 1952 describing the festival of that year as being "completely beautiful" and referring to himself as having "borne up well throughout this annual miracle".

In February 1953 he wrote:

> . . . I keep going, miraculously it seems. My capacity for work surprises everyone, not least myself, despite unpleasant headaches from time to time. . . . The fever of the festival has started here. . . . I have until 20 May to study and complete the orchestral scores for all the works. This will be followed by a month of rehearsals and then the concerts, from 15 June to 5 July. I wish you could come and enjoy it with us! . . . The atmosphere at these festivals is unique. . . .

In 1954 my second daughter Montse, was married, and

again I invited him to the wedding—only to receive the same
reply as before.

> I would love to be present at the event, but you know of
> my self-imposed ban on visits to England and other countries
> which have done us so much harm. . . . Your impressions on
> your trip to Spain, and particularly to Catalonia, agree with
> what I have heard from others regarding the situation in our
> country. Although it is sad, we ought to be glad at the
> corruption brought about by the present régime, as we can
> logically assume that this will one day be the cause of the
> collapse and replacement of Francoism. Perhaps you are
> right in saying that American-style occupation may, on the
> one hand, restrict Franco and his mob somewhat, and, on
> the other, give our people a little more courage. However, I
> am not prepared to thank the Americans for anything, as I
> consider them to bear prime responsibility ever since
> Britain allowed itself to have its influence usurped in certain
> areas, Spain in particular.

From then on my correspondence with Casals lost some of its
intimacy. We all knew by then that there was nothing we could
do to alter the course of the fateful destiny of our country. The
influence of the USA, contrary to what I had suggested, did
not serve as a moderating influence on Franco; on the contrary,
it enabled him to continue to asphyxiate our country and to
suppress the formation of Catalan as well as Spanish youth.
Casals was right.

In 1954 I was approached by the organizers of the Edinburgh
Festival, which at that time was already set on a fully ascendant course, asking me if I would once again intercede with
Casals with a view to getting him to reverse his decision not to
accept their invitation to play at the festival on the grounds
that while Britain continued to recognize Franco he would not
play there. I took advantage of the opportunity to write to him,
telling him that he should take into account that the Edinburgh
Festival was not an English festival but precisely an effort to
restore to the ancient capital of the Scottish kingdom the
importance which the imperial preponderance of London had
removed from it, and that the organizers were, for the most

part, local patriots who saw in him the possibility of paying homage to a Catalan irredentist who would not bow to tyranny. It seems my letter may have had some slight effect, for Casals took time in replying; but when the answer came, it was as on previous occasions: he did not want to make exceptions.

About this time the BBC in London were trying to get Pau Casals to do an introduction to a film on his life which had been filmed by NBC in Prades. It had been a great success in the United States, where its showing had to be repeated. The BBC had approached Casals directly, but he showed little interest.

Through his friendship with my son-in-law, Michael, Tim Holland-Bennett, the television booking manager of the BBC, got in touch with me to try to get Casals to record an introduction to this film, prior to its being shown on BBC television. In answer to my appeal, Casals said: "I am glad the BBC are going to show the film on television, and I hope you will be able to see it. I saw it at Charlie Chaplin's house, and liked it a great deal. Chaplin was enthusiastic. . . . I leave tomorrow for Puerto Rico (the island where Casals lived until his death) . . ." However, no introduction to the film was made. An opportunity had to be found for the film to be projected by the BBC— and this was to hand: the eightieth birthday of the Master.

Late on 30 December 1965, the BBC put on extracts from *Conversations with Pau Casals*, together with part of a French film called simply, *Pau Casals*. In informing me of this, Holland-Bennett said in his letter: "I am so glad that all our combined efforts have at last borne fruit, and I know you and your family, together with Christina [Holland-Bennett's wife] and myself will be watching our screens with the utmost interest on December 30th."

The programme, indeed, was a great success. This despite the opposition, I am quite sure, of a bureaucracy offended by Casals' refusal to play in the country for so many years. Men like Holland-Bennett, who had promoted the project as if they were friends of Casals and, through him, of Catalonia, had achieved their aim.

After the maestro had gone to live permanently in Puerto Rico, and to give concerts in Mexico and throughout South

America, my contact with him diminished. But my affection for him was not lessened, nor, I am sure, his towards us.

Finally, in 1963, we had the immense pleasure of seeing him again in England. Political circumstances had not altered, but Casals had composed the music for the nativity poem of his friend Joan Alavedra, "El pessebre" (The crib), and he came to conduct the orchestra and choir in a work which he had composed as a great message of peace for the world. On the occasion of its presentation, Amelia and I went to greet him at a packed Festival Hall. We talked to him and once more were able to witness, with the utmost emotion, the impact of his music, and perhaps even more his personality, on the minds of music lovers in Britain, even though he was not playing his 'cello. It was then that we first met his wife Martita, his faithful companion until his death.

We saw them again together in Puerto Rico some years later. She was a charming, intelligent woman and a great musician in her own right. Notwithstanding the disparity in their ages, it was moving to see them together. She looked after him, arranged his cushions, gave him the right medicine at the right time, and had no compunction in escorting guests to the door with great tact when she considered their visit to the maestro had lasted long enough. In short, a surprise for us taking into account the difference in their ages, a disparity which was negligible after one had been with them a while and you started to see her in the rôle of a mother looking after her child. This alliance lasted eighteen years and I believe, having seen them together in London and Puerto Rico, that it is thanks to Martita that he lived to the age of ninety-six.

In Puerto Rico they took us to see their country house at the other end of the island. Sitting next to him, he said to me: "Look, doesn't this remind you of Tarragona? . . . See how the green and the blue blend together . . ." Then, suddenly, with his characteristic realism, he pointed to a sugar plantation where some black people were cutting cane, and said: "They are not like our peasants. Ours would cut the cane close to the root, but these people cut it one metre from the ground, because they do not want to make the effort of bending down."

In Puerto Rico he had tremendous moral authority. He did a lot of good there; like all men of absolute integrity, he radiated goodness and probity. He quickly saw through the sycophantic charlatan out for the advantages to be found in his friendship, and lost no time in sending him on his way. On the other hand, there is no doubt that people of deep sincerity would be his friends for ever. As is well known, the Prades Festival moved to Puerto Rico with him, which was logical since, as the years drew on, he could travel less and less.

The last time we saw them was again in Puerto Rico in 1973, when he was feeling unwell and not far off his end. A tumour had been diagnosed and it was suspected that he had rampant internal cancer. I had some complementary X-rays made and realized that what in fact he was suffering from was Paget's disease—a degeneration of the bone which can be very painful, especially at night. Fortunately, there is a drug which I was able to prescribe for him to ease the pain, and Martita wrote later that he felt more comfortable. He lived for another eight or nine months.

I saw Martita later in Barcelona, when she came to settle various affairs connected with her husband's will. She came to our home, charming and beautiful as ever. Some time later she married the great pianist Istomin. The last time I saw her was when she attended the formal unveiling of the statue of Casals playing the 'cello, which now stands on the mountain of Montserrat, to the north-west of Barcelona. That was in November 1976.

Chapter 3

AROUND THE WORLD WITH AMELIA

FOR YEARS I had been promising Amelia that before I retired
from the Chair, we would do a world tour free from any
academic obligations, in other words very different from overseas journeys we had done up to then. In the event I was
unable to keep my promise, but in May 1970 I received an
invitation from the University of British Columbia at Vancouver to take part in a one week's course. They were paying
for my return fare from Barcelona to Vancouver, an honorarium for the course and all expenses. It seemed to be the
perfect opportunity for me to keep my promise, although not
to the letter, for one week's work was involved. But we could
go round the world, via Asia and the Pacific on the outward
journey and back across Canada and the Atlantic.

We flew via Paris to our first stopping place, Athens, where
my old assistant Cavadias met us at the airport. We knew
Athens well from previous visits and left, after a very short
stop-off, for Tel Aviv. Israel is really well worth visiting—at
least the Israel that we saw. Wherever you look, the impression is one of activity, civilization, order, creative desire.
Looking towards the Israeli/Jordan frontier, it is not necessary
to enquire where one nation ends and the other starts. On one
side are green, cultivated fields and well-kept roads; on the
other side is the typical Biblical scene of Palestine at the time
of Jesus Christ, with the goatherd and his goats and lack of
vegetation: in short a wide contrast between the one nation
and the other.

My ex-assistant, Myer Makin, now professor and head of the
orthopaedic department at the University of Jerusalem, was
waiting for us at the airport at Tel Aviv. He looked after us for
three days taking us to the sacred spots in the northern part
of the country and showing us the modern city of Haifa,

industrially very active, particularly in the port area. We were extremely agreeably impressed, except for the excessive number of military uniforms to be seen all around one, regardless of sex. Naturally enough, we were affected most of all by the holy places, bringing to life the divinity studies of our childhood, and which, nowadays, due to Jewish organizing capacity, are seen in an impressive state of upkeep and order.

We night-stopped en route to India, in Teheran, where all we saw were the lights of the city and, at the airport itself, masses of jewels being offered for sale by Persian merchants to the American tourists who filled our aircraft. In New Delhi it suited us to join a group of Spanish tourists who were being convoyed by a Barcelona tourist company all the way to the World Fair at Osaka, and who found themselves with vacancies.

The Spanish ambassador in New Delhi, an old patient of mine, advised us what to see in the city: the old part, the Red Fort and the fortifications about twenty-five to thirty kms away, which had protected the city from Mongol invaders. He also recommended us to fly to Kajuraho, the city of temples. There is no city there today, only the temples and a small hotel put up by the Ministry of Tourism for the convenience of travellers. The temples are testimony to the artistic capacity of the Indians of seven to eight hundred years ago, their façades being covered in small figures, sculpted in the minutest detail portraying the act of procreation in all its imaginable variations. It is remarkable that, whilst individually they are obscene, in conjunction they constitute a marvel of art. Artists and believers went there to pray for fertility and certainly inspiration should have come to them from contemplating the temples.

We had been told that it was a place of extreme heat; so much so that it was necessary to visit the temples at six am and be back in the hotel by ten am. This we did, and were back before ten, completely exhausted. The shade temperature outside was 48°C; the atmosphere was completely dry, with no movement of air, so that to breathe seared one's throat.

From Kajuraho we flew in about two hours to Benares on the Ganges, the river that washes up against the steps of the palaces of the great Indian maharajas, and leaves, on the tiny strand at its edge, the places where the dead are incinerated and their ashes thrown into the river so that their spirits can go straight to their nirvana without interruption. We watched this ceremony, at five in the morning, from a boat, as the bereaved are extremely irritated by the curiosity of foreign tourists and one has to leave as soon as it starts to get light. It was really very impressive to see three mounds of logs burning, each with a body atop, and the families turning the bodies with long sticks, so that they burn evenly all over. Looking up from this spectacle we beheld in contrast the maharajas' palaces, still existing, notwithstanding the fact that social conditions appear to have changed vastly in the last few years. We walked through the city, duly making way for the sacred cows we encountered, and coming across vast numbers of beggars, many with striking physical defects, some using tree branches as improvised crutches, all of whom had come from far distances, according to our guide, to be near the river when their time comes to die.

From New Delhi, with the Barcelona tourist group, we flew to Japan, stopping en route for one night in Thailand. The river market in Bangkok was interesting, with its floating shops moored on both banks, and the buyers being poled up and down the river in small boats, bargaining and discussing prices and changing from one place to another in a very curious manner; the whole scene had an air of extraordinary primitiveness.

In Hong Kong, where we also stopped briefly, we were accompanied by a doctor who showed us all the interesting places and even took us to the frontier with China. Naturally, the ladies were able to close several satisfactory business deals, buying authentic Chinese goods in the shops set up by Mao in Hong Kong to earn American dollars in the free trade colony.

I made the mistake of buying what purported to be a new, Japanese camera of first-class make; however, it turned out not to be so new, having apparently been exposed to high temperatures in the shop window for several months, with the result that the photo-electric cell had burnt out. Fortunately, I was able to have it mended, first in Japan and later in Barcelona. I certainly burned my fingers; like a good Catalan looking for a bargain, I thought I was saving some $25 but getting the "brand new" camera repaired cost me far more.

The flight from Hong Kong to Japan was remarkable for a strange occurrence. The captain of the aircraft sent a member of the crew to ask if I was a doctor. When I admitted to this, I was asked to have a look at a little boy of about seven or eight years of age who had been taken seriously ill. I found him lying on his mother's lap, with a high temperature of well over 103°F (43°C). The mother, an English woman, told me they had come from Arabia where her husband worked and were returning to the United Kingdom via the Pacific route. The child had been playing normally at Hong Kong airport but about half an hour after take-off had become drowsy and developed this dangerously high temperature.

The captain asked me what I thought he should do. He told me Japan was still three-and-a-half hours' flying time away. I told him I did not think the child would survive that long without medical attention and that in these conditions I could not hold myself responsible. He went off to consult his maps and discovered that there was an island with a hospital and an airport not too far off our route. The hospital and the airport were duly alerted and all was ready when we landed shortly afterwards. By coincidence, the head of the hospital, known to me by correspondence, was a surgeon interested in my work on Perthes' disease and I had even quoted him in a book on this infirmity. He took over the child, but, unfortunately, we never heard what became of the patient.

We flew on to Japan and stayed, not in Osaka, which seemed to us to be greatly overpopulated, but in nearby Kyoto, a city which still preserves the magic of old Japan, with its little lamps in the streets, bamboo houses, raffia curtains, silence, cleanliness and, of course, the delicate custom of removing one's out-of-doors shoes before entering houses. The first duty of the visitor is to divest himself of European garb and put on a kimono. We visited several houses and a couple of doctors were kind enough to take us to their homes. One of them invited us to lunch, which, taken sitting cross-legged on the floor, was not the most comfortable of meals for us. We were all therefore to enjoy vision a of the Japan of before westernization. The Osaka Fair was an exhibition of the industrial power of the country: a mixture of beauty and functional efficiency, and most of the buildings, at least in our view, were extraordinarily graceful.

9

Particularly interesting and nostalgic to us Catalans was to find in the government pavilion, dedicated to gas, a panel some twenty metres long by Joan Miró, which was clearly a centre of attraction judging by the long queues forming to see it. It gave us great satisfaction to be able to say: "We come from this gentleman's country." After three visits to the fair, we travelled to Tokyo in the famous express in which each carriage has a speedometer, so that we were vastly entertained watching the needle go up to 225 kms per hour and wondering if it would even reach 230—and all this time the train seemed to be motionless. All this explained the difference between practical efficiency and high-falutin talk. The Japanese are a people who work and get things done, which explains how in a relatively few years, from being a wholly beaten and partially devastated country, they have rebuilt it and incorporated into it what we call the Western way of life.

An amazing sight were the droves of uniformed school children, all more or less of the same age, commanded by a leader with a small flag, who orders them around like soldiers. "Stop!"—and they stop. "Walk!"—and they walk. "Fall out!" and then comes the danger. When they break ranks they rush towards you, dozens of them, all with a note-book, to ask you for your signature! I do not know what this means to them, as they rush from one to the other without asking who they are. They are just interested in the signatures of people from the West. I suppose it indicates the prestige brought to the country by American influence. This may also have brought the undesirable in its train, but the observable standard of living and general well-being gives one an impression of marked improvement.

With the rest of the group we visited the area of the lakes and various centres of interest on the outskirts of the capital, all very attractive, because one can still see Japanese-type gardens, looked after to the last most delicate detail, with their rivulets and miniature waterfalls, admittedly artificial but nonetheless exceptionally graceful.

The city of Tokyo itself is totally uninteresting but vast in area, incredibly so when one considers that the houses are low and the population is some twelve to fourteen millions. We took leave in Tokyo of our Barcelona group, who were returning home via the North Pole, whilst we went on to Honolulu. Unfortunately, we spent eight hours at Tokyo Airport, ostensibly for technical reasons, but really because at the advertised time for take-off we were only some one hundred passengers, an uneconomical payload for our Jumbo. We finally took off, still not full, with almost two hundred aboard after other connecting flights had come in.

In Honolulu Amelia had the time of her life. This part of the South Pacific although not that far south is still tropically influenced. The American lady tourists lost no time in buying the typical Hawaiian multicoloured long dresses which at evening parties are so becoming even to the least attractive of women. There was golf and tennis to play; interesting places to see on the island; we bathed and swam; and in the evenings the men turned out in white dinner jackets and the ladies in their newly acquired Hawaiian dresses. We even found time in our three days to visit Pearl Harbor where Japanese bombers had wreaked such havoc on the US fleet in the early hours of 7 December 1941.

We flew direct from Honolulu to Vancouver where I had to fulfil my commitment: to lecture at a course on osteology and orthopaedics organized by the University of British Columbia.

Vancouver, which we knew from a previous visit, is a very attractive city with pleasant surroundings. It is situated below wooded hills which are the forerunners of the Rockies though not actually part of the range. The bay, on a sunny day, reminds one of the Mediterranean. Vancouver is a great salmon centre and this was a factor in the discovery by one of my friends, Professor Cobb, of calcitonin, a very important hormone for bone metabolism. It is taken from a gland in the throat of the salmon, so the researchers found plenty of raw material at hand.

Cobb and a Professor Patterson took me salmon fishing one night. We took off at 3 am, and half an hour later I felt a great pull: unfortunately it turned out to be a species of small shark. The same thing happened twice again—and, after much sweating to land a fish which is not even good to eat, I got discouraged.

A strange coincidence occurred while we were in Vancouver. During the war, I had treated in Britain a photographer by the name of Shiffer for a leg wound, after which I completely lost touch with him. In 1950, while in Buenos Aires, I was asked to pose for the university photographer—and there was my ex-patient, by then with a reputation as the best photographer in South America. He took some splendidly flattering pictures of me at fifty-three. We said goodbye, expecting it to be for ever. However, in Vancouver I was again asked to pose for a photographer said to be one of the best in the States and Canada. I put myself at his disposal and who should it turn out to be but my friend Mr Shiffer again. At seventy-three years of age, in Vancouver, I had the best colour photographs I have ever had taken of myself.

Our stay in Vancouver over, we took the polar route back to London. The flight in itself is not in the least bit interesting—all you see below you is a continuous milky fluff. We stayed in London only long enough to change planes and fly on to Barcelona, where we arrived safe and sound, forty days after we had left, our world tour happily and finally accomplished at last.

Epilogue

AMELIA'S DEATH

DURING OUR LAST trip to Italy Amelia started having pains in one of her legs, so when we returned to Barcelona I had her examined and it was found that she had a circulatory deficiency of the lower limbs, which was the beginning of arteriosclerosis. Slowly, the discomfort increased, but despite this she continued to live a normal life until one day, on her way to the airport to see our youngest daughter Julie off back to Madrid, she had a sudden heart attack. Montse, who was driving, rushed her to the intensive care unit of the Quiron Clinic, where she survived for three days. I do not have to say what the loss of my life's companion meant to me.

As if this tragedy were not hard enough to bear, a month later my sister Júlia also died of a heart attack and I suddenly found myself within four weeks without either of the two women who had been the principal mainstays throughout my life. Alone with three daughters—two of them living in Madrid—my life cycle seemed to have come to an end then and, as if it were a premonition, I was found to have a malignant tumour, which I doubt I shall survive. Whether I come through it or not, this is the end of a long succession of adventures which I have written as memories, rather than an autobiography.

I should revise these papers, but if I am not allowed the time I feel sure one of my daughters will do so and perhaps put them in some sort of order. I know a great deal is missing from them, interesting anecdotes which unfortunately will have to disappear with me. On reflection though, I have no cause to complain. At the end of my life I have been honoured by HM King Juan Carlos I with the highest honour the country can bestow; my old University of Barcelona has made me a doctor honoris causa and the city where I was born has given me its gold medal. I have been blessed with honours and good wishes from Narcis Jubany, Cardinal of Barcelona, to the city's humblest inhabitant. I pray to God the time has not yet come to say goodbye, but if it has, I welcome the hour.

Barcelona, 7 January 1977

Appendix
and
Index

Appendix

"TRUETA'S MESSAGE"

IN 1941 THE meeting of the British Orthopaedic Association, under the presidency of Professor Girdlestone, was held in Oxford. My book, *Principles and Practice of War Surgery* had not yet been published but the association had made me an honorary member in 1940 so that I could take part in its meetings and other activities despite the fact that I was not British and my medical qualifications had no validity in the country. (In 1951, when professor at Oxford, I relinquished my honorary membership and became a full member of the association.)

The following May, 1942, *The British Medical Journal* published an article of mine on the "five points" on which I based my technique, and it was well received to such an extent that the editorial of the current *Journal of the Royal Army Medical Corps* was entitled "Trueta's Message". It said:

> Great men always manage to express great truths in the shortest possible space. . . . And was it not John Hunter who replied to the cogitation of a colleague "Don't think! Try!" Something of the same brevity and wit is evident in Trueta's manner of dealing, in five sentences, with the short treatment of war wounds and fractures, as detailed in the *B.M.J.* for May 16, 1942. They are expressed as follows: 1. Prompt surgical treatment; 2. Cleansing of the wound; 3. Excision of the wound; 4. Provision of drainage; 5. Immobilization in a plaster-of-Paris cast.

In October that same year, the *Sunday Express* published an article by their Moscow correspondent, Paul Holt, headed "80 out of every 100 Soviet wounded go back to battle". He was writing after visiting the famous Botkin Hospital where

9*

they had increased the number of beds from the initial 500 to 2,300. The article contained the following words: "Satisfactory progress has also been made with the use of plaster casing over open wounds. This remarkable method of avoiding spreading sepsis was discovered by accident during the Spanish Civil War, when the Republicans, lacking medical supplies, packed linen rags round the wounds and left them for long periods." There is no doubt that the advantages of encasing wounds in plaster became evident to the Russians, as can be seen later, from the treatises and papers I had published on the subject in England.

My book *Principles and Practice of War Surgery* in English was preceded by the publication in Barcelona in 1938 of my first small tract on the subject (*Tractament de les Fractures de Guerra*); this, as explained elsewhere in this book, was published in English in 1939 with certain additions made in London (*Treatment of War Wounds and Fractures*). Both in the Catalan original and in the English translation there appears a passing historical reference, citing especially Winnett Orr and Ollier but omitting reference to Pirogoff. This was rectified in my later book *Principles and Practice of War Surgery*, in which a detailed reference to the Russian surgeon was made. It is true that I commented that Pirogoff had used plaster bandages when he had nothing else with which to cover wounds, but that no sooner had the Crimean War ended than he stopped the use of plaster. My book must have been available in Moscow shortly after it was published, years before it was translated into Russian and published in Moscow without my knowledge. The reference to Pirogoff was noticed, among others, by my acquaintance Yudine and ever since then the treatment which the Russians had called "this remarkable method . . . discovered by accident during the Spanish Civil War [by] the Republicans . . ." (though my name is conspicuous by its absence) thereafter became known as Pirogoff's, just as in France it was called Ollier's and in Italy Magatti's. It is not to be wondered at therefore that famous British surgeons visiting Russia found to their surprise that Pirogoff had preceded me by nearly one hundred years! With somewhat more reason, the Americans claimed their compatriot Winnett Orr as the originator of the method. This confusion in fact gave rise to many American soldiers not benefiting from the treatment as it should have been practised, due to the fact that Winnett Orr had never treated a war wound himself and was therefore unaware of the decisive value of excision of dead tissue before enclosing the wound in a plaster of Paris cast.

My personal position was conditioned by the fact that although I was in a country which had welcomed me warmly, it was not my native land and I was little known here. The whole affair could have aroused suspicions that I was a mere plagiarist, intent on turning to my own advantage the work of others.

The first signs of this scepticism came in a comment on my book in the *BMJ* in which the writer referred to me as a person "who had developed the Winnett Orr method during the Spanish Civil War". Shortly after, the famous orthopaedic surgeon Reginald Watson-Jones wrote to the editor of the *Journal* complaining, in some indignation, that, according to him, I had used Winnett Orr's method and done nothing more.

Girdlestone and Seddon overrode my natural wish to defend myself personally and insisted on replying to Watson-Jones' letter in the *BMJ* themselves. The text of Watson-Jones' letter published on 9 November 1940 was:

"Closed Plaster Technique for Infected Fractures and War Wounds".

Sir, I must protest once more. We are failing to pay credit where credit is due. In the latest publication "Surgery of Modern Warfare", edited by Hamilton Bailey, are these words: "The closed plaster method was developed from Böhler's technique by surgeons engaged in the Spanish war, particularly Trueta . . . It must be considered to be still on trial."

Nothing could be further from the truth. Trueta did not develop the technique. Böhler abhors it. It is the Winnett Orr technique. It was developed in the last war, a quarter of a century ago. The cases were fully documented in 1929. Some surgeons may not have heard of it until the Winnett Orr method was used in Spain, but if so they have only themselves to blame. During the last six years the British

Medical Association has been circulating a film which illustrates every detail. Most orthopaedic surgeons in this country have used it routinely for over ten years. I am, etc.
R. Watson-Jones, Liverpool, 1 November.

It was obvious that Watson-Jones was lamentably confusing my method—for dealing with recent wounds—with Orr's, which was for the treatment of chronic bone infections, among them infected and old fractures.

I was prepared to clear up the confusion because Watson-Jones was recommending initial suturing of fresh wounds; but, as I say, Girdlestone and Seddon insisted on answering themselves. They wrote in the *BMJ* on 16 November 1940, under the same title:

Sir, We agree with Mr R. Watson-Jones (9 November p. 648): it is important "to pay credit where credit is due". He is right in ascribing the closed plaster treatment to Winnett Orr; Trueta does the same (vide his manual on the "Treatment of War Wounds and Fractures" p. 13), and in the most generous terms.

Then Mr Watson-Jones adds: "Trueta did not develop the technique". Perhaps he would agree that he applied it most successfully and on a very large scale to the injuries encountered in modern warfare, worked out the details of the method from hard experience, defined its scope and limitations, and brought about a revolutionary improvement in the treatment of war wounds first in Spain, later in France, and then in this country, often in the face of indifference and sometimes active opposition. Mr Watson-Jones may not call this a development, in which case the word as he uses it has lost its usual meaning. At any rate, those who have had the privilege of seeing Trueta at work are convinced that he has carried the method far beyond the place claimed for it by its originator, and made a most valuable contribution to the surgery of war. I am, etc. . . .
G.R. Girdlestone
H.J. Seddon
Wingfield Morris Orthopaedic Hospital,
Oxford. Nov. 11.

APPENDIX 269

Watson-Jones' brusqueness did not completely surprise me bearing in mind the mixed thinking on the subject which still existed in the minds of many Anglo-Saxon doctors. This gave me the opportunity to state the facts clearly once and for all because by then I already had proof that Winnett Orr had not only never used his treatment in the 1914 war, but that moreover he had never placed a plaster on a recent open fracture— fortunately for the patient, be it said. My method was based on a sequence of principles which in importance ranged from radical enlarging of the wound, meticulous excision of pieces of damaged tissue, the cleansing of the wound, the placing of dry absorbent gauze on the cleaned tissues and, only at the very end of this sequence, the applying of a plaster of Paris in contact with the actual surface of the wound. It is obvious therefore that only the plaster of Paris was coincident with Orr's method: everything else was different, and even in radical opposition, since Orr rejected the excision of damaged tissue saying that "nature"(?) would see to the elimination of all that was dead and that there was therefore no need for surgeons to concern themselves with this aspect.

The number of cases of gas gangrene and infections of all kinds resulting from the application of Orr's recommendations only the Americans themselves know. That is why I felt put out when my friends and professional colleagues Girdlestone and Seddon, alongside whom I worked, asked me to say nothing lest the British might think I was trying to "glorify myself".

As regards Watson-Jones personally, we lived many years thereafter in close friendship, especially after the trip we made to Brazil in 1957, on which Amelia came and to which reference is made earlier in this book. Although from his physique one would not have thought Watson-Jones to be Anglo-Saxon, his fervent patriotism and the quality of his prose and oratory made him a worthy spokesman for the British world I came to know.

All the polemics over the "paternity" of the treatment came to an end with the publication of my book *Principles and Practice of War Surgery* in 1943. An expert in the subject such as S. M. Cohen, for instance, wrote to me on 22 January 1943 saying:

. . . I honestly believe that [Orr] did nothing at all for war

wounds; that he never understood or described the principles of wound excision; that although he used plaster for Osteitis cases, and later some compound fractures, he never really understood or made any attempt to explain the rationale of immobilisation. He simply believed that to leave tissues to "stew in their own juice" was a good thing, and his emphasis was that repeated dressings were harmful. One has only to remember the high temperatures over quite a long period that some of his early cases ran, to know that he didn't appreciate that adequate drainage was important. I think myself that you have brought an entirely new conception into the treatment of war wounds in your ideas about wound excision. People spoke about wound excision previously, and thought that excision meant that all the "Bacteria" should be removed. Emphasis was laid on changing forceps and instruments and in that way avoiding leaving any organisms behind. Your conception was—remove all dead material and no organisms will then flourish. One has only to see that your principle was not at first accepted by the fact that excision was limited to six hours at first, then a lot of people started saying ten hours—and handed credit for the latter possibility to Sulphanilamide. I well remember, however, your declaring at the Royal Society of Medicine, that there was no time limit for wound excision, and that even up to forty-eight hours you did full excisions and found that safe, provided there was subsequent immobilisation. Now only, is this fact being accepted, and I understand that in the forthcoming new gas gangrene booklet by the M.R.C., excision even after many days will be advocated. I understand also that they are adopting your suggestion that to put the limb suspected of gas gangrene into plaster even at that date is to be recommended. . . .
Yours sincerely,

Sol. M. Cohen, London County Council,
Public Health Dept., Southern Hospital,
Dartford, Kent.   January 22, 1943.

My distinguished dissident, Watson-Jones, reverted to the subject in an article on "Bone and Joint Injuries" in *The Lancet* of 6 February 1943 in which he manifested his agreement with what I had predicted at the time of the discussion we had had, on the occasion of my address to the British Orthopaedic Association years before.

At that time he had suggested that war wounds as well could be sutured provided there were sufficient skin for the purpose. Now he wrote:

> ... An essential step is the free division of deep fascia in order to permit subsequent swelling of muscles without strangulation and ischaemia; and in no circumstances is it permissible to suture fascia, muscles, periosteum or other deep layers of the wound. Similarly—with the very few exceptions of sucking wounds of the chest, open wounds of the brain and some penetrating wounds of the joints—the skin should not be sutured. Only two purposes are served by suture of the skin; to occlude the wound and prevent secondary infection; and to gain a neater scar. Occlusion can be secured no less effectively and much more safely by a plaster cast. The neatness of the scar is to be balanced against the risks of infection: tension within a sutured wound causes spreading infection, possibly gas gangrene, amputation or death.

The most conclusive and for me personally the most satisfying acknowledgment of the efficacy of my surgical method was its application by the Canadian Expeditionary Forces in the Dieppe raid. As is well known, the Canadians were chosen to test the effectiveness of the German coastal defences facing Britain. I had been superficially consulted on what would be the best course to take with casualties in the case of an attack starting from Britain. After a violent assault in which it suffered heavy casualties, the expeditionary force returned to England, as planned. Some time later Colonel J. A. Mac-Farlane, Consulting Surgeon at Canadian Overseas Military Headquarters, published a medical report on the raid. His article appeared in *The Lancet* of 17 April 1943, from which the following extract is quoted:

> Of the soft-tissue wounds, 97% were explored, and varying degrees of excision and drainage carried out. Nearly all of

these were left open and then packed. Some sulphonamide drug was used locally in all cases. A relatively small number were immediately enclosed in plaster because of pressure of work, but many of the large soft-tissue wounds were immobilized after three or four days. One was impressed by the much greater degree of comfort and general well-being of those men who were immobilized.

In summing up the experiences of Dieppe, MacFarlane went on to say: "The incidence of serious wounds of the extremities is high but is comparable to figures from other theatres of war. The experience in this group of cases confirms the value of the principles laid down by Trueta—wide exploration and debridement; packing the open wound; immobilization and infrequent dressings."

The recognition of the difference between my method and that of the American Winnett Orr put surgery—good technical surgery—at the heart of the method which some had called "revolutionary", and relegated the less responsible factor—immobilization by plaster cast—to a complementary rôle and not one that was in itself responsible for the "miracle".

Shortly before my book *Principles and Practice of War Surgery* came out in 1943, penicillin had started to be used in treating war wounds. Professors Howard Florey and Hugh Cairns, the latter then Professor of Surgery at Oxford University, went to North Africa to study the benefits of the first antibiotic on wounds, used in combination with surgery. Cairns was a first-class neurosurgeon, but with little experience of traumatology; Florey was an eminent laboratory scientist. The first thing they tested was the effect of penicillin used locally, for the sterilization of wounds.

The results were to be expected, as they were when we initially tried to cure osteomyelitis by the use of penicillin alone; that is to say, we found ourselves obliged to help the action of the antibiotic, eliminating the subperiosteal pus, which means placing penicillin at the service of good surgery, enabling it to reach the infected foci since penicillin, carried in the blood stream, was vital for the eradication of sensitive bacteria in the infected part. This was even more apparent in the case of war wounds, jagged in shape and filled with fragments of dead tissue. I recall the arrival from North Africa of a Belgian soldier with a shattered thigh, the entry hole in the middle third of the thigh being the size of a ten-penny coin, and the exit wound twice that size. A rubber tube had been placed in the entry hole and was lost in the depths of the wound; through this tube penicillin was being introduced at frequent intervals. Despite this, the progress of the patient was not in the least satisfactory, and we had to explore the wound, remove many pieces of ischaemic muscle fragments and small pieces of bone splinters and drain the wound. We immobilized the limb with a plaster, and gave him penicillin injections and finally, somewhat slowly, the fracture consolidated and the patient recovered normal movement of his leg. For many years, the sister in charge of the ward and I used to receive Christmas cards from the very first war casualty we had treated after penicillin alone had been used. The rôle of the first antiobitic therefore was to serve as a complement to good surgery. This fact seemed so obvious to me that I wrote a letter on the subject to the medical press saying that, no matter how much one might wish it to be so, neither sulphonamides nor penicillin could ever be considered substitutes for good surgery.

I knew that this letter would not please everyone, as was to be expected, and the first indication of this was given to me by Professor Cairns. The first edition of my book, in which I had commented favourably on the use of penicillin, always provided it were accompanied by good surgery, was nearly sold out and I was putting finishing touches to the text for the second edition. Cairns asked me if I had changed my mind regarding the rôle of penicillin, and whether I was amplifying the chapter I had dedicated to it. With regard to the second point, I was able to assure him that he would be pleased with the extra pages dedicated to it; as regards the first, unfortunately, I could not differ greatly from what I had said in the first edition as I was aware of many cases in which surgeons, relying on the "miracle" of the new drug, had neglected surgical principles, with disastrous results. I fear that, despite his traditional kindness and courtesy, this interview with Sir Hugh Cairns ended on a strained note.

It was already obvious that, perhaps somewhat irrationally, successes were being attributed wholesale to the use of penicillin.

Nevertheless, in an article published in the *News Chronicle* of 27 May 1943 by their war correspondent, S. L. Solon, Major-General Ernest Marshall Cowell, Director of Allied Medical Services in North Africa, was quoted as saying that the plaster encasement method was universally used. "We were getting on to it from the developments of the last war," he said. "I saw Trueta in Barcelona during the Spanish Civil War. . . . Lives have been saved which in the last war would have been absolutely lost. . . . In one hospital where we took care of 1,500 severely wounded we had only five deaths."

Meanwhile, the day arrived when I was to receive a D.Sc. honoris causa which brought to Oxford many friends and compatriots. In a letter from Amelia to my mother, she tells her that we were expecting to sleep five guests in the house and wine and dine twenty—it was an underestimate.

The honour bestowed on me had an impact on the medical world and came at an opportune moment so far as I was concerned, since the ceremony took place when the inordinate acclaim of the merits of penicillin had not yet started to distract the attention of surgeons from what really counted: strict observance of the five points of my technique. The event was made much of by the British press, and we were flooded with congratulations, among them, albeit in an indirect way, those of the Spanish ambassador, the Duke of Alba, who wrote to Madariaga telling him that he had read with great interest the letter which my friend had written to *The Times* about my honorary doctorate. He added: "Every Spaniard worthy of the name should rejoice that it should be a Spaniard who has put at the disposal of science and humanity as a whole his intelligence and his efforts." My mother wrote from Barcelona saying that many friends had sent her flowers as a result, and that innumerable people had gone to congratulate her. The fact that the BBC mentioned the ceremony in their Spanish-language programme was of even greater satisfaction to them.

The ceremony took place in the vast Gothic hall of the Divinity School on 6 May 1943, and I was deeply moved when, after the traditional processional walk in pairs to the hall, the public orator in his inaugural speech in Latin, said as my turn came to be introduced to the university members: "The Romans crowned a man who saved the life of another.

Today we are honouring a man who has saved the lives of many."

This great honour led to no relaxation whatsoever in the tempo of my activities. I continued to travel from one hospital to the next; from one lecture to another; always worrying about emergencies and the diminishing availability of assistants, all of which kept me away too long from Amelia. She, poor woman, frequently wrote to my mother, complaining of the fact that I was so rarely at home. In one letter, full of joy, she wrote: "He has promised me that at least once a week we shall go to the theatre! But several weeks have gone by, and he has forgotten his promise . . ." Rereading some of these letters now, it seems impossible to me, in view of my temperament and my love for Amelia, that the weight of my responsibilities and the anxiety I felt about our future should have put her out of my mind so much at a time when she most needed me to help her face a hard climate, economic difficulties and, most of all, uncertainty; all this, apart from the obvious daily wartime worries and, above all, the fear of air raids, which were a nightly occurrence. Fortunately, no bombs fell on Oxford, but it seemed that the city was a concentration point for German bombers. Successive waves of them came over us the night Coventry was destroyed and the glow of the burning city was clearly visible in the Oxford sky fifty miles away.

Amelia's hereditary tendency towards depression worsened with solitude, and although it did not seem to be a rational remedy, I am sure that cycling around the place as she did tended to compensate in the form of exercise for the lonely hours she spent alone, while our girls were at school at Rye St Antony and at university at Somerville.

In a letter which she wrote to my mother in November 1943, Amelia told her about the exceptionally cold weather we were suffering at home and she mentioned that one day the wind had been so strong that, unable to ride her bicycle, she had been obliged to push it all the way home from the shopping centre. For economic reasons, central heating was out of the question, and we kept ourselves warm as best we could with electric stoves and, during the day, pulled ourselves up close to the coal-fire in the sitting-room.

Testimonies of affection and recognition followed one on the

other from my British colleagues and, in fact, continued right
up to the time we left Britain to spend the rest of our days at
home. I have a letter from the Head of the Military Hospital
at Shaftesbury, Lt.-Col. W. G. Lister, dated 14 October 1943,
in which he wrote, among other things: "We all feel that it is
due to you perhaps more than to any other that the treatment
of wounds and fractures during this war has been so vastly
more successful than ever before." On 16 October 1943, the
writer of an editorial in *The Lancet* was kind enough to write:

> . . . In his fine book [*Principles and Practice of War Surgery*] he
> [Trueta] points out the way to the correct philosophical
> approach to war surgery. . . . Trueta's theme is respect for
> the body's healing capacity . . . for, as the President of the
> Royal College of Surgeons recently pointed out, the
> principles of how nature works don't have to be invented:
> they are there to be discovered. Trueta finds plaster the most
> convenient immobilising agent to obtain rest, but he insists
> that early surgery, excision and drainage are all necessary
> for success. His good early results were achieved before the
> days of local sulphonamides. . . .

As 1943 progressed, my continual contact with Colonel
MacFarlane proved more fruitful than I could have hoped.
He used to send me young officers of the Canadian medical
corps to work with us for six weeks in the Accident Service. In
this way, Canadian surgeons could put into practice our
techniques prior to going to the battle fronts and at the same
time they helped us to treat the constantly arriving casualties
since we had no other source of assistance, despite ineffectual
requests which I put in through Professors Seddon and Cairns.
My main grievance was that the provisional hospital for head
injuries at St Hugh's, under the directorship of Cairns and
Pennybacker, had over fifteen qualified medical men to cope
with fewer beds than I had, whereas at that particular time at the
Accident Service we were just Francis Masina, two assistants
and myself with over eighty beds to attend to; and, to cap it
all, at the end of 1943 Masina was called up for army medical
service. The arrival of the Canadian officers was a God-send.
They were all very well selected, as was proved by their later

work in the war and we were able to look after our casualties better as well as to instruct Canadians in the details of my technique. I recall with affection and gratitude the names of so many of these young men, in particular those of Captains Bigelow and Pennel, whom I later met again after the war, well established in their careers in their native Canada. As a small testimony of my gratitude for their help, I gave a lecture at the No. 12 Canadian General Hospital (Horley) commanded by Colonel W. A. Fraser, from whom I received a letter thanking me "for the excellent and inspiring talk" and hoping I would be able to visit them again.

Towards the end of 1943, Major-General Philip Mitchiner, so well known to me, wrote in an article in *The Medical Press and Circular* entitled: "War Surgery—a Retrospect after Four Years":

It would appear to be more economical in man-power if greater attention and prompt treatment were given to the more lightly wounded cases in the front line, where adequate and early surgery would permit of a far earlier return to duty in these cases. . . . The early treatment of all wounds is essential if infection is to be avoided. The relief of tension and the excision of a narrow margin of skin and all damaged muscle must be thoroughly carried out, whilst in any case seen after six hours of the infliction of the wound, adequate drainage from its most dependent part is an essential to successful treatment. Primary suture of any wound is absolutely contra-indicated, but secondary suture can frequently be carried out in the course of a few days.

All these good counsels, which are repetitions of those given in my books, are complemented by an erroneous deduction derived from my later book. Mitchiner says:

In the case of all wounds, the closed plaster technique, originally and successfully used in the Crimea, and recently resuscitated and popularised by Trueta, is comfortable to the patient, promotes quick healing and gives satisfactory results, provided oedema or infection is allowed for by bivalving of all plasters applied in those cases where transport to another hospital has to be undertaken within five days of application of the plaster, otherwise infection and oedema under the rigid case will cause pain, loss of limb and often life.

It can be seen that the long-standing prejudice of Mitchiner and Cowell stated in their earlier book, that plasters cause gas gangrene, is reiterated in Mitchiner's article but now only as regards cases where compression has been allowed to occur. On the other hand, probably because they had read about my reference to the Crimean War, Mitchiner adds that I "resuscitated and popularized" a method which Pirogoff had originated with success(?). It is quite clear however that my method has nothing in common with Pirogoff's, which consisted of nothing more than covering a wound with pieces of cloth soaked in a plaster paste.

The problem with the Americans was slightly different as it was I myself who, in the foreword of my book, had given prominence to Winnett Orr on the question of plasters. But his technique in the treatment of recent fractures was unknown to me or anyone else, since Orr had no such experience, as became clear when World War II was already in its second year. I had discovered this much earlier when Orr, knowing through me about the results I obtained in the Spanish Civil War, insisted that all I was doing was merely applying his method to war surgery, with "simple adaptations . . ." This induced senior American surgeons to follow Orr's advice (incision and drainage with packing of gauze soaked in vaseline or paraffin) followed by the application of a plaster. The results were all too soon apparent: the incidence of serious infections and gas gangrene forced the Americans to stop using the technique which they named "Trueta-Orr", and to start thinking again about what should be done. The head surgeon of the US army, Colonel Churchill, published in 1944 an unequivocal paper: the "Trueta-Orr" technique must be abandoned and wounds must be operated on as soon as they are produced, enlarging them fearlessly, excising the damaged tissue meticulously, draining them with dry gauze and immobilizing them, if possible, by the application of a plaster. In other words, exactly my technique, as rediscovered on the battlefield by American experts!

Canadian medical headquarters asked Orr what importance he himself attributed to the excision of damaged tissue, and he was candid enough to reply that he did not believe in excision; that excision took place anyway under the plaster, the dead tissue being eliminated through sphacelus, in other words, putrefaction. He made no allowance for the fact that there might not be time for sphacelus to be produced, because before then the patient would have died. Orr believed that excision was a dangerous technique, only to be undertaken by expert surgeons, and consequently inconceivable in the majority of cases. I had a copy of Orr's report sent to me, and the matter ended there because the essential difference between my method and his was not a question of technical detail, but of fundamental principles.

It was one of the greatest satisfactions of my life when, after the war, Colonel Churchill acknowledged the error they had made in linking my name with Winnett Orr's, or rather, my technique with Orr's. Even so, not many years ago, in a history of American orthopaedic surgery in time of war, my name once again appeared paired with Orr's.

Index